P9-BZI-667

Devotions for Kindred Spirits

Devotions for Kindred Spirits

Edited by Roy B. Zuck

VICTOR BOOKS®
A DIVISION OF SCRIPTURE PRESS PUBLICATIONS INC.
USA CANADA ENGLAND

Unless otherwise noted, Scripture quotations are from the *Holy Bible, New International Version*, © 1973, 1978, 1984 by the International Bible Society. Used by permission of Zondervan Bible Publishers. Other quotations are from the *New American Standard Bible* (NASB), © The Lockman Foundation 1960, 1962, 1971, 1972, 1973, 1975, 1977; and the *King James Version* (KJV).

Library of Congress Cataloging-in-Publication Data

Devotions for kindred spirits : 365 daily inspirations from faculty members at Dallas Theological Seminary / edited by Roy B. Zuck.
p.   cm.
ISBN 0-89693-243-5
1. Devotional calendars. I. Zuck, Roy B. II. Dallas Theological Seminary.
BV4810.D46   1990
242'.2–dc20
90-35720
CIP

1   2   3   4   5   6   7   8   9   10   Printing/Year   94   93   92   91   90

© 1990 by Scripture Press Publications, Inc. All rights reserved. Printed in the United States of America. No part of this book may be used or reproduced in any manner whatsoever without written permission except in the case of brief quotations embodied in critical articles and reviews. For information address Victor Books, Wheaton, IL 60187.

CONTENTS

F O R E W O R D

A Christian man remarked while packing his suitcase for a trip in the presence of a friend, "I've still a little corner left, and I'm saving it for a guidebook, a lamp, a mirror, some letters, and a sword."

"Ridiculous!" exclaimed his friend. "You can't possibly get all those things in."

"Yes, I can," replied the traveler. Then he deposited his Bible in the empty place.

The Bible is indeed an amazing book with many purposes. Its first purpose, of course, is to make men and women "wise for salvation through faith in Christ Jesus" (2 Tim. 3:15). Having received this salvation, we need to grow spiritually and be equipped to serve the Lord. Paul affirms, "All Scripture is God-breathed and is useful for teaching, rebuking, correcting, and training in righteousness, so that the man of God may be thoroughly equipped for every good work" (2 Tim. 3:16-17). The reading and study of the Bible then is a prime requisite for the Christian who wants to lead an effective and fruitful Christian life.

Devotional books can help us feed on the Scriptures but perhaps you have found—as I have—that many of them are superficial and experience-centered. This one is not. Select members of the Dallas Seminary faculty have written daily devotionals that are biblically based and apply the truths of Scripture to daily life.

Journey with us through 365 days of the year as we explore the faith of Abraham, the providence of God in the life of Ruth, the life and psalms of David, the outlook on life in Ecclesiastes, the messages of the Minor Prophets and the messages of New Testament writers, John, Paul, and James. I promise a rewarding trip.

We do well to remember the words of an unknown devotional writer,

> "These hath God married and no man shall part,
> dust on the Bible and drought in the heart."

It is my prayer that your use of this book will bring daily refreshment to your heart and renewed strength to your soul.

Donald K. Campbell,
President, Dallas Theological Seminary

January

Devotional readings on the life of Abraham
by F. Duane Lindsey

ABRAHAM'S FAME

A brilliant but bitter agnostic writer toured Europe with his wife and small daughter. He received honors from schools, royalty, and friends. After the family returned home, his daughter, impressed with her father's fame, said, "Daddy, I guess pretty soon you will know everybody except God."

The name and fame of Abraham is known by nearly everyone. He received special honors from God. God's promise to him, "I will make your name great" (Gen. 12:2), has been fulfilled. He became to the Jews "our father Abraham" (John 8:53); to the Arabs he is *el Khalil* ("the friend of God"); and to Christians he is the father of all who believe (Gal. 3:6-9, 29). Three world religions look back to Abraham for their roots.

And Abraham knew God and was known by God. So he was called "God's friend" (James 2:23). It is amazing that a mortal human could be a friend of the eternal Creator of heaven and earth. But the eternal Son of God said to His followers, "I have called you friends" (John 15:15).

What a joy! We can develop a friendship with God in Jesus Christ. But that friendship requires knowing God by faith in Christ, and then obeying God, for Jesus said, "You are My friends if you do what I command" (John 15:14). Then, like Abraham, our fame will come not by how many people we know but simply by knowing God.

OVERCOMING A SLOW START

An athlete regularly amazed onlookers when he won the 100-yard dash after being 10 yards behind at the 50-yard mark. His fast finish always made up for his slow start. A caterpillar creeps slowly across the sidewalk, unaware that one day it will be a butterfly flitting from flower to flower overhead. Many Christians plod through life thinking, "My family background, my past sins, and my ignorance of God and His Word keep me from being an effective servant of God."

Abram (later named Abraham) grew up in a pagan family, in a civilized but idolatrous culture in Ur of the Chaldeans (in modern Iran). His religious roots were nothing to brag about. He didn't know the one true God. But one day (as Stephen said), "The God of glory appeared to our father Abraham while he was still in Mesopotamia, before he lived in Haran. 'Leave your country and your people,' God said, 'and go to the land I will show you' " (Acts 7:2-3). Abram started in the right direction when he took his family with his father Terah to the city of Haran, in modern Iraq (Gen. 11:31). But he delayed there until Terah died. At last he set out for the land of Canaan (12:4-5).

Don't be discouraged: Your past background or yesterday's failures need not hold you back. Abram, who later would be featured in the Hall of Fame of Faith (Heb. 11:8-19), almost didn't make it out of the starting blocks in the race of faith. But he did believe God's promise and, after several false starts, he grew in faith to become known as "the man of faith" (Gal. 3:9). And so can you. Live by the words of a New Testament son of Abraham: "Forgetting what is behind and straining toward what is ahead, I press on toward the goal to win the prize for which God has called me heavenward in Christ Jesus" (Phil. 3:13-14).

PROMISES

God's commands are often backed up not by reasons but by promises. When He commanded Abram to leave family and homeland, His promises to him ranged from personal fame to being a channel of universal blessing. The blessing to "all peoples on earth" (Gen. 12:3) is basically spiritual, and it came through Abram's descendant, Jesus Christ. Paul said that Christ "redeemed us in order that the blessing given to Abraham might come to the Gentiles through Christ Jesus, so that by faith we might receive the promise of the Spirit" (Gal. 3:14).

When Crowfoot, the great chief of the Blackfoot confederacy in southern Alberta, gave the Canadian Pacific Railroad permission to cross the Blackfoot land from Medicine Hat to Calgary, he was given in return a lifetime railroad pass. Crowfoot put it in a leather case and carried it around his neck for the rest of his life. There is no record, however, that he ever availed himself of the right to travel anywhere on the CPR trains. We often treat the promises of God in the same way.

The patriarchs looked forward to the coming of Jesus Christ. Today the promise of salvation by God's grace through faith in Christ looks back to His completed provision for us in His death, burial, resurrection, and appearances to witnesses (1 Cor. 15:3-8). Just as sin in all ages has left everyone in a state of condemnation before God, so salvation in every age has been by God's grace (never merited or earned), based on the death of Christ (whether prophetically or historically), and received through faith (reliance on the person, promise, and provision of God).

An invitation: If you have never exercised trust in Jesus Christ regarding His sacrificial, substitutionary death on the cross, act on the promises of God today and become a participant in the blessing of salvation promised through Abraham.

OBEDIENCE IS A LONG HIKE
IN THE SAME DIRECTION

Nate Saint was one of five missionaries who were killed by the Auca Indians. He once said that his life did not change until he came to grips with the idea that "obedience is not a momentary option . . . it is a die-cast decision made beforehand."

Abram chose to obey God and to place confidence in His promise. But his faith did not mature overnight. It began with faltering steps that grew more stable as he walked the pathway of obedience. On a few occasions he stepped aside from the path, but God graciously directed him back to continue the route to the fulfilled promise. God encouraged Abram's faith by periodically appearing to Him with words of reassurance and refinement of the content of the promise.

His initial arrival in Canaan and his trek south on the ridge route to Shechem in the heart of the land was followed by a revelation of God. The Lord appeared to him and said, "To your offspring I will give this land" (Gen. 12:7). In response, Abram built a sacrificial altar to worship the Lord. Then he "called on the name of the Lord," that is, he made public proclamation of the Lord by name. And he did that in the midst of a perverse, pagan Canaanite culture. In this way, he began to fulfill his role of being a blessing.

God may or may not call you to leave homeland and family, but He expects you to believe His Word and follow Him obediently — even in the face of pagan opposition. God will not appear to us as He appeared to Abram, but He will reassure us and reaffirm His promise through His written Word, the Bible. And He expects to be glorified as our worship proclaims our faith to those around us.

It's up to you: Decide today to begin the trek of obedient faith in the promises of God.

FAITH OR FAMINE?

When famine struck Canaan, Abram struck out for Egypt. Humanly speaking, that was a wise decision, though not without its dangers. But Abraham made the decision without consulting God, and so he entered a famine of faith.

Abram had every intention of returning to the land of promise as soon as the famine was over, since he "went down to Egypt to live there for a while" (Gen. 12:10), not forever. But he gave God no other options in the matter. So we'll never know if his trip was God's plan, or just His permission. God might have directed Abram to Egypt and given him clear warnings to protect him from doing what he did there. Or he might have miraculously provided for him in the land of Canaan. Clearly, Abram's spiritual life and walk of faith were not advanced in Egypt.

Think about it: We often make decisions, even important ones, without giving thought to the fact that God might have better options for us in the matter. Since we have the completed revelation of God in His Word, we should not expect Him to appear to us with special instructions. We ought to rely on the commands and principles He has recorded for us in the Bible, and apply those to our daily decisions with spiritual wisdom and faith. We must not rely solely on human wisdom and what seems expedient at the moment of the decision. We must exercise "the wisdom that comes from heaven," the wisdom that is "first of all pure; then peace-loving, considerate, submissive, full of mercy and good fruit, impartial and sincere" (James 3:17).

IS SHE OR ISN'T SHE?

Canada's Justice Landreville of the Ontario Supreme Court admitted before a Senate-Commons investigating committee, "I often lie on minor matters." Many Canadians were shocked. A man who was vested with the responsibility for handing out justice, and who often commanded those before the bar to "tell the truth, the whole truth, and nothing but the truth, so help me God," had himself handled the truth loosely.

One day Abram made the same mistake. He had traveled to Egypt—the land of the Nile, the pyramids, the Great Sphinx. Abram gazed at them like a tourist on a holiday. But his trip to Egypt was no picnic. He knew that his wife Sarai was beautiful in spite of her sixty-five years of age. He knew that Egyptian men had an unusual attraction toward Semitic women. He knew his life was in danger if the wrong person decided he wanted to take Sarai to become his wife. And he knew that Sarai actually was his half-sister (a marriage custom socially acceptable, even praiseworthy, in the Hurrian culture he left behind in Haran). So he told the Egyptians she was his sister, hiding the "whole truth" that she was also his wife.

Perhaps he felt there was no real danger to Sarai. Likely he thought the famine in Canaan would be over and they could leave Egypt before the long process of someone bartering with Sarai's "brother" for a wife could be completed. But he didn't count on the interested suitor being the one person who needed no bartering process to take Sarai for a wife. So Pharaoh took her into his harem. And Abram must have felt very guilty as he went about his business of becoming rich in Egypt.

A lesson for us? How like the Canadian judge and the ancient patriarch many of us are today! Not only bending the truth, or telling a "little white lie," but also being involved in outright deception—of our employer, our husband or wife, our children, the IRS. And sometimes we even think we're fooling God! Repentance and restitution are called for before we get in as deep as Abram.

JEOPARDY OR WHEEL OF FORTUNE?

Abram's strategy in Egypt placed in jeopardy not only Sarai's purity but also the fulfillment of God's plan for a son to be born to her and Abram. Ironically, Abram's participation in the game of jeopardy carried him further to "become very wealthy in livestock and in silver and gold" (Gen. 13:2).

But God intervened to protect both Sarai and His word of promise, which were in jeopardy. He brought severe plagues on Pharaoh and his household. Sarai apparently remained untouched by them, for Pharaoh soon realized that her presence was the cause of the plagues. What a picture this was of God's deliverance of the Israelites from Egypt during the rule of a later Pharaoh!

However, God does not always deliver His people from predicaments, especially those of their own making. This was true a number of times in the history of Israel. And it may be true in our lives today. But God at times still does deliver us from problems — even those we have thrust ourselves into, like Abram did in Egypt.

Abram did not escape unscathed. He received an embarrassing rebuke from Pharaoh who expelled him from Egypt with all his family and belongings.

Something to watch: Our deceitful, manipulative strategies may cause us to prosper for a season, but they will eventually overtake us and lead at least to very embarrassing results, if not to outright disaster. God protected Sarai and Abram because of His jealousy to fulfill His promise. But we cannot presume. We should turn away from such deceptions at once and resume the walk in faith that is pleasing to God.

BACK TO BETHEL

Abram brought home three F's on his report card from the school of faith. The first F was in a survival course entitled "The Sufficiency of Faith in Famine." In that course he failed the midterm exam by going to Egypt without God's direction. He also failed the final exam by lying about Sarai (Gen. 12:10-20).

Later Abram received an F in a course on "The Patience of Faith," when he took things into his own hands to fulfill God's promise of an heir, and he fathered Ishmael (16:1-16). The third F came in a course on "The Integrity of Faith" in which Abraham* turned in a report that previously got him an F, telling a pagan ruler (this time the king of Gerar) that Sarah* was his sister (20:1-18).

But God overruled the F's to make them steppingstones in Abram's growth in faith. When Abram exited from Egypt, he went back to Bethel ("House of God") "where he had first built an altar. There Abram called on the name of the Lord" (13:4). His worship and testimony for God were renewed and his walk of faith resumed. He also faced the daily issues and problems and stresses (such as the strife with Lot in Genesis 13). But we will see that through these God refined his faith.

About our failures in faith: They may differ from Abram's, though there are probably many similarities. We must show our report cards to our Heavenly Father, confessing our sins and receiving His parental forgiveness and restoration (1 John 1:9), and resume positive growth in our walk of faith.

See reading for January 15 relating to this spelling that begins in Genesis 17.

FAITH RELINQUISHES RIGHTS

Quarreling Christians should remember the words of Lord Nelson at Trafalgar who, coming on deck and finding two British officers quarreling, whirled them about and—pointing to the ships of their adversary—exclaimed, "Gentlemen, *there* are your enemies!"

Abram and Lot had become tribal chiefs with many "flocks and herds and tents" (Gen. 13:5). Their herdsmen quarreled over pasturage and water rights. Moses, the sacred historian of Genesis, found it noteworthy to record that their enemies "the Canaanites and Perizzites were also living in the land at that time" (v. 7).

For the sake of peace Abram suggested they part company. Instead of insisting on his rights as the one to whom God had promised "this land" (12:7), he graciously offered Lot the first choice of the land. Lot based his decision on appearances—"Lot looked up and saw that the whole plain of the Jordan was well watered. . . . So Lot chose for himself the whole plain of the Jordan" (13:10-11). That decision turned out to be Lot's undoing, for it led him to the wicked city of Sodom.

But God appeared to Abram and promised to him and his offspring forever all the land he could see north and south, east and west (vv. 14-15). So he embarked on the prototype Holy Land tour in response to God's command, "Go, walk through the length and breadth of the land, for I am giving it to you" (v. 17).

Regarding rights: God honored Abram's willingness to relinquish his rights, and He reaffirmed His covenant promise with him. Relinquishing rights may be an especially important lesson for us to learn in modern litigious America. Christlikeness requires of us that we "look not only to [our] own interests, but also to the interests of others" (Phil. 2:4).

KINGS IN CONFLICT

The first war mentioned in the Bible is found in Genesis 14. Four powerful city-states from the northeast came to punish rebellious vassals that included five city-states located just south of the Dead Sea. One of the defeated cities was Sodom, where Lot lived. Thus he was taken captive with other inhabitants of the city. When news reached Abram, he gathered 318 of his own fighting men along with a sizable force belonging to three tribal chiefs with whom he was in league, and pursued the invaders northward beyond Damascus. The surprise attack under the blessing of God brought victory to Abram and freed Lot and the other captives.

The invaded land was, at least in part, land promised to Abram, and his victory was a result of the divine promise (Gen. 12:1-3). That Abram's victory was given by God was confirmed by the blessing he received from Melchizedek.

Amazing: Paul tells us that God "has blessed us in the heavenly realms with every spiritual blessing in Christ" (Eph. 1:3). God promised a physical land to Abraham and his descendants. During the time of Joshua, God told the Israelites, "I will give you every place you set your foot on" (Josh. 1:3). Likewise Paul instructs us in Ephesians 4–6 how to "set our foot" on our spiritual blessings in Christ and make them our own. Part of that practical possession is our spiritual warfare. We are to "be strong in the Lord and in His mighty power" and to "put on the full armor of God" to "stand against the devil's schemes" (Eph. 6:10-11). We must stand firm in the victory Christ achieved for us on Calvary. We must constantly be clothed with the full armor of God—the belt of truth, the breastplate of righteousness, the shoes of readiness that come from the gospel of peace, the shield of faith, the helmet of salvation, and "the sword of the Spirit, which is the Word of God" (vv. 14-17).

KINGS IN CONTRAST

How would you feel if your spouse, needing something for the house, went to the next-door neighbor and got some money? It would break your heart. That is what we do to God when we go the world's way in meeting our needs. It's as if we're saying, "Lord, You aren't adequate. You don't know the best way for me. I'll have to get what I want by myself."

Two kings met Abram when he returned from victory over the forces of Kedorlaomer. They could not have been more different in personality, moral and social values, or religious beliefs.

The pagan king of wicked Sodom was delighted to regain the freed prisoners and redeemed property of his city (including Lot), and offered Abram the rightful spoils of war. Melchizedek, king of Salem (an early name of Jerusalem) and priest of "God Most High, Creator of heaven and earth" (Gen. 14:19), brought out refreshments to Abram, pronounced God's blessing on Abram, and worshiped God for delivering Abram's enemies into his hand. Abram accepted the divine blessing by giving Melchizedek one-tenth of all his possessions. But he refused the king of Sodom's gift of the spoils of war, not wanting the blessing in any way to be tarnished. Abram's encounter with Melchizedek, a true spiritual brother in a pagan world, had a profound and positive influence on his faith in the nature and promise of God. Abram rejected the opportunity for worldly riches from the king of Sodom and waited for the enrichment promised by God.

How about it? Like Abram, we need to depend on God so that we do not confuse worldly benefits with divine blessing. We must depend on our Heavenly Father for meeting our needs, rather than relying on the ways of the world.

FAITH IS THE VICTORY

People disagreed about who deserved credit for the Allied victory at the Marne in World War I, and some reporters asked Field Marshal Joffre of France about it. "I don't know who deserves credit for the victory," he said, "but I know that if it had been a defeat, they would have blamed it on me."

God was the one who gave Abram the victory over the invading armies. But from the human perspective it was Abram who was offered (and who rejected) the spoils of victory by the king of Sodom. And the threat of the enemies would certainly not be the last. So Abram's exhilaration after victory may have passed, leaving him fearful and feeling unrewarded.

Then the Lord spoke to Abram in a vision. "Do not be afraid, Abram. I am your shield, your very great reward" (Gen. 15:1). How simply but profoundly does the great God meet our deepest needs!

Yet Abram questioned God's fulfillment of His promises, since the only heir to receive those promises was one of his household servants. But God graciously submerged Abram's doubts in greater clarification of the promise, "A son coming from your own body will be your heir" (v. 4). Not only that, but "your offspring" will be as numberless as the stars (v. 5).

In response to this great confirmation of the promise, we are told that "Abram believed the Lord, and He credited it to him as righteousness" (v. 6). This verse is quoted in the New Testament to illustrate justification by faith (Rom. 4:3).

For you: You too may feel fearful and unrewarded. But from the God who was Abram's shield and reward, you too may receive by faith the greatest gift God can give—a righteous standing before Him because of what Christ did on the Cross.

THE PROMISE CONFIRMED

The Lord confirmed His promise to Abram first by word ("a son coming from your own body will be your heir," Gen. 15:4) and then by a solemn covenant grant ceremony to assure Abram that his descendants would gain possession of "this land, from the river of Egypt to the great river, the Euphrates" (v. 18).

Abram was still experiencing growth pains in the life of faith — "O Sovereign Lord, how can I know that I will gain possession of it?" (v. 8) The Lord responded to his desire for evidence by ratifying a covenant to guarantee the fulfillment of the promise. He also warned Abram that the fulfillment would be preceded by a period of enslavement, a reference to the period when Israel was in Egypt.

The fact that Abram was in a deep sleep when the Lord ratified the covenant illustrates that its fulfillment rests on God, not on Abram's or the nation's obedience. And the specific boundaries of the Promised Land indicate that God has a future for His people Israel in the land of Israel since they have never yet in history possessed all the land ratified in the covenant.

Good news: we can have the same assurance that Abram had about God's faithfulness to fulfill His promises. For example, we have the promise of a completed salvation — "Christ is the mediator of a new covenant, that those who are called may receive the promised eternal inheritance" (Heb. 9:15). Though the fulfillment may be preceded by apparent delays, "The Lord is not slow in keeping His promise, as some understand slowness. He is patient with you" (2 Peter 3:9). Though suffering and even death may precede the ultimate fulfillment, the Lord will be faithful to keep His promises (Rom. 8:31-39).

WEAK FAITH AND IMPATIENCE

Madalyn Murray O'Hair was not the first atheist to gain great public attention on the American scene. Generations ago Robert Ingersoll drew large audiences for his lectures on atheism. He liked to shock his hearers by taking out a big pocket watch and announcing, "I give God—if there is one—five minutes to strike me dead." When someone called this to the attention of the English evangelist Joseph Parker, who was conducting revival meetings in America at the time, Parker responded with typical English aplomb, "And did the gentleman presume to exhaust the patience of the eternal God in five minutes?"

Genesis 16 directs attention to two tensions—the barrenness of Sarai and the conflict between Sarai and Hagar. Neither tension is resolved in the story, and Abram is virtually passive throughout.

God's program for Abram was on schedule, but Abram was getting impatient with the apparent delay. After all, he was eighty-five years old, and an heir was not yet born. So impatience brought about the birth of Ishmael and resulted in Abram's second deflection from walking by faith.

Just as famine in the land tested Abram's faith and resulted in using human strategy in Egypt, so also the barrenness of Sarai was a test of faith, and again Abram reverted to human reasoning. In harmony with the social customs of the day, and at Sarai's suggestion, Abram had union with Sarai's maid, Hagar, to bear a child for Sarai and Abram. But further tension developed from Hagar's maternal pride and Sarai's jealousy. When Hagar fled into the wilderness, the Angel of the Lord responded to her affliction and promised her descendants through Abram's son, Ishmael.

Let's take note: We often become impatient and use worldly methods to accomplish God's plans. This frequently puts us in tension with ourselves, our family and friends, our church, and even with God Himself. Let's learn patience from the impatience of Abram. God's time schedule is best. And so are His methods to accomplish it.

WHAT'S IN A NAME?

People change their names for a number of reasons — marriage, religious conversion, adoption of a new culture or homeland, embarrassment at or dislike of an unusual name, or even admiration of or a desire to be like a particular person. A man in Britain recently changed his name (as well as his dress and behavior) to that of a well-known Hollywood movie actor.

God changed the names of a number of prominent biblical persons, including Abram and Sarai. Such name changes normally denoted a change in status or circumstances. They also indicated the sovereign authority of the one granting the new name.

God gave Abram a new name when He reaffirmed His covenant promise to him: "This is My covenant with you: You will be the father of many nations. No longer will you be called Abram [meaning 'exalted (with respect to) father']; your name will be Abraham [sounding like *abhamon*, 'father of a multitude'], for I have made you a father of many nations. . . . As for Sarai your wife, you are no longer to call her Sarai; her name will be Sarah [meaning 'princess']. I will bless her and surely give you a son by her. . . . She will be the mother of nations; kings of peoples will come from her" (Gen. 17:4-5, 15-16).

Thus those name changes constituted another pledge that God would fulfill His promise. And every time Abraham and Sarah heard their new names they would be reminded of God's promise and they would be encouraged to count on His faithfulness.

A reminder: As believers in Jesus Christ we have come under His authority, and go by His name, being known as Christians. In fact, we have been reborn into the family of God, and so we should behave as His children. When we hear the name *Christian,* let us remember God's faithfulness to keep His promises to us.

HE WHO LAUGHS LAST

The Lord's appearance to Abraham in Genesis 17 raised him to a new level of trust in God to fulfill His promises. After 13 years of thinking that Ishmael was the son of promise (in 17:18 Abraham still saw the possibility of Ishmael fulfilling the promise), God specified that a son would be born to Sarah (v. 16). That announcement brought Abraham to his knees in laughter. The exact reason for the laughter is not stated, but it apparently reflected some degree of unbelief. Similarly, Sarah later laughed to herself when the Lord announced that she would soon be pregnant (18:12). Ironically, the Lord chose for the son of promise to be named Isaac (meaning "he laughs").

Yet Abraham responded in obedient faith as he carried out the stipulations that God announced about the covenant sign of circumcision (17:23-27; cf. vv. 9-14). The act of physical circumcision would identify the descendants of Abraham as those who shared in the covenant promise, reminding them to be separated, pure, and loyal to the covenant, and to avoid marital impurity so as to produce a godly seed (see Mal. 2:10-17).

Moreover, God expected them to accompany the physical ritual with spiritual circumcision of the heart, and so to be devoted to Him (Deut. 30:6; cf. Rom. 2:29).

It's a fact: As New Covenant believers today we are to be pure and separated persons devoted to God and trusting in His promises (Col. 2:11-15). The new identity God has given us in Christ Jesus, and the signs of our identity with Him and with the New Covenant (i.e., baptism and the Lord's Supper) should encourage us to walk in faith and expectation that God will fulfill all His promises to us.

25

THE GOD OF THE IMPOSSIBLE

In the final analysis the narrative of Abraham's growth in faith as he responded to God's covenant promises is not primarily a story about Abraham's faith but rather a revelation of God's incredible power and gracious purpose. The hospitality narrative of Genesis 18:1-8 describes a fellowship meal between Abraham and the Lord, and it introduces the whereabouts of Sarah ("Where is your wife Sarah?" [v. 9]) in connection with a further annunciation of the birth of Isaac ("Sarah your wife will have a son" [v. 10]). The Guest from heaven obviously knew the new name of Sarah— "Where is Sarah, Princess [i.e., the mother of many nations, the corecipient of the promises]?" The focus on Sarah was an emphasis on the Lord's power to bring about all He had promised.

Laughter by ninety-year-old Sarah was a natural reaction, but it prompted the divine response, "Is anything too hard [literally, 'too wonderful'] for the Lord?" (v. 14). The supernatural ability expressed by the Visitor's knowledge that Sarah laughed in her heart was just a small example of His mighty power. Could not the Creator of the universe, who brought all living things into existence by the power of His word, bring forth life from the dead womb of Sarah to demonstrate His wonderful Person, and cause all who heard it to wonder in worship of Him?

The Lord's promise, "I will return to you at the appointed time next year, and Sarah will have a son" (v. 10), indicated His incomparable intervention to bless. Thus the promised seed would be recognized as the Lord's provision.

Good advice: As we read the promises of God in His Word, we should not view them as incredible, because He has power and knowledge and wisdom and love beyond compare. It is His Person, not His promises, that is beyond our comprehension; that should lead us to believe and worship with Abraham the wonderful God who is beyond compare.

THE RIGHTEOUS JUDGE

James I of England once tried his skill as a judge, but was so perplexed after hearing both sides in a case that he abandoned the profession in despair, saying, "I could get on very well hearing one side only, but when both sides have been heard, by my soul, I know not which is right."

Abraham expected a positive answer to his question to the Lord, "Will not the Judge of all the earth do right?" (Gen. 18:25) The patriarch knew that the Lord was just and that His omniscience and perfect wisdom enabled Him, in contrast to James I, to "know which is right."

Abraham's question was evoked by the Lord's stated purpose to investigate the wickedness of Sodom (where Lot lived) and Gomorrah for impending judgment. The Lord said, "I will go down and see if what they have done is as bad as the outcry that has reached Me" (v. 21). This anthropomorphic description shows that the Lord's judgment is just, for it is based on full and accurate information.

The Lord informed Abraham of His purpose because His promise to Abraham included blessing to all nations, the number of which He was about to decrease by two. The Lord also saw this as an opportunity to teach Abraham a lesson to pass on to his descendants on "what is right and just" (v. 19). Abraham's descendants would enjoy the blessings of the promise if they would be characterized by righteousness (living in conformity with the will of God) and justice (making decisions based on His will).

Don't forget: The righteous and just Judge of all the earth expects us also to uphold and exemplify righteousness and justice in our lives, as well as teach those qualities to our children. Though we may share with James I an inability to "know who is right" in a case of law, we have the foundation of the Word of God to guide us toward a lifestyle in which righteousness and justice play a significant role.

GOD CARES FOR THE RIGHTEOUS

Monica prayed many times for the conversion of her wayward son Augustine. When he decided to leave for Rome. she prayed that God would prevent him from going to that wicked city. But he went to Rome where he was converted to Christ. God denied Monica's prayer of the moment that He might grant her prayer of a lifetime.

When Abraham learned that the Lord was going to destroy Sodom and Gomorrah, his concern for his nephew Lot took the form of a negotiation with God regarding the inhabitants of Sodom. Though his negotiation with the Lord about Sodom does not fit the pattern of other intercessions in the Bible, it functions generally as an intercession. Yet the emphasis in Genesis 18:22-33 is on the justice of God, not on the intercession of Abraham. Abraham asked God to spare the city of Sodom, based on an appeal to God's justice not to destroy the righteous with the wicked (vv. 22-25).

The progress of the negotiation indicated that the Lord was willing to spare wicked persons for the sake of the righteous. Yet the actual outcome of God's judgment on Sodom indicated that even though the righteous were fewer than Abraham negotiated for, God did not destroy the righteous (Lot and his family) with the wicked inhabitants of Sodom. Rather He delivered the family of Lot out of the city. (The judgment on Lot's wife was another matter—an individual case of judgment for disobedience to a specific divine command.)

Abraham wanted God to manifest His justice, deliver Lot, and spare the city. Yet God manifested His justice and delivered Lot while destroying the city of Sodom.

Isn't it true? We sometimes want God to act in a certain way. But He can manifest His power and goodness in ways different from the limited options we place on Him. And He can answer our prayers in ways that grant the object of our requests without using the method of our requests.

THE FOLLY OF WORLDLINESS

A preacher was shown the sights of New York City by friends he was visiting. That night he prayed, "Thank You, Lord, for letting me see all the sights of New York. And thank You most of all that I didn't see a thing that I wanted!"

Lot was a righteous man (2 Pet. 2:7) who saw and loved the world and the things in the world. His compromising and hypocritical lifestyle caused the wicked men of Sodom to scoff at him (Gen. 19:9), his sons-in-law to laugh at him (v. 14), two angels of the Lord to drag him kicking and screaming out of Sodom (vv. 15-20), his wife to look back toward Sodom (v. 26), and his daughters to conceive by him (vv. 30-38).

You could take Lot out of Sodom, but you couldn't take Sodom out of Lot. Sodom died in a conflagration from the Lord but was born anew in a cave near Zoar. Lot offered his daughters to the wicked men of Sodom who rejected his offer and his hypocrisy. Lot's daughters initiated incestuous relationships with Lot as the only solution (they thought) to bearing children.

We may generally shun the outright wickedness of the world in which we live, but the more subtle influence of its affluence has great effect on us. We have become too content in the world to heed the call of the Apostle John, "Do not love the world or anything in the world. If anyone loves the world, the love of the Father is not in him. For everything in the world—the cravings of sinful man, the lust of his eyes, and the boasting of what he has and does—comes not from the Father but from the world. The world and its desires pass away, but the man who does the will of God lives forever" (1 John 2:15-17).

A good idea: Let's reflect the attitude of the preacher who thanked God that he didn't see a thing he wanted.

WILL WE EVER LEARN?

A small boy gazed into a gorge at a river far below. He saw a boat floating along with the current. Not accustomed to the visual perspective at that distance, he cried out to his father, "Look, some boy lost his toy boat!" His father explained that it was a real boat and that it appeared so small because they were so far above the river below. The boy seemed to understand, but then replied, "But how will the boy ever find his toy boat?"

It takes a while to learn some lessons. Even Abraham seemed to take too long to learn some very important spiritual lessons.

By the time Abraham and Sarah moved to the city of Gerar (Gen. 20:1), they had made substantial progress in the walk of faith. But old fears raised their ugly head in the heart of Abraham and caused him to have a wrong perspective. He told Abimelech, king of Gerar, regarding Sarah, "She is my sister" (v. 2), so the king took Sarah into his harem. As in the parallel case concerning Pharaoh in Egypt (12:10-20), the Lord preserved the purity of the mother of the promise, this time warning Abimelech in a dream (v. 3). The Lord accepted Abimelech's plea of innocence — that he had taken Sarah "with a clear conscience and clean hands" (v. 5). But the Lord still held Abimelech accountable for having Sarah in his harem and indicated that he should return her to Abraham and ask Abraham to pray for him so that he would live and not die (v. 7).

Once again Abraham's faith was rebuked by a pagan king. As far as we know, Abraham finally learned his lesson, for no third occurrence such as this is recorded for us (though the scenario was repeated in the life of Isaac and Rebekah, 26:1-11).

It's so true: We also are sometimes slow to learn lessons in the life of faith because we have not developed spiritual perspective regarding the fears and distresses that threaten us. We need to obey God's Word and depend on His promises.

A MIRACULOUS BIRTH

Luke 2:1-7 records the birth of a miracle Baby—Jesus the Son of Mary. Genesis 21:1-7 also records the birth of a miracle baby— Isaac the son of Sarah and Abraham. Both babies were named before they were conceived (Luke 1:31; Gen. 17:19). Both conceptions required the supernatural activity of God (Mary was a virgin, Sarah was over ninety-years old—well beyond child-bearing age).

Both infants were sons of the Abrahamic promise. Isaac was the initial son of the Abrahamic promise in whom God's promise began to be fulfilled. Jesus, a descendant of Isaac, was the ultimate Son of the promise through whom blessing would come to all nations of the earth. Of course, Jesus was unique because He was not only the son of Abraham through Mary but also the Son of God born of a virgin without a human father, the eternal Word become incarnate (cf. John 1:1-18).

The birth of Isaac was linked to the previous promise, "the Lord did for Sarah what He had promised" (Gen. 21:1). Though no angels appeared to glorify God at the birth of Isaac, Sarah offered praise by declaring what God had done—"God has brought me laughter." And that laughter, with (no doubt) a rehearsal of the act of God that prompted it, would be contagious—"and everyone who hears about this will laugh with me" (v. 6). Though God's promise of the birth of Isaac (whose name means "he laughs") may have prompted Abraham (17:17) and Sarah (18:12) to laugh in mild unbelief, God's fulfillment of His promise brought a laughter of joy and praise. Thus Isaac's name would recall not the unbelief of his parents but rather the faithfulness of God.

For us: As modern-day participants in the blessing promised through Abraham, we should rejoice in and praise God for the births of both miracle babies. Both births are testimonies of God's faithfulness to His promise and of His intention to manifest His grace to us.

PROTECTING THE INHERITANCE

"Get rid of that slave woman and her son, for that slave woman's son will never share in the inheritance with my son Isaac" (Gen. 21:10). Those words of Sarah rang in Abraham's ears and distressed his heart because "it concerned his son" Ishmael (v. 11), born to him by Hagar. Abraham no doubt realized the potential threat that Ishmael was to Isaac and the fulfillment of the promise through him. He must have been aware, like Sarah, that Ishmael "was mocking" Isaac (v. 9). But it seemed so hard-hearted to expel Ishmael and Hagar from the camp. What would the Lord think of him for doing that?

But God relieved his anxiety: "Do not be so distressed about the boy and your maidservant. Listen to whatever Sarah tells you, because it is through Isaac that your offspring will be reckoned" (v. 12). So Abraham sent Hagar and her son off into the desert near Beersheba.

On the human side Sarah sought to avoid any potential threat to the inheritance of Isaac. On the divine side God affirmed the wisdom of Sarah's desire, but also miraculously provided for Hagar and Ishmael and told Hagar, "I will make him [Ishmael] into a great nation" (v. 18).

Paul saw an analogy between the experience described in Genesis 21 and Christian experience as he described it in Galatians 4:21-31. As Ishmael was a threat to the fulfillment of the promise through Isaac, so is the Law a threat to the freedom we have in Jesus Christ. We, "like Isaac, are children of promise" (Gal. 4:28). So we must "get rid of the slave woman [the Mosaic Law] and her son [those who seek to be in bondage to the Law]" (v. 30).

A challenge: Let us, with Paul, not use our freedom "to indulge the sinful nature," but rather to "serve one another in love" (Gal. 5:13).

LIVING IN PEACE

John Foster Dulles was reported as saying, "The world will never have lasting peace so long as men reserve for war the finest human qualities. Peace, no less than war, requires idealism and self-sacrifice and a righteous and dynamic faith."

As Abraham's expulsion of Ishmael and Hagar removed internal threats to the fulfillment of the promise and Isaac's inheritance in the land, so Abraham's peace treaty with Abimelech assured external peace so that the Abrahamic line might dwell in peace and prosperity in the land.

The peace treaty came on the heels of strife between Abraham's herdsmen and the herdsmen of Abimelech regarding water rights in the Beersheba area. Abraham viewed Abimelech's desire for peaceful coexistence in a positive light, especially since it grew out of Abimelech's awareness that God was with Abraham (Gen. 21:22).

When a dispute occurred about ownership of a water well, Abimelech accepted seven lambs from Abraham as a witness to Abraham's ownership of the well. Thus the place was called Beersheba (v. 31), meaning "well of seven" or "well of the oath." After Abimelech returned home, Abraham planted a tree near the well as a lasting landmark to the provision of God, whom he then worshiped (v. 33).

Abraham's peaceful settlement of disputes should be an example to believers today. Paul exhorted us, "Live in harmony with one another. . . . If it is possible, as far as it depends on you, live at peace with everyone" (Rom. 12:16, 18). "Be of one mind, live in peace" (2 Cor. 13:11). "Live in peace with each other" (1 Thes. 5:13). The author of Hebrews even linked peacefulness with holiness: "Make every effort to live in peace with all men and to be holy" (Heb. 12:14).

How about it? Let's translate these commands into daily behavior, to impact our society in which genuine peace is so noticeably absent.

HOW FAR DO WE OBEY?

Abraham's spiritual journey consisted of steps of faith, weak at first but becoming stronger as the Lord renewed the promise and made it more explicit. That journey included several major sidetracks from the pathway of faith, but God faithfully brought Abraham back to continue the trek. Then God's promise reached its initial fulfillment in the birth of the heir (Isaac).

But that was not the end of Abraham's struggles in becoming the father of faith. For the first time in those struggles "God tested Abraham" (Gen. 22:1). The test was whether he would obey a clear command from God: "Take your son, your only son, Isaac, whom you love, and ... sacrifice him ... as a burnt offering" (v. 2). Would Abraham revert to some scheme of his own to retain the son of promise? Or would he obey God in spite of the apparent unreasonableness of the command?

When Field Marshal Bernard Montgomery was called in to remedy the continued Allied loss of battles in North Africa in World War II, he expected his commands to be carried out. He later described how he turned defeat into victory: "Orders no longer formed the basis of discussion, but for action."

For Abraham, God's orders were not the basis for discussion but for action. Abraham's commitment to obey God is immediately evident: "Early the next morning Abraham got up and ... took ... his son Isaac" (v. 3). There is no hint that Abraham doubted God or wavered in faith. Abraham had matured in faith to the point of trusting God to fulfill His promise. Abraham's task was only to trust and obey God.

Be reminded: The tests God allows in our lives may differ from Abraham's test. But some of them may seem as unreasonable. Our proper response must be to trust and obey Him.

THE OBEDIENCE OF FAITH

Faith relies on God to fulfill His promises. Faith looks beyond the present to God's carrying out those promises. Faith is not selfish—it is willing to sacrifice to be obedient to God or serve others. That is why faith, hope, and love are often linked together in the New Testament (e.g., 1 Cor. 13:13).

The climax of Abraham's walk of faith coincided with his arrival on Mount Moriah to sacrifice Isaac, the son of promise. Abraham willingly obeyed. All else, including the fulfillment of the promise through Isaac, was up to God. Thus in faith the patriarch told Isaac that "God Himself will provide the lamb for the burnt offering" (Gen. 22:8), knowing that the lamb God would provide was apparently Isaac.

Seeing Abraham's willingness to obey, the Lord provided "a ram caught by its horns" in a thicket (v. 13). So Abraham "sacrificed it as a burnt offering instead of his son" (v. 13). The theme of a substitutionary sacrifice is brought together with the theme of the Lord's provision. In fact Abraham named the place "The Lord Will Provide" (v. 14).

We can only guess what went through Abraham's mind as he trudged up Mount Moriah with Isaac at his side. We know he trusted God to fulfill the promise in Isaac, and that he was obeying God in sacrificing Isaac. The writer to the Hebrews concluded that "Abraham reasoned that God could raise the dead, and figuratively speaking, he did receive Isaac back from death" (Heb. 11:19).

Take notice: Paul may have had this story in mind when he wrote to the Roman Christians about God's provision of His Son Jesus Christ in our place: "He who did not spare His own Son, but gave Him up for us all—how will He not also, along with Him, graciously give us all things?" (Rom. 8:32) We should give Him the best we have because He has given us the best He has.

HOPE BEYOND THE GRAVE

When Sarah died at the age of 127 "Abraham went to mourn for [her] and to weep over her" (Gen. 23:1-2). With the death of Sarah, Abraham must have realized that the promises of God would not all be fulfilled during his lifetime. So he had to start thinking about the future. Someone has said that Enoch dreamed of heaven, Noah dreamed of a land beyond the sea, and Abraham dreamed of "a land beyond the years."

The first step in Abraham's estate-planning was to purchase a burial place for Sarah. Instead of returning her body to their ancestral home in Mesopotamia, he sought a site to become a new ancestral burial spot in the land of promise. Abraham went through all the necessary legal requirements to obtain the cave at Machpelah (vv. 17-18). "Afterward Abraham buried his wife Sarah in the cave in the field of Machpelah near Mamre (which is at Hebron) in the land of Canaan" (v. 19).

Sarah's death gave Abraham another occasion to exercise faith in God's promise. This plot of ground was the first portion of Canaan to which Abraham received legal title. The future for Abraham's descendants was in the land of Canaan.

Like Abraham, we should view the time of the death of a loved one as one of our greatest opportunities to exercise faith and confidence in God and His promises. The greatest fulfillment of God's promises to us lies in the future. That is why the object of Christian hope, though future, is certain. God's promises extend into the life to come.

PREPARING TO PASS ON THE PROMISE

Abraham played only a supporting role in the events recorded in Genesis 24. After commissioning his servant to find a bride for Isaac, Abraham is absent from the story. The Bible includes no record that he even showed up for the wedding.

But the chapter provides a significant advance in the fulfillment of God's promise to Abraham. Now that Abraham was thinking about passing on the promise to the next generation, he faced a dilemma. Should he let Isaac marry a woman from the land of Canaan? Or should Isaac return to Mesopotamia to seek a bride? The chapter resolves the dilemma by showing how Abraham (through his servant) faithfully sought and the Lord providentially provided a bride for Isaac to continue the Abrahamic line. But more than that, the chapter indicates Abraham's faithfulness to preserve the purity of his descendants by not allowing Isaac to "get a wife . . . from the daughters of the Canaanites" who lived in the land (24:3).

When the servant heard Abraham's charge, "Go to my country and my own relatives and get a wife for my son Isaac" (v. 4), he immediately realized the potential problem in finding a woman willing to come back to Canaan. If that were the case, he asked, "Shall I then take your son back to the country you came from?" (v. 5). Abraham's emphatic objection ("Do not take my son back there, " v. 9), suggests that Isaac's leaving the land of promise would be even worse than staying in the land and marrying a Canaanite woman. Either option would have been a threat to the preservation of the Lord's promise. Nevertheless, Abraham in faith assured the servant that the Lord would "send His angel before you so that you can get a wife for my son from there" (v. 7).

Be advised: We need to approach our daily dilemmas with Abrahamic faith, confident that God will go before us and prosper those activities that will promote His purpose in our lives.

FAITH IS CAUGHT MORE THAN TAUGHT

Many believe that the servant whom Abraham commissioned to bring back a bride for Isaac was "Eliezer of Damascus" (Gen. 15:2-3), whom Abraham viewed as his heir before the birth of Ishmael. If so, then Eliezer had known Abraham and observed his faith in the Lord (along with his failures) for many years. So the servant undertook the long journey—not only with Abraham's promise that God would send His angel before him to give him success but also with the example of Abraham's faith. Arriving at the town of Nahor in northwest Mesopotamia, the servant prayed at the town well that God would prosper his mission (24:10-14).

The servant's prayer concerned immediate and specific guidance to locate the girl whom God had chosen to be the bride of Isaac. The servant demonstrated full confidence in Abraham's God and in Abraham's word that the Lord was preparing the way. His close relationship to Abraham seems to have taught him much about the life of faith.

Indeed God was providentially preparing the way, for "before he had finished praying, Rebekah came out with her jar on her shoulder" (v. 15). The servant spoke to her and soon learned that she was of the family of Nahor, from which the servant was to seek a bride. His response was immediate and vocal worship of the Lord (vv. 26-27).

Be challenged: Like Abraham's servant, who lived in the 20th-century B.C., we A.D. 20th-century servants of the Lord should also follow Abraham's example of faith. The author of Hebrews devotes more discussion to Abraham and Sarah than to any other individuals in his portrayal of the Old Testament Hall of Faith (Heb. 11:8-19). They are among the cloud of witnesses who have finished their course and are observing "the race marked out for us" (12:1). With our eyes on Jesus, let us run the race in faith as Abraham and Sarah ran.

DOING THE WILL OF GOD

When some ministers urged Abraham Lincoln to free all slaves, he responded, "It is my earnest desire to know the will of Providence in this matter. And if I can learn what it is, I will do it . . . I suppose . . . I am not to expect a direct revelation; I must study the . . . facts of the case . . . and learn what appears to be wise and right."

The faithfulness of Abraham's servant and the providence of God had brought him to Rebekah. Then her brother Laban welcomed him into his home. But the servant would not eat until he disclosed his mission, which he rehearsed in full, including his prayer and encounter with Rebekah at the spring. Laban and his father, Bethuel, immediately recognized the providential hand of God in the matter: "This is from the Lord; we can say nothing to you one way or the other. Here is Rebekah; take her and go, and let her become the wife of your master's son, as the Lord has directed" (Gen. 24:50-51).

The next morning the servant departed with Rebekah, who affirmed her willingness to go. The long trip ended one evening in the Negev when Isaac, who was meditating in a field, saw the camels approaching, and caught the first glimpse of his bride, who had veiled herself for the occasion. The marriage took place and Rebekah became the wife of Isaac.

Abraham's servant, Rebekah, her family, and Isaac all appear in the story as persons who are committed to doing the will of God. In their case God made His will known through His providential workings in answer to the faith and prayer of Abraham's servant.

What about us? We too need to be committed to knowing and doing God's will. Prayer, common sense, and providence are avenues God uses to guide us. Besides these, we now have a resource that those in this story did not have—the complete Word of God, the Bible. As we obey His will as revealed in the Bible, we can experience His guidance.

GOD FULFILLS HIS PROMISES

A young girl told her friend she had ten pennies. When her friend saw only five pennies in her hand she said, "No, you have only five pennies." The girl responded, "I have five, and Daddy told me he'd give me five more tonight, so that's ten." She understood that her father's promise was as good as done.

Abraham also accepted God's promises as "good as done." These promises included his becoming progenitor of many nations (Gen. 17:4) and living a long life (15:15). Genesis 25 begins with a genealogical report that identifies nations descended from Abraham (vv. 2-4) and then turns to the inheritance passed on to Isaac (vv. 5-6). Verses 7-10 indicate that Abraham died at age 175. Ishmael joined Isaac as they buried their father in "the cave of Machpelah . . . with his wife Sarah" (vv. 9-10).

In succeeding generations God proved faithful to His promises to Abraham by preserving a line of promise and blessing through Isaac, Jacob, Judah, and on down to King David, and eventually on to "Jesus Christ, the son of David, the son of Abraham" (Matt. 1:1).

Through His death on the cross, Jesus inaugurated a New Covenant by which Gentiles as well as Jews would be saved, thus beginning the fulfillment of the part of the Abrahamic promise that states, "All people on earth will be blessed through you" (Gen. 12:3). The national and land promises to Abraham yet await their fulfillment at the Second Coming of Christ when He will rule from the land of promise over a redeemed national Israel and peace and righteousness will fill the earth.

A glad thought: God's Word contains many promises to believers today—promises we need to know. Let's depend on Him to fulfill these promises in our lives this day and this week.

February

Devotional readings in the Book of Ruth
by F. Duane Lindsey

DIVINE PROVIDENCE IN RUTH

Two books in the Bible are named for their leading female character—Ruth and Esther. Both books trace God's providential actions
at critical points in Israel's history. Ruth was a foreigner (a Moabitess) who immigrated to the land of Israel. Esther was a Jewess in
exile in a foreign land (Persia). Through Ruth, God provided a
lineage to the Messiah; through Esther, He delivered the exiled
nation Israel from extermination.

In both books we see the providence of God operative in His
behind-the-scenes activity through precise timing of everyday
events to guide His people into the experience of His will. Unlike
the Book of Esther in which the name of God is not mentioned and
His providence is implicit, the Book of Ruth clearly reveals the
Lord's presence in the daily life and conversation of His people and
His name is on their lips in their decisions and relationships. But
God's actions in Ruth are not manifested by supernatural activities
or by priests or prophets. God is at work in the events of Ruth, but
mainly through His people who manifest righteousness and loyalty
in character and conduct. He is also the provider of food and life
(Ruth 1:6; 4:13).

The Book of Ruth links the Abrahamic and Davidic covenants by
providing the bridge between God's promises to Abraham and His
covenant with David. Also Ruth the Moabitess is an example of
God's blessing through Abraham to all nations of the earth (Gen.
12:3).

Questions: Have you ever been delayed in traffic so that you
missed traveling on a plane or bus that was involved in a serious
mishap? Have you somehow been prevented from seeing a friend
to tell him certain information, only to find out later that the
information would have been very disturbing or discouraging to
him? We are not always aware of the reason certain things happen
to us. But we can trust our all-knowing, good God to dovetail
happenings together and to accomplish His purpose in our lives
(Rom. 8:28).

THE TIMES OF THE JUDGES

Though the book of Ruth was probably written during the time of David the king (whose name is the last word in the book), its unknown inspired author tells us that the story took place "in the days when the judges ruled" (1:1).

The significance of that time reference is more moral than chronological (though it informs us that the events of Ruth happened between the death of Joshua and the beginning of the monarchy), for in the days of the judges "Israel had no king; everyone did as he saw fit" (Jud. 17:6). But in that dark period of apostasy, immorality, and anarchy, some Israelites still lived in righteous obedience to the Law and were faithful in their relations to God and man.

As an example of that dark period, we read in Judges 19 that a Levite from the hill country of Ephraim journeyed south to Bethlehem to persuade his runaway concubine to return home with him. On their return journey, they were housed overnight in Gibeah in Benjamin by an old man who also was from Ephraim. "Some of the wicked men of the city surrounded the house" and eventually the concubine was sent out to fulfill their pleasure (vv. 22, 25). The next morning the Levite took her dead body from before the door, completed his homeward journey, and then cut up her body, "limb by limb, into twelve parts and sent them into all the areas of Israel" to arouse people's feelings against the Benjamites (v. 29).

Such wickedness and violence is absent from the story of Ruth. Though she was a foreigner, Ruth received growing acceptance and praise by the inhabitants of Bethlehem (see Ruth 2:8-16; 4:15).

Think about it: We live in days of moral failure and growing anarchy that increasingly resemble the period of the judges in Israel. But as believers in Jesus Christ, we should be light and salt in the world. Like Ruth and Boaz, our lifestyle, attitudes, and commitments should contrast with the immorality and lawlessness that surrounds us.

WRONG SOLUTIONS TO LIFE'S PROBLEMS

You may remember Dagwood Bumstead's misdirected efforts to fix his kitchen sink. After he had botched the job and was standing knee deep in water, his wife Blondie offered the solution he should have started with—call the plumber!

In the spiritual realm as well as the physical, we often make a problem worse by trying to solve it ourselves. Elimelech's family lived in Judah in the town of Bethlehem (meaning "house of bread"). But the "house of bread" was empty, for "there was a famine in the land" (Ruth 1:1). Like their ancestors—Abraham (Gen. 12:10), Isaac (Gen. 26:1-3), and Jacob (Gen. 46:1-7)—the family of Elimelech left home to dwell in a foreign land because of a famine in the land of Canaan. Elimelech, his wife Naomi, and their two sons, Mahlon and Kilion, "went to live for a while in the country of Moab" (1:2). But unlike the case of Jacob, whom God told "I will go down to Egypt with you, and I will surely bring you back again" (Gen. 46:4), Elimelech had no promise of the presence or blessing of God on his visit to the breadbasket of Moab.

Perhaps that is why Naomi found herself some ten years later facing an unknown future with two widowed and barren Moabite daughters-in-law, while the bones of Elimelech, Mahlon, and Kilion lay rotting in the fertile land of Moab. In seeking prosperity outside of God's will, Elimelech had taken his family from a bad situation to one that turned out worse—one in which his wife and two daughters-in-law became widows bereft of the support and protection of an extended family.

Question: How many times in the last week have you faced a problem that you tried to solve in human wisdom without even asking yourself (let alone God) if God had some special purpose or solution for it? Many of our problems are aggravated not by foolish solutions but by not even giving a thought to God's possible involvement in the solution. Let's follow the example of James who said, "If it is the Lord's will, we will live and do this or that" (James 4:15).

GOD RESTOCKS "THE HOUSE OF BREAD"

Three women couldn't have been more destitute than Naomi, Orpah, and Ruth. Though the Lord was the protector of widows (Ps. 68:5) and executed justice on their behalf (Deut. 10:18; 27:19), the general status of a childless widow in Israel was one of social and economic destitution. With no male heir she would become isolated from the land that provided a home and food. A younger widow might return to the home of her parents. But Naomi had no parental home to become her shelter, and she was too old to bear sons to carry on the inheritance of the family of Elimelech and to plant and harvest the grain to support life.

Hopeless and homeless in the land of Moab, Naomi heard news that "the Lord had come to the aid of His people by providing food for them" (Ruth 1:6). Her thoughts turned homeward and Godward, and she decided to return to Bethlehem. Her realization that "the Lord" (Yahweh, the covenant name of God in His gracious relation to Israel) was blessing His land and people with prosperity implied her awareness that she and Elimelech had been disobedient when they had fled the famine. She also became aware of the chastening hand of God in her misfortunes in Moab ("the Lord's hand has gone out against me," v. 13), and she probably hoped that a return to the land of Judah was the next step in her restoration to the blessings of God.

George Whitfield, the famous Methodist preacher, noted in his journal on a voyage to Georgia that the ship's cook had a bad drinking problem. When reproved for that and other sins, the cook boasted he would be wicked until the last two years of his life, and then reform. But within six hours the cook had died of an illness related to his drinking.

Don't delay: Naomi had put off returning to "the house of bread" for over ten years. Perhaps you have delayed from returning to a place of God's blessing in your life. If so, don't put it off any longer.

GOD IS FAITHFUL

The good news Naomi heard from Judah motivated her to return to her homeland and to the Lord. It also shows us one of the avenues of the providence of God—His activity in accomplishing His purpose through natural causes and events. Two such actions of God are mentioned in the Book of Ruth—His provision of food following famine (1:6) and His enablement for birth following barrenness (4:13). We thus learn that the issues of life (birth and sustenance) are in the sovereign hand of God. The Lord's grace, covenant faithfulness, and loyal love to His people were the sources of the restored prosperity.

As the journey of the three widows brought them closer to the Jordan River, which then formed the border between Judah and Moab, Naomi counseled her daughters-in-law to return to their maternal homes so they might find "rest [marital blessing and security] in the home of another husband" (Ruth 1:9). She accompanied her counsel with the prayer, "May the Lord show kindness [loyal love] to you, as you have shown to your dead and to me" (v. 8).

Each major person in the story of Ruth is the object of a prayer that the Lord would manifest His loyal love to those who had demonstrated similar faithfulness in their relations to others (see 2:12, 20; 3:10; 4:11-12). So Naomi viewed Orpah and Ruth as having demonstrated faithful loyalty to their husbands and now to her.

It would have seemed logical for Orpah and Ruth to remain in Moab. Why did Naomi, who knew the true God, want to send them back to their pagan culture? Perhaps her prayer for the Lord to manifest His covenant faithfulness to these foreign women implied her hope that they would worship the God of Israel, even in Moab.

To contemplate: God's providence in our lives is sometimes manifested in natural causes and events—birth and death, seedtime and harvest, summer and winter, drought and flood, war and peace, night and day. We need not experience unusual timing of events to realize that God is at work in our lives each day.

A PARTING OF THE WAYS

When Orpah and Ruth affirmed their goal to return with Naomi to her people (Ruth 1:10), Naomi further objected that she was too old to remarry, and even if she did remarry and could bear sons it would be too long before Ruth or Orpah could marry them and bear children of their own. Naomi probably had in mind the ancient custom of levirate marriage that would be significant later in the Book of Ruth (4:5, 10).

The term *levirate* comes from Latin for "brother-in-law." It is used by scholars to describe an ancient marriage custom whereby a brother (or other near relative) would marry his relative's widow to beget children that would perpetuate the name and inheritance of a man who died childless (see Gen. 38:1-26; Deut. 25:5-10). Thus the purposes of the levirate law were to perpetuate male descent, to prevent loss of the family property, and to provide for the care and protection of the widow.

Naomi apparently convinced Ruth and Orpah that they had no possibility of finding acceptance or security in the land of Judah. So Orpah weighed her loyalty to Naomi against the logical counsel of Naomi and made the decision to return to her Moabite culture and religion. Thus Naomi pointed out to Ruth that "your sister-in-law is going back to her people" (Ruth 1:15). Naomi encouraged Ruth to do the same.

When seeking the guidance of God: We should not automatically rule out choices that make "good common sense," for reasoned solutions may be used by God in His providential direction. However, in the case of Ruth, reason would have directed her to make the same decision Orpah made, and it would have been the wrong decision. Likewise, we need to be aware of the limits of reason and remember that "the foolishness of God is wiser than man's wisdom" (1 Cor. 1:25). We will see that God's guidance for Ruth involved faith in things not seen.

FAITH IN THINGS NOT SEEN

One child's definition of a relative was "a person who comes to dinner who isn't a friend." It seems that some adults apply that same definition to relatives who are in-laws.

In contrast to those attitudes of indifference, or even hostility, Ruth showed a high degree of devotion to her mother-in-law, as well as a commitment to Naomi's people and God.

Ruth gave six reasons why Naomi should stop urging her to remain in Moab. Ruth was committed to go with Naomi, to remain with her, to adopt her people, to accept and worship her God, to die with her, and to be buried in her family burial place (Ruth 1:16-17). While including personal devotion to Naomi, Ruth's statement emphasized her new identification with Naomi's nationality and religion. Ruth's concluding oath—"the Lord deal with me, be it ever so severely, if anything but death separates you and me" (v. 17)—indicates that the Lord (Yahweh) was to be her God. By naming Him in her oath, she was making Him the object of her faith. By placing her trust in Yahweh, she was identifying herself with the people whose God was Yahweh.

Ruth's conversion was brought about on the human side by at least two factors—the personal adversity she had endured (the death of her husband and her barrenness), and Naomi's positive example in adversity and Naomi's testimony about the Lord. Ruth's deliberate action (1:17; 2:12) reflected her knowledge of Israel's God.

Since one of the purposes of human suffering is to bring the sufferer to a personal knowledge of God's saving grace, God had been working providentially in the adversity of both Naomi and Ruth. And it culminated in her statement of faith in the Lord.

Remember: The suffering that God allows in our lives may also indicate His purpose to bring us to a greater level of faith in our walk with Him.

NAOMI'S RESPONSE TO ADVERSITY

Naomi's statement to the women of Bethlehem seems to be a bitter complaint against God for the adversity in her life. When Naomi said, " 'Don't call me Naomi . . . Call me Mara' " (Ruth 1:20), she was making a play on words with her name, for Naomi means "pleasant" and Mara means "bitter." In modern expression, it was as though she said, "Don't call me Sweetie, call me Sourpuss."

Naomi confessed that "the Almighty has made my life very bitter" and "the Lord has afflicted me; the Almighty has brought misfortune upon me" (vv. 20-21). Was Naomi blaming God for her misfortune? Or was she naming God as the Sovereign Lord who had justly punished her disobedience? Perhaps the answer lies somewhere in between, for it would have been natural for Naomi to feel that God could have made life much more bearable for her. Yet she must have realized that calamity as well as blessing (see 1:6; 2:20) comes from God—that He is the Sovereign of all of life. She must have sensed that God's actions toward her were like that of a father disciplining a disobedient child.

Think it over: Sometimes we become bitter at life and at God. Perhaps God has brought adversity into your life as chastening for disobedience to His Word and will. On the other hand, suffering is sometimes allowed by God for other reasons, such as to suppress pride and develop faith (Job. 42:5-6; 2 Cor. 12:7-10), to teach patience (James 1:2-4), to foster fellowship with Christ (Phil. 3:10), or to experience God's comfort to share it with others (2 Cor. 1:3-5).

RUTH'S RESPONSE TO ADVERSITY

God included in the Law a provision for the poor to obtain grain left by reapers during the harvesting process (Lev. 19:9-10; 23:22; Deut. 24:19). The perfect timing of God's providence brought destitute Naomi and Ruth back to Bethlehem in April/May "as the barley harvest was beginning" (Ruth 1:22), just in time to take advantage of the law of gleaning in the fields for grain.

Though Ruth was an alien in the land, she did not wait passively for Naomi to act. She requested permission from Naomi to "go to the fields and pick up the leftover grain behind anyone in whose eyes I find favor" (2:2). As she walked into the fields near Bethlehem, she chose a field where the harvesters were active and, after obtaining permission from the foreman of the harvesters (vv. 6-7), she "began to glean in the fields behind the harvesters" (v. 3).

Naomi's deceased husband, Elimelech, had a close relative (according to some Jewish traditions, a nephew) who owned fields of grain near Bethlehem. In another demonstration of divine providence, Ruth "found herself working in a field belonging to Boaz" (v. 3). Her "chance" decision to enter that field was later that evening regarded by Naomi as an expression of God's kindness, or loyal love (v. 20).

It became obvious that in spite of her adversity Ruth was a resourceful, self-confident woman who had great expectations and hope in the new homeland she had chosen.

In times of adversity: We should follow Ruth's example and actively direct our lives toward the future. Paul reflected a similar hope when he wrote, "We are hard pressed on every side, but not crushed; perplexed, but not in despair; persecuted, but not abandoned; struck down, but not destroyed. . . . We do not lose heart. . . . For our light and momentary troubles are achieving for us an eternal glory that far outweighs them all" (2 Cor. 4:8-9, 16-17).

THE ARRIVAL OF BOAZ

With the arrival of Boaz from Bethlehem, the final major character is introduced, and the tempo of the story increases. The exchange of greetings between Boaz and his workers may have been a conventional blessing ("The Lord be with you! The Lord bless you!" Ruth 2:4), but it reflected genuine dependence on the Lord in the daily affairs of life, as well as a positive relationship between the landholder and his laborers.

Ruth's presence drew the immediate attention of Boaz, who was informed by his foreman of Ruth's identity ("the Moabitess who came back from Moab with Naomi," v. 6). The foreman also indicated Ruth's polite, unassuming request to glean in the fields, along with his observation about Ruth's diligence (v. 7).

Probably a skilled harvester from the fields of Moab, Ruth felt confident in her work. Though she worked hard, she felt secure in resting with the other workers under the shelter provided for that purpose.

Boaz had already heard about Ruth and formed a favorable impression of her because of her dedication to Naomi (cf. vv. 11-12). But now he had seen her with his own eyes and observed her diligent labor. Boaz was impressed. The providence of God was demonstrated again not only by Ruth's positive reception by the foreman, harvesters, and landholder, but especially by the identity of the landholder, who, Ruth will soon learn, was a close relative of Elimelech.

Consider: In spite of adversity we may experience, God can enable us to rise above our circumstances and to attain fruitful goals. Like Ruth we may be unaware of how God is working behind the scenes in our lives, but we need to work diligently and rest securely at the appropriate times, confident of God's leading.

GRACIOUS BOAZ MEETS GRATEFUL RUTH

Boaz wanted to confirm personally what he had heard about and seen in Ruth. Approaching her, he invited her to continue gleaning in his fields rather than going to other fields (v. 8). He encouraged her to follow his female workers who gathered the cut grain into sheaves, and informed her that he was giving his male harvesters instructions to treat her with the same respect they would a Jewish woman. He also encouraged her to "drink from the water jars" provided for the hired harvesters (v. 9).

Ruth's response was full of gratitude but also curiosity, for she realized that Boaz had acted in grace far beyond what was required by the law of gleaning: "Why have I found such favor in your eyes that you notice me—a foreigner?" (v. 10)

Boaz's reply contained an explanation and a blessing. The explanation concerned the favorable report apparently being spread throughout Bethlehem about Ruth, "all about what you have done for your mother-in-law since the death of your husband," how she had left all to be with Naomi in a new homeland (v. 11). The blessing was a prayer that Ruth would "be richly rewarded by the Lord, the God of Israel, under whose wings you have come to take refuge" (v. 12).

Thought for today: Boaz recognized the value of interpersonal communication with Ruth in order to establish a relationship for encouraging and strengthening her. We also need to establish such relationships with those we desire to help so that our efforts will be most effective.

BOAZ THE ENCOURAGER

The blessing on Ruth by Boaz made reference to "the God of Israel, under whose wings you have come to take refuge" (Ruth 2:12). The image of taking refuge under God's "wings" probably refers to the Lord's special care of His covenant people (Deut. 32:11; Ps. 91:4). Boaz recognized that Ruth's commitment was spiritual as well as personal and national.

Ruth's response to Boaz indicated her humble thankfulness as she accepted Boaz's favor and expressed her confidence about her future well-being. She acknowledged that Boaz had provided much encouragement to her, that he had "spoken kindly to [literally, to the heart of] your servant" (v. 13). When the time for the midday meal arrived, Boaz invited Ruth to eat with the harvesters. She ate her fill and had leftover roasted grain for a later meal.

As the meal concluded, Boaz instructed his young men not only to allow Ruth to glean anywhere she chose without rebuking or embarrassing her, but also to "pull out some stalks for her from the bundles and leave them for her to pick up" (v. 16).

Famous football coach Bear Bryant explained his philosophy of coaching by summarizing what he told his players: "If anything goes bad, then *I* did it. If anything goes semi-good, then *we* did it. If anything goes real good, then *you* did it." That kind of encouragement helped him win football games.

Think about it: Can you imagine how Ruth would have felt if Boaz had berated her for assuming she could glean in his fields just because she was Naomi's in-law? What if he had told his workers to snub their noses at this ungodly Moabitess? Ruth might have risen above that treatment, but how much better that she was affirmed and encouraged by the godly words and actions of Boaz. "Let us encourage one another—and all the more as you see the Day approaching" (Heb. 10:25).

RUTH'S REPORT TO NAOMI

Ruth's face must have been radiant as she carried her heavy load of threshed barley (probably about one-half bushel weighing around thirty pounds) back to Bethlehem. She must have been tired but joyful as she reflected on her first day in the fields of Boaz.

When Naomi saw the large amount of grain, along with the leftovers from the noon meal, she knew something unusual had taken place. The questions poured from her lips: "Where did you glean today? Where did you work?" (Ruth 2:19). Before Ruth could reply, Naomi added, "Blessed be the man who took notice of you!" (v. 19). With all due respect to Ruth's diligent labor, Naomi realized someone had granted special favor to Ruth.

Ruth informed Naomi that "the name of the man I worked with today is Boaz" (v. 19), not yet knowing that the man was well known to Naomi as one of Elimelech's relatives.

Naomi made her blessing more specific by saying, "The Lord bless him!" (v. 20) Realizing that God was at work that day, she expressed her praise to God before Ruth by declaring, "The Lord has not stopped showing His kindness to the living and the dead" (v. 20). She realized that the covenant God of Israel was providentially carrying out His plan, a plan that involved Ruth and herself ("the living") and also, in some way, the preservation of the name and inheritance of their deceased husbands.

Do you agree? Like Naomi we need to be alert to the providential actions of God in our daily activities. That awareness should lead us to declare God's praise concerning what He has done for us. Praise Him today for what He is doing in your life.

THE AWAKENING OF HOPE

Ruth learned from experience that Boaz was a generous man of noble character. Next she learned from Naomi that he was a relative: "That man is our close relative; he is one of our kinsman-redeemers" (Ruth 2:20).

The concept of the kinsman-redeemer (Hebrew *gō'ēl*) is central in the story of Ruth. The *gō'ēl* was a close relative who would defend the rights of a person in trouble. That could happen in several ways. The *gō'ēl* might redeem property that had been lost (or needed to be sold) because of poverty (see Lev. 25:23-28; Jer. 32:1-15). Or he might redeem persons who had to sell themselves into slavery for indebtedness (Lev. 25:47-55). The "avenger of blood" duty might also fall on the shoulders of the *gō'ēl* (Num. 35:19-21; Deut. 19:1-3; Josh. 20:1-9). The Book of Ruth assumes that the *gō'ēl* also could fulfill the levirate marriage duty of providing an heir for a deceased relative (Ruth 4:5-10; cf. Deut. 25:5-10).

Naomi identified Boaz as a potential kinsman-redeemer for herself and Ruth. When Ruth mentioned Boaz's invitation for her to continue with his harvesters "until they finish harvesting all my grain" (v. 21), Naomi confirmed the wisdom of that, lest Ruth come to potential harm in someone else's fields.

So Ruth gleaned in the fields of Boaz not only through barley harvest but also through the succeeding wheat harvest, a period of about seven weeks that culminated in the Feast of Weeks (cf. Lev. 23:15-21).

Praise God: We also have a Kinsman-Redeemer—Jesus Christ. He met the qualifications to be our *Gō'ēl*, for as Man He was our Kinsman (John 1:14; Rom. 1:3; Phil. 2:5-8; Heb. 2:14-15), as the sinless One He was free from the curse of sin (Heb. 4:15), as God the price of redemption He paid by His death was infinite in value (1 Peter 1:18-19)—and so He willingly redeems those who trust in Him (Matt. 20:28; John 10:15, 18; Heb. 10:7). Thank Him today that He is your Kinsman-Redeemer.

GOD'S USE OF HUMAN PLANS

Naomi prayed in the land of Moab that the Lord would "find rest in the home of another husband" for Ruth (Ruth 1:9). Now God began to use Naomi to answer her own prayer.

Naomi asked Ruth, "Should I not try to find a home [literally, 'rest'] for you?" (3:1). Naomi was undertaking the parental responsibility of arranging marriage for Ruth. But for circumstances left unstated she proposed an unusual manner of seeking to arrange the marriage. Their kinsman-redeemer Boaz would be "winnowing barley on the threshing floor" that very night (v. 2). Perhaps the afternoon winds had just become sufficiently favorable to separate the husks, chaff, and stalks from the heavier kernels of grain as it was tossed into the air. At any rate, Naomi viewed this as the opportune time to enact her plan, which called for private conversation between Ruth and Boaz.

Naomi's plan involved Ruth's preparation to look (and smell) her very best for Boaz. It also involved secrecy until the right moment—after Boaz had finished dinner! And after he had then gone to sleep at the threshing floor (perhaps as a deterrent to any thievery). The plan called for Ruth to "uncover his feet and lie down" (v. 4). This was a symbolic action, not a sexual act. Yet Naomi was asking Ruth to enter a potentially compromising situation. The manifest purity of Boaz and the further outcome of the story confirm the wisdom of Naomi's plan.

The last step in Naomi's plan was left to Boaz (and the providence of God): "He will tell you what to do" (v. 4). The ball would be in his court!

Think about it: Like the lady who prayed for rain and began to carry her umbrella under a cloudless sky, we need to entrust our needs to God and then be available to accomplish God's providential action. Naomi did just that.

GOD'S BLESSING ON OBEDIENCE

Jesus spoke a parable of a father who told his two sons to "go and work today in the vineyard" (Matt. 21:28). The first said, " 'I will not,' " but later "changed his mind and went" (v. 29), whereas the second answered, " 'I will, sir,' but he did not go" (v. 30). Promises may not produce performance, though their absence may not preclude ultimate obedience.

In the case of Ruth we find a promise (she told Naomi, "I will do whatever you say" [v. 5]) matched by a performance ("she went down to the threshing floor and did everything her mother-in-law told her to do" [v. 6]). That is consistent obedience, the kind Jesus desires from us (John 15:14).

Ruth was a barren widow. God had a plan to bless Ruth. That plan included marriage-rest in the home of Boaz, a kinsman-redeemer. It also included motherhood, for she would give birth to an ancestor of King David. God's plan for Ruth included her in the genealogy of Jesus Christ. The grace of God would provide redemption to Israel and the whole world through the descendant of this Moabite woman (see Matt. 1:5-6).

Divine providence in the history of Ruth was to accomplish all that. But God in His sovereignty chose to work through human responsibility. The other side of divine providence is the response of men and women to be obedient to God and cooperate with His activity in bringing about the realization of His will.

Demonstrating obedience, Ruth was effectively involved in bringing a Redeemer to the world.

To think about: Are we obedient to Jesus' plan to "go and make disciples of all nations, baptizing them . . . and teaching them to obey everything I have commanded you" (Matt. 28:19-20)? Is our obedience a consistent obedience, like that of Ruth? Or do we make a pretense at working in the Father's vineyard, but do not go?

RUTH'S REQUEST FOR MARRIAGE

Ruth obediently followed Naomi's plan. She remained hidden until Boaz finished winnowing, ate dinner, and went to sleep. She quietly lifted the corner of his garment, exposing his feet to the cool night air. She lay down at his feet until "something startled the man [cold feet?], and he ... discovered a woman lying at his feet" (Ruth 3:8).

After identifying herself, Ruth inserted another step in Naomi's plan. Instead of waiting for Boaz to tell her what to do, she invited Boaz to function as her kinsman-redeemer. She understood the Israelite custom and the significance of Naomi's plan more than Naomi realized.

Ruth requested Boaz, "Spread the corner of your garment over me, since you are a kinsman-redeemer" (v. 9). "Spreading the corner of the garment" over someone was symbolic of extending shelter, protection, and marriage (see Ezek. 16:8). Ruth was requesting from Boaz a proposal of marriage, linked to his responsibility as a kinsman-redeemer.

Like Naomi earlier in the day, Boaz was to be involved in God's answer to his own prayer on a previous occasion. In his first recorded meeting with Ruth, he had prayed, "May you be richly rewarded by the Lord ... under whose wings you have come to take refuge" (Ruth 2:12). God was going to answer that prayer through Boaz. Ruth may have implied as much, for the Hebrew word used by Boaz for "wings" was also the word Ruth used for "corner [of the garment]."

Ruth's obedience was consistent (she did what she said she would do), and it was also informed (it was not blind obedience, for she understood fully what her actions symbolized).

Consider this: There may be times when God seems to request "blind obedience" from us. But normally He expects us to be very knowledgeable about the obedience we give Him. Paul spoke of the plight of those whose "zeal is not based on knowledge" (Rom. 10:2). Let's be obedient to God, with an obedience based on a knowledge of His Word.

ASSURANCE OF MARRIAGE

Boaz was overjoyed at Ruth's request for marriage. He compared her earlier expression of loyal love toward Naomi with her present desire that he would fulfill the role of kinsman-redeemer. He viewed her loyal love toward him as excelling that expressed toward Naomi, since Ruth could have legitimately sought the attention of younger men.

Boaz assured Ruth that he would carry out the responsibility of kinsman-redeemer, understood in the Book of Ruth to include levirate marriage, because the elders of the city "know that you are a woman of noble character" (Ruth 3:11).

Boaz had apparently anticipated fulfilling the role Ruth requested, because he was aware of a potential roadblock—the existence of "a kinsman-redeemer nearer than I" (v. 12). Not wanting to circumvent another man's opportunity to act responsibly, Boaz informed Ruth he would interact with the nearer kinsman as soon as the town gate opened in the morning. If the latter would be unwilling to serve as a kinsman-redeemer, Boaz gave his oath that he would do so.

Boaz instructed Ruth to remain at his feet until morning. Many thoughts must have filled their minds during the sleepless hours as they waited for the dawn.

Boaz arose before sunrise and sent Ruth back to Naomi with "six measures of barley" poured into her shawl (v. 15). Boaz headed for the town gate as Ruth returned to Naomi.

If you were in Boaz's sandals: Would you have exercised moral restraint toward Ruth on the dark Judean hillside? Would you have been willing to sacrifice marriage to Ruth (whom Boaz obviously loved) for the legal rights of the nearer kinsman? The countryside near Bethlehem was the scene of many lessons we need to learn in our modern world.

HE'S AS GOOD AS HIS WORD

After Ruth had met Boaz for the first time, she had returned home to report to Naomi all that had happened to her on that first day of gleaning (Ruth 2:18-22). How much more excited she was to report to her mother-in-law about the outcome of her night on the threshing floor!

Once again, Naomi was the one with the question: "How did it go, my daughter?" (3:16) Ruth's full report left out no detail of the night, for "she told her everything Boaz had done for her" (v. 16), including the gift of barley, which seemed to be meant as a tangible assurance for Naomi that he would indeed be their kinsman-redeemer.

Naomi's next statement indicated her insight into human nature, particularly when a couple is in love! Ruth needed to be patient and sit tight: "Wait, my daughter, until you find out what happens"; that is, when Boaz would meet the nearer kinsman. Boaz, on the other hand, would not rest until the matter was settled (v. 18). Naomi knew that Boaz was as good as his word.

This scene reminds us of the patience (Ruth) and impatience of love (Boaz), the providence of God ("what happens") and the agency of man ("the man will not rest"). It ends with a tension—how will the matter be resolved?

There are times when we become impatient—very impatient, even with God. Like Ruth we need to "sit tight" and wait for action by our Kinsman-Redeemer who, like Boaz, is as good as His word. This does not mean that the Christian life is one of passivity. Ruth demonstrated active and knowledgeable obedience in her encounter with Boaz. Then it was time for her to rest patiently for what he would do for her.

Note carefully: As we read the Word of God and commit ourselves to obey it, God will give us the good sense to have a balance between activity and rest. Both require faith in Him and His promises to us.

ALL TO NO AVAIL?

Boaz had a goal and a plan to achieve that goal. He proceeded to fulfill his sworn oath to Ruth (3:13) according to the customary legal procedures of the day. He assembled a legal judicial body and then put the case before the nearer kinsman-redeemer: "Naomi ... is selling the piece of land that belonged to our brother [i.e., relative] Elimelech. I ... suggest that you buy it.... If you will redeem it, do so. But if you will not, tell me ... [for] I am next in line" (4:3-4).

Since the right to hold property passed through the male line (Num. 27:8-11), it seems odd that Naomi was selling the piece of land belonging to Elimelech. But the Old Testament is silent about the inheritance rights of widows. Apparently, by custom, the property remained in possession of the widow as long as she lived, or she could sell it if in dire need.

If Elimelech had entrusted the use of the land to a friend or relative when he took his family to Moab, that person would have had the right to harvest the crop he had planted in the year Naomi returned to Bethlehem. Now that harvest season had ended, local custom apparently allowed Naomi to proceed with the sale.

As readers who have witnessed the growing romance between Boaz and Ruth, are we suddenly brought to a disappointing climax in the story with the reply of the nearer kinsman, "I will redeem it" (v. 4)? Was the goal of Boaz to remain unachieved? Were his carefully laid plans destined to failure? Did God bring about so many providential events merely to teach disappointment to Ruth and Boaz?

Is it true of you? Similar questions arise in our minds when we face apparent disappointments. But we need to realize that initial disappointments may be God's test of our faith and perseverance. In the case of Boaz, he would use the apparent roadblock to his plan to accomplish his goal of acquiring Ruth.

PERSEVERANCE BRINGS SUCCESS

Florence Chadwick, the first woman to swim the English channel in both directions, set out to be the first woman to swim the twenty-one miles from Catalina Island to the coast of Southern California. She persevered for fifteen hours through bone-chilling cold, increasing fatigue, and dense fog that prevented her from seeing even the boats beside her. She finally gave up and was lifted into one of the boats, only to learn that she was only a half-mile from the shore, invisible because of the fog. She said, "If I could have seen the shore, I might have made it." She was defeated not by the cold or even the fatigue, but by the fog, which obscured her goal.

Boaz did not give up when his goal was obscured by the willingness of the nearer kinsman to be the redeemer. He persevered with his plan to inform the man, "On the day you buy the land from Naomi and from Ruth the Moabitess, you acquire the dead man's widow, in order to maintain the name of the dead with his property" (Ruth 4:5).

That levirate function was not agreeable to the kinsman. So he immediately responded, "Then I cannot redeem it because I might endanger my own estate. You redeem it yourself" (v. 6). Boaz must have been delighted that God had blessed his plan to accomplish his goal.

For you: The Word of God provides many goals for Christians. One of those goals is to become more conformed to the image of Christ (Rom. 12:2; 2 Cor. 3:18). We must not let "the world or anything . . . in the world—the cravings of sinful man, the lust of his eyes and the boasting of what he has and does" (1 John 2:15-16) create a fog that obscures our goal of being transformed into the image of Christ.

BAREFOOT KINSMAN

Boaz had called a legal town meeting, demonstrating his commitment to righteousness and proper legal procedures. Since the nearer kinsman did not display much knowledge of Naomi's situation, Boaz probably could have gone ahead and functioned as kinsman-redeemer without the legal proceeding. But Boaz was committed to act justly. That also was an act of divine providence, for the legal line to King David was of no small importance.

After the near kinsman declined to act as redeemer, "he removed his sandal" (Ruth 4:8), for the legal surrender of the right of redemption was symbolized when "one party took off his sandal and gave it to the other" (v. 7; see Deut. 25:7-10).

Boaz attested his legal acceptance of the rights and responsibilities of kinsman-redeemer by calling on the witnesses present: "Today you are witnesses that I have bought from Naomi all the property of Elimelech, Kilion, and Mahlon. I have also acquired Ruth the Moabitess, Mahlon's widow, as my wife, in order to maintain the name of the dead with his property, so that his name will not disappear from among his family or from the town records. Today you are witnesses!" (vv. 9-10).

The purpose of the witnesses was to notarize the oral transaction. No money changed hands since the property had not been purchased by another party when Elimelech left Bethlehem. Through this transaction Boaz acquired all and any property that had belonged to Elimelech or his sons; he also acquired the right and responsibility to marry Ruth (see v. 13) and to convey to their firstborn son the right to inherit all Elimelech's property in the name of his father, Mahlon.

For today: Boaz's commitment to following prescribed legal procedures is commendable. In a lawless age, when legal procedures are often used by those who think their rights have been violated, we should be people of integrity.

BLESSING ON RUTH, BOAZ, AND THEIR DESCENDANTS

Most of today's young adults seem committed to limiting the number of children born in each family. The culture and economy of the ancient Near East made large families desirable, for many children meant a larger work force in earning the family livelihood. Thus marriage, family, and children were highly significant in biblical narratives.

When Boaz accepted the legal responsibility to marry Ruth and provide an heir to Elimelech's estate, the elders and people who witnessed the transaction offered a spontaneous blessing on Ruth, Boaz, and their descendants.

The blessing on Ruth was that she would be fertile like Rachel and Leah, the wives of Jacob who, with their maidservants, were the founding mothers of the twelve tribes of Israel. Marriage to Boaz was the final step in granting to Ruth full membership in the covenant community of Israel.

The blessing on Boaz was that he might "have standing in Ephrathah [another name for Bethlehem] and be famous in Bethlehem" (Ruth 4:11). Such prosperity was, no doubt, related to Ruth's fertility, for many children produced greater family wealth and respect.

The blessing transcended Boaz's immediate children to his "family" (v. 12), his line of descendants who were envisioned as being like those of "Perez, whom Tamar bore to Judah" (v. 12). The family of Perez was the clan from which Boaz and most of the people of Bethlehem descended. The comparison of Ruth to Tamar is striking, for both were foreigners whose family line was threatened with extinction. And both are included in the genealogy of Jesus Christ (Matt. 1:3-5).

Ponder: Though our culture may favor some limitation on the size of our families, the general decadence of moral values makes it all the more important for us to place high biblical priorities on marriage, children, and family life.

A CHILD IS BORN IN BETHLEHEM

Two months ago we were thinking of Jesus' birth in Bethlehem. Under normal circumstances Jesus would have been born in Nazareth in Galilee, far to the north of Bethlehem in Judea. But in the providence of God, Caesar Augustus issued a decree for a census that required Joseph and Mary to travel to Bethlehem because that was the hometown of their ancestor David. Of course, Matthew recorded Jesus' birth in Bethlehem as the fulfillment of prophecy (Matt. 2:5-6; cf. Micah 5:2).

Neither Jesus nor his ancestor David would have been born in Bethlehem if their ancestor Obed (David's grandfather) had not been born in Bethlehem to Ruth and Boaz. And that is just what happened, for "Boaz took Ruth and she became his wife. And the Lord enabled her to conceive, and she gave birth to a son" (Ruth 4:13).

We do not know why Ruth and Mahlon, who were married about ten years before Mahlon died (1:4-5), did not have any children. Nor do we know the age of Ruth; the Bethlehemites obviously regarded her as child-bearing age, and the "elders" of the town viewed her as a "young woman" (4:12). In any case, she must have had some uncertainty about her ability to bear a child. But God was accomplishing His purpose ("the Lord enabled her to conceive," 4:13), and Ruth gave birth to a boy she named Obed.

The providence of God, active in the births of two special babies in Bethlehem, is also active in our lives today. The God who "holds the little tiny baby in His hands" is in charge of where we (or our children) were born. And where we will die. Or perhaps where (and when) our child has died. God is in control of all life's activities from birth to death.

Also in the spiritual realm: He is the agent of our new birth into His family, and the director of those things He allows in our lives to mold us and make us more like His Son. Let us rejoice and praise Him for His sovereign care and direction in all He does.

NAOMI AGAIN REFLECTED HER NAME

When Naomi returned to Bethlehem from Moab, she was greeted by women who exclaimed, "Can this be Naomi [Pleasant]?" (Ruth 1:19). Her response was "Call me Mara [Bitter], because the Almighty has made my life very bitter" (v. 20).

Contrast that scene with the rejoicing by the women when Naomi's grandson was born: "Praise be to the Lord, who this day has not left you without a kinsman-redeemer. May he become famous through Israel! He will renew your life and sustain you in your old age. For your daughter-in-law, who loves you and is better to you than seven sons, has given him birth" (4:14-15).

Naomi had attributed her misfortune in Moab to the Lord. Now the women attributed Naomi's good fortune to the Lord. She had returned from Moab empty. Now she was being made full. She was no longer bitter, she was Naomi.

Though Boaz was the kinsman-redeemer who acted on behalf of Naomi and Ruth, the women called the child Naomi's kinsman-redeemer because he would sustain her in her old age. The wish that he would "become famous throughout Israel" (v. 14) was certainly fulfilled when Obed's grandson David became king.

Earlier when Ruth arrived in Bethlehem with Naomi, the women of the city apparently paid her little regard. But now they lavished praise on her by saying she was better to Naomi than "seven sons" (v. 15), for "seven sons" was proverbial for a perfect family.

A reason to rejoice: The covenant faithfulness of the Sovereign God transformed Naomi from weeping to rejoicing, from emptiness to fullness, and from destitution to deliverance. God is still faithful today in lifting His wayward children from spiritual destitution and emptiness to spiritual fullness and blessing. Let us daily praise Him for that work in our lives.

ASK ME ABOUT MY GRANDBABY!

Asked if she had yet made a long trip to visit her son and his new wife, a woman replied, "No, I've been waiting until they have their new baby." When her friend thought the delay was to save money, she explained, "No, it isn't that. You see, I have a theory that grandmothers are more welcome than mothers-in-law."

Ruth and Boaz were no doubt delighted in their new baby. And Naomi was certainly welcome to lavish her love on her grandson. Like any doting grandmother, Naomi "took the child, laid him in her lap, and cared for him" (Ruth 4:16).

Because of his special legal status as the heir of Elimelech and Mahlon, the neighbors said, "Naomi has a son" (v. 17). She no doubt treated him as her own son. In fact, the childcare that Naomi provided may have been on a more or less permanent basis. Ruth may have given Obed over to Naomi to raise as her own son, for he was the legal heir to the estate of Elimelech.

The name given to the child was Obed, meaning "servant," perhaps in anticipation of the comfort he would be to Naomi in her old age.

Naomi found in her grandson Obed all that she had lost in Moab. In fact, she gained more than she lost, for she was back in Bethlehem with joyful family surroundings and a secure future.

Compare: That situation is like our condition as sinners lost in Adam and then redeemed in Christ. God the Father has not only restored to believers all that we lost in Adam, but He has also given us so much more through our position in Christ. Through the grace He has bestowed on us, we have forgiveness for the past, joy for the present, and security for the future. What a cause for rejoicing!

LINKED TO ROYALTY

A genealogist in London, who noticed the large number of Americans trying to trace their British ancestors, said, "Often they're elderly people without relations who want to recreate a sense of family feeling by learning about their forebears."

Biblical genealogies also recreated a sense of family continuity over the generations. The genealogy found in Ruth 4:18-21 is more significant than an appendix tacked onto the end of the book. It forms a literary and historical bridge connecting Israel's patriarchal past with her monarchical future. Moreover, it is a connecting link between Abraham, "God's friend" (James 2:23), and David, "a man after [God's] own heart" (1 Sam. 13:14; Acts 13:22). The genealogy is a key to unlock the theological significance of God's providential dealings in the story of Ruth—to provide a godly ancestry for David the king.

Thus the story of redemption in the Book of Ruth is a logical link between the Abrahamic Covenant, in which God promised to Abraham a land and a people, and the Davidic Covenant, in which God promised to David a dynastic succession or line of descendants that culminated in Jesus Christ, and an everlasting throne and kingdom.

The genealogy is selective, listing only ten generations in the period of about 800 years from Perez the son of Tamar (Gen. 38:27-30) to David. The inclusion of Boaz, the natural father of Obed, may seem peculiar since Obed was the legal son of Mahlon. Perhaps the narrator was stressing God's grace to Boaz as well as to Ruth.

Inclusion in the line to David meant inclusion in the line to Jesus Christ. How fitting that Boaz, the kinsman-redeemer of Naomi and Ruth, was reckoned in the line to the Kinsman-Redeemer of all mankind. More important than the *feeling* of belonging to a physical family is that of *belonging* to the family of God with other believers as our brothers and sisters.

For us: Let's recognize that spiritual kinship because of what Christ has done for us.

LESSONS FROM THE BOOK OF RUTH

The story of Ruth has taught us many lessons—lessons revolving around God and His people, His promises, and His providence.

An important truth running through the Bible is God's plan to bless both the physical and spiritual descendants of Abraham. The promise of blessing on Abraham's physical descendants relates to the nation Israel. The promise of blessing to Abraham's spiritual descendants extends to all nations of the earth. Ruth was an example of God's blessing extending beyond the borders of Israel. God chose to include her in the line leading to Abraham's ultimate descendant, Jesus Christ, who is the agent of the blessing to all nations. Thus Ruth was a link in God's chain from Abraham to Christ to bring worldwide blessing.

That line to Christ in which Ruth was a link also passed through David, because God purposed that Christ would be the son of David, one who would rule on David's throne over a restored physical national Israel in a future period of divine blessing on the earth.

The hiddenness of God's providence is highlighted in the story of Ruth. He worked mostly behind the scenes to use selected people and events to accomplish His purpose.

At the heart of the narrative of Ruth is the concept of redemption. Boaz illustrated the functions of a kinsman-redeemer and also exemplified the godliness, grace, and love later manifested in *the* Kinsman-Redeemer, the Lord Jesus Christ.

Of the many practical lessons in Ruth, that of friendship stands out. Ruth's devotion to Naomi and Naomi's concern for Ruth frame a beautiful tapestry of feelings and events.

A suggestion: Read the Book of Ruth again, and make changes in your life to reflect the grace and glory found in that delightful story.

March

Devotional readings on the life of David
based on portions of 1 & 2 Samuel and 1 Kings
by F. Duane Lindsey

MAN LOOKS ON THE OUTWARD APPEARANCE

God sent Samuel, his chosen kingmaker, to anoint Saul as king of all Israel (1 Sam. 10:1). When Saul was introduced publicly as king, "he was a head taller than any of the others" (v. 23), so Samuel affirmed, "There is no one like him among all the people" (v. 24). But later, when Saul disobeyed the command of the Lord at Gilgal, Samuel informed him that the Lord would replace him with "a man after His own heart" (13:14; see also 15:1-11).

Eventually God sent Samuel from Ramah to Bethlehem, to the house of Jesse, a grandson of Ruth and Boaz. As Jesse paraded his seven stately sons before Samuel, the man of God may have been impressed, like he had once been with Saul, but the prophet said, "The Lord has not chosen these" (16:10). Finally David was brought in from the shepherd's fields, and Samuel "anointed him in the presence of his brothers" (v. 13). Though David had "a fine appearance and handsome features" (v. 12), God's choice of David was not based on outward appearance, for "the Lord looks at the heart" (v. 7). God's choice of David was based on inner qualities, such as faith in Him, a quality later demonstrated by David.

Has it occurred to you? Rightly or wrongly we are often judged by others on the basis of appearance. The impressions we make on another person can be used by God as a lever to open a door for the Gospel to penetrate his or her heart. How we appear in conduct can also turn someone off from hearing our verbal message. Unloving behavior can easily lead another to reject our claims about the love of God. So appearances are not to be ignored, but God's Word places the emphasis on matters of the heart — "love, joy, peace, patience, kindness, goodness, faithfulness, gentleness, and self-control" (Gal. 5:22-23). Are you reflecting these inner qualities?

"WELL DONE!"

The Lord had endowed Saul with His Spirit to enable him to serve as leader over His people Israel. In disobeying the Lord, Saul had rejected Him as the ultimate King of Israel. So God rejected Saul as the earthly leader of His people. Along with that rejection "the Spirit of the Lord ... departed from Saul" (1 Sam. 16:14). That departure apparently coincided with the anointing of David, since "from that day on the Spirit of the Lord came upon David in power" (v. 13). To fill the vacuum left by the Spirit's departure from Saul, the Lord allowed "an evil spirit" to torment him (v. 14). Saul's subsequent fits of depression and rage demonstrated his lack of fitness to serve as king of Israel.

Saul's importunity, however, was David's opportunity. Among the many skills David had developed as a shepherd boy was that of playing a harp, or lyre. When Saul requested his attendants to "find someone who plays well" (v. 17), one of them immediately thought of David. So David entered the service of Saul. Whenever Saul was depressed, "David would take his harp and play. Then relief would come to Saul" (v. 23). Also "David became one of his armor-bearers" (v. 21).

God used David's gifts and skills as an entree for placing David in the royal court of Saul. David had already been faithful in developing his gifts in the humble role of a shepherd boy. God was providing an enlarged opportunity for him to prepare to shepherd the flock of God's people.

Think about it: We too need to be faithful in exercising the gifts and opportunities God gives us where we are. We will then be like the servant to whom the master said, "Well done, good and faithful servant! You have been faithful with a few things; I will put you in charge of many things" (Matt. 25:23).

A PROMISE OF REWARD

The youngest son of Jesse may have had abilities that qualified him for service in the court of Saul; but could he demonstrate the fearless military leadership needed to shelter Israel from its aggressive neighbors? A Philistine intrusion into the Valley of Elah (located in the fertile foothills between the coastal plain where the Philistines dwelt and the mountainous heartland of Judah) gave David an unexpected opportunity to demonstrate his military prowess.

Single combats between selected warriors often decided battles in ancient times (cf. 2 Sam. 2:12-17). The Philistines had a hero well-suited for such conflict. Goliath was nearly ten feet tall, was protected by a bronze helmet and armor weighing about 125 pounds, and wielded a huge spear with an iron point that weighed over fifteen pounds.

As a reward to motivate an Israelite warrior to face Goliath, Saul promised great wealth, the hand of his daughter in marriage, and a family tax exemption to anyone who would kill Goliath.

David, returning from a leave from Saul's court to tend his father's sheep, appraised the situation and regarded the Philistine champion's challenge as defiance against the God of Israel. David convinced Saul that "the Lord who delivered me from the paw of the lion and the paw of the bear will deliver me from the hand of this Philistine" (1 Sam. 17:37). David's motivation was not personal reward but the honor and glory of the Lord God of Israel.

Consider this: God has promised Christians a number of specific rewards, or victor's crowns (cf. 1 Thess. 2:19; 2 Tim. 4:8). However, our service in spiritual warfare for Jesus Christ should not be motivated by reward but by love for Him and a desire to bring honor and glory to God. After all, like the twenty-four elders, believers in heaven will not keep their rewards but will "lay their crowns before the throne" as an act of praise to the Lord God who is worthy "to receive glory and honor and power" (Rev. 4:10-11).

THE BATTLE IS THE LORD'S

When David requested permission to represent Israel in the battle with Goliath, Saul gave David his permission, his blessing, and his armor. David tried on Saul's armor and sword. He gracefully declined to use them: "I cannot go in these . . . because I am not used to them" (1 Sam. 17:39). Because Saul was unusually tall, his armor must have been much too large for David.

David was much more comfortable with his shepherd's staff and his sling, for which he "chose five smooth stones from the stream" (v. 40). As David approached him, Goliath despised and ridiculed David, "cursed David by his gods" (v. 43), and threatened to give his "flesh to the birds of the air and the beasts of the field!" (v. 44) David fearlessly out-threatened Goliath by announcing he would "give the carcasses of the Philistine army to the birds of the air and the beasts of the earth [so that] the whole world will know that there is a God in Israel . . . for the battle is the Lord's, and He will give all of you into our hands" (vv. 46-47).

Though David was depending on the Lord and not on weapons, it should be noted that the sling was a formidable weapon in ancient warfare. For example, a fighting unit of 700 Benjamite slingmen "could sling a stone at a hair and not miss" (Jud. 20:16). As David approached Goliath, swinging the stone in his sling faster and faster, he released one string of the sling, causing the stone to hurl at great velocity directly at Goliath's unprotected forehead. As David next decapitated the fallen Philistine with his own sword, the aroused Israelite army routed the Philistine army.

It's a fact: "The battle is the Lord's" is equally true in spiritual warfare, for we must "be strong in the Lord and in His mighty power" (Eph. 6:10) to overcome the spiritual Goliaths under the command of Satan.

THE JEOPARDY OF JEALOUSY

From the day David killed Goliath, he remained full time in the service of Saul. David seems to have been one of those persons whom people either loved or hated. The problem, from Saul's viewpoint, was that everyone loved David, even his own son Jonathan.

David was such a successful warrior that at first Saul admired him greatly and "gave him a high rank in the army" (1 Sam. 18:5). The people thought highly of David and the women sang, "Saul has slain his thousands, and David his tens of thousands" (v. 7). The comparison displeased Saul, who from that day "kept a jealous eye on David" (v. 9).

The next day Saul made two attempts on David's life by trying to pin David to the wall with his spear "while David was playing the harp" (v. 10) to pacify Saul. Still hoping to do away with David, Saul offered his daughter Michal in marriage to David in exchange for a military exploit against the Philistines. David's success dashed the hopes of Saul, who then "realized that the Lord was with David and that his daughter Michal loved David" (v. 28). So "Saul became more afraid of him and . . . remained his enemy the rest of his days" (v. 29).

Saul's behavior illustrates the destructive effects of jealousy. His initial admiration for David gave way to fear and jealousy, which promoted anger and attempted murder. Only God's providential protection of David spared his life.

Thought for today: Hopefully you have not tried to murder anyone. But even the anger promoted by jealousy (the fear of being replaced) was viewed by Jesus as a form of murder. Just as "anyone who murders will be subject to judgment," so also will "anyone who is angry with his brother" (Matt. 5:21-22). Let's stamp out the sparks of jealousy before they turn to anger. That requires dependence on God, for "the acts of the sinful nature" that include jealousy can be replaced only by "the fruit of the Spirit" that includes love (Gal. 5:20, 22).

A HELPING HAND

When "David met with more [military] success than the rest of Saul's officers, and his name became well known," Saul issued the command to "Jonathan and all the attendants to kill David" (1 Sam. 18:30; 19:1). Though Saul's enmity against David became more blatant, Jonathan's friendship toward David became more courageous. Jonathan warned David about Saul's intent. He also successfully interceded for David before Saul, who took an oath that David would not be put to death.

Of course that oath was forgotten by Saul the next time David repeated his military exploits. Saul was again jealous, and for the third time he drove his spear into the wall as "David eluded him" (19:10).

David fled to his home where, during the night, his wife Michal helped him escape from her father's men who were sent to capture David. David fled to Samuel in Naioth at Ramah, where Samuel apparently directed a school of prophets. Three times Saul sent men to capture David, but each time Saul's men began to prophesy. When Saul himself finally went to seek David, he too began to prophesy. This event was rumored among the people so that the saying spread about, "Is Saul also among the prophets?" (v. 24)

Three times David's agility delivered him from the murderous spear of Saul. But then he began to experience the help of others in escaping Saul's enmity. Jonathan warned him and interceded for him. Michal manipulated his escape by night. Finally God miraculously protected him by placing the spirit of prophecy in Saul and his soldiers. David was forced to learn the lesson of dependence on others, especially dependence on God.

Consider this: In our spiritual conflicts we must learn to depend on other Christians who can help us escape the devices of the devil. Most of all we must learn to depend on God, to "be strong in the Lord and in His mighty power," so that we will "stand against the devil's schemes" (Eph. 6:10-11).

A FRIEND IN NEED

Jonathan had proved to be David's friend. He had pledged his love, loyalty, and allegiance to David by giving him "the robe he was wearing . . . along with his tunic, and even his sword, his bow, and his belt" (1 Sam. 18:4). He had interceded for David and "spoke well of David to Saul his father" (19:4). So David fled to Jonathan for advice and encouragement in his time of persecution. Jonathan reaffirmed his "covenant with the house of David" (20:16). Also he agreed to test his father's attitude toward David's absence from court during "the New Moon festival" (v. 5). When Saul hurled his spear at Jonathan to kill him for protecting David, Jonathan realized that his father would not be dissuaded from seeking David's life.

Two days later David waited by a large stone in a designated field. Jonathan came to the field as though for archery practice. Then he shot an arrow beyond the boy picking up arrows, a prearranged signal to David that he should flee because Saul indeed planned to kill him. But David felt he must risk saying good-bye to Jonathan, so the experienced and hardened warriors "kissed each other and wept together" (v. 41). And then David departed as Jonathan said to him, "Go in peace, for we have sworn friendship with each other in the name of the Lord, saying, 'The Lord is witness between you and me, and between your descendants and my descendants forever' " (v. 42).

What about it? Do you know a person who, like David, has been wrongfully mistreated? Have you, like Jonathan, sacrificed your own interests to defend and affirm that person? Jonathan's friendship to David was one that he knew would cost him dearly, perhaps even his own life. Are you willing to enter into friendships like that of Jonathan and David "in the name of the Lord" (v. 42)? Begin today to seek a relationship that will lead to that kind of friendship.

A LITTLE WHITE LIE?

David's flight from Saul took him south to Nob, on Mount Scopus just north of Jerusalem. David deceived the priest Ahimelech by saying he was on a secret mission for the king. Ahimelech's cooperation with David would later cost him and many others their lives. Ahimelech gave David food (the consecrated "bread of the Presence" that was normally eaten by the priests [1 Sam. 21:6]) and "the sword of Goliath the Philistine" (v. 9).

Then David left the kingdom of Saul and sought asylum in the Philistine city of Gath. It seemed foolhardy for David to enter the hometown of Goliath with that hero's sword swinging at his side! He was immediately recognized and captured by the Philistines. He had to pretend insanity (another deception) to facilitate his exit from the city.

David escaped to the cave of Adullam, about 10 miles southeast of Gath, where his brothers visited him, and his band of fugitives increased to about 400 men. David then took his parents east of the Dead Sea to a city in Moab (the homeland of David's ancestor Ruth) where they would be safe from Saul's persecution. David sought refuge in "the stronghold" (22:4), possibly Masada, towering 1,320 feet above the eastern shore of the Dead Sea. At the Prophet Gad's advice, he "went to the forest of Hereth" in the land of Judah several miles southeast of Adullam (v. 5).

Think it over: We sometimes feel like we have been hounded by our enemies and isolated from our friends. We may feel that everyone and everything is against us, and then we may resort to some scheme for survival. Like David, we may lie to others, or resort to some other "little sin" to aid our survival. But David's "little white lie" had disastrous effects for the village of Nob. Regardless of the outward effects of deception, it is sin against God. "Do not lie to each other" (Col. 3:9).

A ROOT OF BITTERNESS

As Saul continued to harbor bitterness in his heart against David, he complained to his officials about their lack of cooperation in capturing David. Saul's head shepherd (cf. 1 Sam. 21:7), Doeg the Edomite, seized the opportunity to ingratiate himself with Saul. He came forward and reported that he saw the priest Ahimelech give "provisions and the sword of Goliath the Philistine to David" (22:10).

Saul then accused Ahimelech of conspiracy and ordered the execution of his entire village. When Saul's "officials were not willing to raise a hand to strike the priests of the Lord" (v. 17), Doeg the Edomite willingly obeyed Saul's command to do so. He killed eighty-five priests, along with the inhabitants of Nob, "its men and women, its children and infants, and all its cattle, donkeys, and sheep" (vv. 18-19).

Saul had once failed to destroy completely the Amalekites and all their livestock (15:1-26). For that reason the Lord rejected him as king over Israel (v. 27). In contrast, through Doeg, Saul did completely destroy the priests of the Lord and the other inhabitants of Nob. That incident seems to indicate that Saul's growing bitterness was not only against David but also against the Lord. Saul had disobeyed God and refused to honor the man whom God chose to replace him. In spite of many opportunities for repentance, any changes in Saul were temporary. He seemed driven to keep his appointment with divine judgment.

Abiathar, a son of Ahimelech, was the sole survivor of the attack on Nob. He "escaped and fled to join David," who accepted responsibility for the deaths of Abiathar's whole family (22:20, 22).

Sad to say: There are times when some professing believers seem bent on destroying the work of God rather than attacking the strongholds of Satan. When God chastens us for disobedience, we must allow that discipline to drive us to repentance. Let us confess and forsake any bitterness toward God or other believers, and take positive steps to obey God and to promote godly living.

A FRIEND CLOSER THAN A BROTHER

Still avoiding Saul, David delivered the Judean city of Keilah (located just south of Adullam on the eastern edge of the hill country) from Philistine raids on its threshing floors. Saul learned David's location and gathered his army "to go down to Keilah to besiege David and his men" (1 Sam. 23:8). The Lord revealed to David that the ungrateful Keilites would surrender him to Saul. So David moved southeast, beyond Hebron, and "stayed in the desert strongholds and in the hills of the Desert of Ziph" (v. 14)

Saul again pursued David, but Jonathan found David and "helped him find strength in God" (v. 16). During this last recorded meeting with David, he encouraged him and reminded him, "You will be king over Israel, and I will be second to you. Even my father Saul knows this" (v. 17).

Meanwhile the people of Ziph plotted to betray David into Saul's hands. David fled southward to the Desert of Maon, with Saul in pursuit. Just as Saul was closing in on him (with only a mountain ridge separating them), a messenger informed Saul of a Philistine attack; so, in the providence of God, Saul had to cease his pursuit of David to fight the Philistines.

Jonathan stands out in Scripture as an example of a faithful friend. He set aside his natural rights (as Saul's heir to the throne) and recognized God's choice of David to be the next king of all Israel. When others showed ingratitude or treachery toward David, Jonathan continued to manifest loyalty and love toward the man he had chosen to serve.

Consider this: Jesus Christ, the Son of David, was chosen by God to rule on the throne of David forever. Jesus said to His disciples, "You are My friends if you do what I command. . . . This is My command: Love each other" (John 15:14, 17). Are we obedient to that command, or do we treat one another with ingratitude and even treachery? Let's demonstrate sacrificial love to other believers today.

HONOR TO WHOM HONOR IS DUE

When he finished pursuing the Philistines, Saul again took up his pursuit of David. He learned of David's presence in the Desert of En Gedi. En Gedi is an oasis at the edge of the cliffs overlooking the western shore of the Dead Sea. Saul took 3,000 of his best troops and looked for David with his 600 valiant followers "near the Crags of the Wild Goats" (1 Sam. 24:2).

In the providence of God, Saul selected the same cave in which David was hiding as a place "to relieve himself" (v. 3). When David's men asked him to attack Saul, he crept up behind Saul, but merely "cut off a corner of Saul's robe" (v. 4). "Afterward, David was conscience-stricken" for cutting Saul's robe, because Saul was "the Lord's anointed" (v. 6).

Saul left the cave, but shortly he heard David call out behind him. "Look at this piece of your robe in my hand! I cut off the corner of your robe but did not kill you. . . . May the Lord avenge the wrongs you have done to me, but my hand will not touch you" (vv. 11-12). Saul recognized David's righteous behavior, and he confessed, "I know that you will surely be king and that the kingdom of Israel will be established in your hands" (v. 20). David agreed to a request by Saul to preserve Saul's family and his family name. So Saul temporarily repented from pursuing David's life.

Think about it: Showing respect to God-ordained civil leaders was not limited to Old Testament times. Paul urged prayer, intercession, and thanksgiving for "all those in authority" (1 Tim. 2:2) and pointed out that "it is necessary to submit to the authorities" (Rom. 13:5). Too often Christians show disrespect for leaders with whom they disagree.

A FOOL IN HIS FOLLY

After the death of Samuel (1 Sam. 25:1), David protected the flocks of Nabal, a wealthy herdsman of Maon. When David sent men to collect their wages, Nabal (whose name means "fool") lived up to his name by refusing payment, even denying that he knew David.

David took 400 men to collect his just wages from Nabal, but he was met on the way by Abigail, Nabal's wise, intelligent, and beautiful wife. Acting to spare bloodshed, she said, "Nabal . . . is just like his name—his name is Fool, and folly goes with him" (v. 25). Abigail confessed Nabal's wrong action and made restitution to David. She affirmed that "the Lord will certainly make a lasting dynasty" for David "because he fights the Lord's battles" (v. 28). Using two comparisons (binding valuables in a protective bundle, and hurling a stone from a sling), Abigail affirmed David's destiny—"the life of [David] will be bound securely in the bundle of the living by the Lord your God. But the lives of your enemies He will hurl away as from the pocket of a sling" (v. 29).

David praised her good judgment and accepted her request and her payment. He told her to "go home in peace" (v. 35). There she found Nabal in a drunken stupor. Later, when she told him all she had done, he apparently became so angry that he had a stroke from which he died ten days later.

David responded to Nabal's death by ascribing to the Lord the bringing of "Nabal's wrongdoing down on his own head" (v. 39). Also he asked Abigail to become his wife, a request to which she responded without delay.

Think it over: An instructive lesson for us is attached to each person in this story. Nabal demonstrated the hardening effect of a morally foolish life. Abigail, by contrast, showed the healing effect of wise and righteous action. And David became the object of God's loving care by being providentially prevented from taking vengeance on Nabal. We should learn repentance, faith, and patience in adversity from this story.

BROKEN PROMISES

Saul's repentance about killing David did not last, and so he sought David in the Desert of Ziph. David and Abishai (Joab's brother) sneaked into the center of Saul's camp at night. They found Saul asleep with "his spear stuck in the ground near his head" (1 Sam. 26:7). When Abishai requested permission of David to kill Saul with his own spear, David told him not to "lay a hand on the Lord's anointed" (v. 9), since "the Lord Himself will strike him; either his time will come and he will die, or he will go into battle and perish" (v. 10).

"So David took the spear and water jug near Saul's head" (v. 12), and they slipped out of the camp without awakening anyone. Then David stood on a hill some distance away and called out to mock Abner, Saul's captain, for allowing someone to infiltrate the camp and take Saul's spear and water jug. Saul recognized David's voice and said, "I have sinned. . . . I have acted like a fool and have erred greatly." He praised David's righteous actions in sparing his life, and promised, "I will not try to harm you again" (v. 21). The Philistines kept Saul too busy to break that promise, until David's affirmation came true that "Saul will go into battle and perish" (v. 10). David's decision to "escape to the land of the Philistines" (27:1) also prevented Saul from chasing him again.

A matter to consider: When others break their promises to us, especially time after time, we usually stamp "untrustworthy" across their foreheads, and cease to give them the benefit of the doubt. Though David distrusted Saul personally, he continued to respect and treat him with dignity. In our relationships, such as between husband and wife or parent and child, we need to manifest patience and respect similar to what David showed toward Saul.

TRIBULATION PRODUCES PATIENCE

David really didn't trust Saul, even after his recent promise not to harm David. So David went to the Philistine city of Gath with his 600 men and their families. He entered into an agreement with its king, Achish, whereby David would serve him, and he would give David the city of Ziklag for his small army.

During the sixteen months David lived in Ziklag, he led his men on raids against the Geshurites, the Girzites, and the Amalekites. Those peoples, living in the Negev, the area surrounding Beersheba south of the hill country, were enemies of Israel. Though Achish thought David was serving him and destroying Israelites on his raids, David was actually destroying the enemies of Israel. Thus he was getting a "head start" on his future responsibilities as king. He was also capturing property to distribute among cities in Judah to gain their allegiance in anticipation of his becoming king.

Even before Samuel anointed David to be Israel's future king, God had been preparing David for the task of leading His people Israel. As a shepherd boy he learned to trust the Lord for provision and protection. As a servant and soldier in the court of Saul, he learned royal and military affairs. As a fugitive fleeing in the wilderness from Saul, he learned survival tactics, leadership qualities, and continued respect for authority. As a vassal of Achish, he learned the geography of the Philistine plain and began destroying the enemies of Israel. In all that, David was learning the lesson of patience as he waited for God's timing to place him on the throne.

Is it your need? Sometimes the lessons God desires to teach us before we can enter a position of service to Him are many and varied. Inevitably patience is one of the lessons we all need to learn. Fortunately patience is included in the fruit of the Spirit (Gal. 5:22). Let us live by the Spirit so that the fruit of the Spirit will be manifest in us.

GOD'S PROVIDENCE AND PLANS

While Saul consulted the medium of Endor because of his fears about the forthcoming battle with the Philistines (1 Sam. 28:3-25), David's army was incorporated into Achish's army to fight with the Philistines against Israel (28:1-2; 29:1-2). But the other Philistine rulers refused to allow David's men to accompany them lest they turn and fight on the side of Israel. So in the providence of God, David was viewed as reliable by Achish, yet he was excused from entering a battle that would have shown his true loyalty to Israel.

David's men returned home to discover that the Amalekites had burned Ziklag and captured all their families. David's men were ready to stone him, but he "found strength in the Lord his God" (30:6). David was assured by God that they should pursue the Amalekites, and they would recover all that had been lost. Because of exhaustion, 200 of David's men could not cross the Besor Ravine, but the other 400 continued the pursuit. After they defeated the unsuspecting Amalekites, they recovered everything that had been taken as well as plunder that belonged to the Amalekites. When they met the 200 men who were too exhausted to complete the pursuit, some of David's men said, "We will not share with them the plunder we recovered" (v. 22). However, David established a precedent for future Israelite policy: "The share of the man who stayed with the supplies is to be the same as that of him who went down to the battle. All will share alike" (v. 24). David also sent some of the plunder to the elders of Israel in areas "where David and his men had roamed" (v. 31).

Seek to find: God helped David avoid a battle and strengthened him to win a battle. We need to seek God's will, as David did, about undertaking tasks that appear necessary. God might have had other plans for David than chasing the Amalekites. David was open to God's guidance and at the appropriate time he received victory from the Lord.

A LIFE OF DISOBEDIENCE

Three days after David defeated the Amalekites, news reached Ziklag about the victory of the Philistines and the deaths of Saul and Jonathan. The Amalekite warrior who reported to David was apparently a mercenary who fought for the Israelites on Mount Gilboa. He claimed that he killed the dying king Saul at his request. As proof of his story, he gave Saul's crown and arm band to David.

David took him at his word (which was probably a fabrication in expectation of reward), and had him executed (2 Sam. 1:15). Actually, after Saul was wounded critically, he "took his own sword and fell on it" (1 Sam. 31:4). Then his "armor-bearer saw that Saul was dead" (v. 5).

David and his men tore their clothes and "mourned and wept and fasted till evening for Saul and his son Jonathan" (2 Sam. 1:12). David composed a lament psalm called the "lament of the bow" (v. 18) to be taught to the men of Judah in remembrance of Saul and Jonathan.

In highly poetic language, David's lament commemorated the deaths of Saul and Jonathan on Mount Gilboa. He called on the "daughters of Israel [to] weep for Saul" (v. 24), while he grieved for Jonathan as a brother.

Instead of rejoicing that Saul who treated him as an enemy was dead, David mourned Saul's passing as a great leader. Yet there was a sense in which Saul's death was long overdue. Saul's life was characterized by disobedience to God. In the process of God's patient dealings with him, Saul had rejected many opportunities for repentance.

What can I learn? Disobedience to God's Word is always a temptation we face as Christians. We need to commit ourselves in advance to obeying God's Word. Then, as situations arise to test our commitment, we should obey Him in dependence on the Spirit of God. When we do disobey, we should go to God for forgiveness and cleansing (1 John 1:9). Saul's example is a negative one we must avoid.

CONFLICT BEFORE VICTORY

At the direction of the Lord, David and his men moved their families from Ziklag and took up residence in Hebron, which was centrally located in Judah on the ridge route in the hill country. People came from all over Judah to Hebron where "they anointed David king over the house of Judah" (2 Sam. 2:4). David ruled from Hebron over Judah for seven and one-half years, and Joab was the commander of his army.

Meanwhile Saul's son Ish-bosheth had been crowned king over the rest of Israel, and Abner was the commander of his army. The two armies met at the pool of Gibeon, located north of Jerusalem on the Benjamin plateau. In another example of ancient warfare by selected warriors, they counted off twelve men from each army who engaged in a conflict that ended in a draw—twenty-four casualties! Thus the full armies had to engage in combat and "the men of Israel were defeated by David's men" (v. 17).

During the battle Joab's brother Asahel was killed by Ish-bosheth's commander, Abner. Eventually Abner called for a cessation of battle and "Joab blew the trumpet, and all the men came to a halt; they no longer pursued Israel" (v. 28). David's men were back in Hebron by daybreak the next morning. But Joab looked forward to settling the score with Abner for killing his brother Asahel. The war between the opposing armies "lasted a long time. David grew stronger and stronger, while the house of Saul grew weaker and weaker" (3:1).

Remember this: Change for the good does not always take place all at once. Seven years of conflict passed before David was crowned king over all Israel. In spiritual warfare that we experience there is often a period of conflict before "the acts of the sinful nature" are replaced by "the fruit of the Spirit" (Gal. 5:16-23). To achieve the desired victory in that conflict, "Let us keep in step with the Spirit" (v. 24).

THE REWARD OF FAITHFULNESS

In the continuing "war between the house of Saul and the house of David" (2 Sam. 3:1), the opposition to David was depleted by several violent incidents. Abner became angry at Ish-bosheth over a personal matter and made an agreement to support David. He arranged for representatives of "Israel and the whole house of Benjamin [Saul's tribe]" (v. 19) to come to Hebron and make a compact with David to rule over all Israel.

Meanwhile Joab returned to Hebron from a military expedition and learned that Abner (who had killed his brother Asahel) had been entertained by David. He accused Abner of spying on David, and Joab sent messengers to bring Abner back under false pretenses to Hebron. Joab took Abner aside and "stabbed him in the stomach, and he died" (v. 27). David mourned over Abner's death and pronounced a curse on those who killed him.

After Abner's death, two Benjamites assassinated Ish-bosheth in his house "while he was taking his noonday rest" (4:5). Then they cut off his head and took it to David, thinking he would be delighted by the gift! But David viewed their act as the murder of "an innocent man in his own house and on his own bed" (v. 11). And so he had them executed.

The groundwork laid by Abner, complemented by the death of Ish-bosheth, came to fruition when all the elders of Israel came to Hebron "and anointed David king over Israel" (5:3). They knew that the Lord had told David, "You will shepherd My people Israel, and you will become their ruler" (v. 2).

So the Lord brought David into the position of prominent service for which he had been anointed by Samuel many years before.

Reflect on this: Like David, God expects us to be faithful during periods of preparation so that we will be faithful in positions of service where He may place us.

THE TRUE SOURCE OF SUCCESS

After being made king over all Israel, David realized the need for a more centrally located capital city. The Canaanite city of Jerusalem, still occupied by the Jebusites, located on the border between Judah and Benjamin, became his goal. It was a fortress city ("the fortress of Zion," 2 Sam. 5:7) surrounded on three sides by deep valleys, had its own water supply (Gihon Spring), and was close to local trade routes.

When David arrived to attack the city, the overconfident Jebusites said, "You will not get in here; even the blind and the lame can ward you off" (v. 6). But David's men, following the leadership of Joab (1 Chron. 11:6), entered the city through "the water shaft" (2 Sam. 5:8) that went up under its walls. So David captured the "fortress and called it the City of David" (v. 9).

He made some expansions in the city, including a palace that Hiram, king of Tyre, built for him. That illustrates the international recognition David was beginning to receive as king of Israel. Unfortunately alliances with foreign countries were sealed by marriages with a daughter of the foreign ruler. Thus David began to accumulate wives and concubines, a sin his son Solomon also committed, and to a much greater degree!

David "became more and more powerful, because the Lord God Almighty was with him" (v. 10). David realized that "the Lord had established him as king over Israel and had exalted his kingdom for the sake of his people Israel" (v. 12). Areas of victory included major defeats of the Philistines (vv. 17-25).

A reminder: When we enjoy success in any area of our lives, whether physical, intellectual, social, or spiritual, we should praise God for providing the enablement to accomplish those achievements.

WORSHIP IS NOT NEGOTIABLE

The ark of God rested in the house of Abinidab at Kiriath Jearim for about a century (see 1 Sam. 7:1). David determined to bring the ark to Jerusalem. But he neglected to follow the divinely pre-scribed method by which the ark was to be carried by the Kohath-ite family of Levites (Num. 7:9). Rather, he transported it on a new cart accompanied by two sons of Abinidab—Uzzah and Ahio. When the oxen pulling the cart stumbled, Uzzah reached out to steady the ark (a direct violation of Numbers 4:15—"they must not touch the holy things or they will die"), and the Lord "struck him down and he died there beside the ark of God" (2 Sam. 6:7).

Then David became angry (probably at himself) and was "afraid of the Lord" (v. 9). After the ark of God remained "in the house of Obed-Edom the Gittite for three months" (v. 11), David renewed his attempt to bring the ark to Jerusalem. This time he had the ark carried properly. Also he wore a linen ephod and "danced before the Lord with all his might" (v. 14).

David placed the ark in a tent in Jerusalem and "sacrificed burnt offerings and fellowship offerings before the Lord" (v. 17), after which he blessed the people and gave each of them a loaf of bread, and cakes of dates and raisins.

When David's wife Michal saw him dancing and leaping before the ark, "she despised him in her heart" (v. 16). When he re-turned home, Michal ridiculed him for "disrobing [wearing only his sleeveless linen garment] in the sight of the slave girls of his servants as any vulgar fellow would!" (v. 20) David pointed out that he was celebrating before the Lord. The narrator notes that Michal "had no children to the day of her death" (v. 23), apparent-ly because of her attitude toward David's act of worship.

Ponder this: Even though David was an activist, he placed a high priority on worshiping the Lord. We sometimes become so wrapped up in religious programs and activities that we neglect to worship God. Let's renew our priority to recognize and celebrate how great God is and tell others what great things He has done for us.

STANDING ON THE PROMISES

As David reflected on the blessings God had given him, it seemed inappropriate that he should live "in a palace of cedar, while the ark of God remains in a tent" (2 Sam. 7:2). However, the Lord revealed to him through Nathan the prophet that he was not to build a house (temple) for the Lord. Rather, the Lord would build a house (dynasty, or ruling line of descendants) for him.

Then the Lord made a covenant with David that included personal promises (a great name, a place for Israel, rest from all their enemies [vv. 9-11]). The heart of the covenant was the dynastic promise, "the Lord Himself will establish a house for you" (v. 11). That was expanded into a fourfold promise to David's posterity: God would provide an eternal descendant (vv. 12, 16), an eternal kingdom (v. 16), an eternal throne (vv. 13, 16), and a Father-son relationship between the Lord and the king (v. 14). The covenant was unconditional since the promise would continue in spite of disobedience (v. 15). It was also promised that David's initial ruling descendant (Solomon) would "build a house for My Name" (v. 13).

The personal promises to David were all fulfilled in his lifetime. The dynastic promise was fulfilled in a line of descendants that culminated in Jesus Christ, the Son of David. In His First Coming, Christ fulfilled the promise of an eternal King (Luke 1:31-33). The ultimate fulfillment of the promises about a kingdom and throne awaits His Second Coming (Rom. 11:26-27; Matt. 25:31-34).

David responded to the Lord's promise to him with a prayer of praise, thanksgiving, and believing expectation (2 Sam. 7:18-29). He emphasized God's sovereign greatness (vv. 22-24) and His trustworthy word (vv. 25-29).

A reminder: The Word of God contains many promises for us believers. We should rely on those promises since God who gave them is fully trustworthy. We should praise and thank Him for who He is and what He has done for us.

MAN'S RESPONSIBILITY
AND GOD'S RELIABILITY

One of God's promises in the Davidic Covenant was "I will give you rest from all your enemies" (2 Sam. 7:11). "In the course of time" (8:1; 10:1), David's army defeated the Philistines, the Moabites, the Arameans, the Edomites, and the Ammonites. This was a fulfillment of the Davidic Covenant, for "the Lord gave David victory everywhere he went" (8:6, 14).

One of the campaigns was precipitated needlessly by the distrust of Hanun who became king of the Ammonites when his father died. David "sent a delegation to express his sympathy to Hanun concerning his father" (10:2). But Hanun believed his nobles' claim that the Israelites were David's spies. So he humiliated them by cutting off half their beards and half their garments. As a result the Ammonites became "a stench in David's nostrils" (v. 6); so they hired mercenary soldiers from the Arameans to help them fight Israel.

As the Israelites drew up their battle lines, David's commander, Joab, said to Abishai, his brother, "Be strong and let us fight bravely for our people and the cities of our God. The Lord will do what is good in His sight" (v. 12). These enemies were defeated and became vassals of David.

Be reminded: David and his military leaders recognized that they must employ the best military strategy they could, but that victory in battle was from the Lord. The spiritual warfare in which we are involved against the hosts of Satan is the same way. We need to be aware of the strategy of our enemy. We must protect ourselves with "the full armor of God" (Eph. 6:11). We are to take the offense with "the sword of the Spirit, which is the word of God" (v. 17). And we must "be strong in the Lord and in His mighty power" (v. 10), knowing that victory in the battle is from the Lord.

THE FIELDS ARE RIPE FOR HARVEST

David's internal policies were as righteous as his military forces were strong. One summary statement of his rule was that "David reigned over all Israel, doing what was just and right for all his people" (2 Sam. 8:15). One example of that was his treatment of Jonathan's son Mephibosheth.

David inquired, "Is there anyone still left of the house of Saul to whom I can show kindness for Jonathan's sake?" (9:1) He learned that a son of Jonathan named Mephibosheth was still alive in the Transjordanian town of Lo Debar. Mephibosheth was "crippled in both feet" (v. 3), due to a childhood accident when his nurse fled at the bad news of the death of Saul and Jonathan (4:4).

David brought Mephibosheth to Jerusalem and gave him all the land that belonged to Saul and his family. Ziba, a former servant of Saul, was designated "to farm the land for him and bring in the crops, so that [he] may be provided for" (9:10). Besides, "Mephibosheth ate at David's table like one of the king's sons" (v. 11).

A glorious truth: Like Mephibosheth, we have become the objects of undeserved favor because of the kindness of Him who will rule as King of kings and Lord of lords. In Jesus Christ we have received full acceptance at the Father's table. We have also been given lands to care for and crops to harvest. "I tell you, open your eyes and look at the fields! They are ripe for harvest" (John 4:35). "The harvest is plentiful but the workers are few. Ask the Lord of the harvest, therefore, to send out workers into his harvest field" (Matt. 9:37-38).

THE SINS OF THE HEART

David's act of adultery with Bathsheba is one of the more familiar stories in the Bible. It illustrates that "a man after [God's] own heart" (1 Sam. 13:14) can still fall deeply into sin. David's multiple sins were eventually followed by remorse, confession, and God's forgiveness (2 Sam. 12:13-14; Ps. 51).

David was tempted during a period of inactivity. Spring was an opportune time of the year for warfare. The Israelite-Ammonite war was continuing, but "David sent Joab out with the . . . Israelite army [while he] remained in Jerusalem" (2 Sam. 11:1). One night as he walked on the roof of the palace, he saw a woman bathing. He found out that she was Bathsheba, the wife of Uriah the Hittite, who was away fighting in David's army. He "sent messengers to get her . . . and he slept with her" (v. 4).

When Bathsheba notified David, "I am pregnant" (v. 5), he conceived a plan to bring Uriah home on leave to be recognized as the apparent father of the child. But Uriah refused to go home while his comrades were in battle, sleeping at the palace entrance instead. Even after David got him drunk, Uriah did not go home to Bathsheba.

So David sent a letter with Uriah instructing Joab to place Uriah in the front line of the battle "so he will be struck down and die" (v. 15). As the battle progressed, Uriah was killed. When the time of Bathsheba's mourning was over, she became David's wife and "bore him a son. But the thing David had done displeased the Lord" (v. 27).

Be alert: Some of us may say, "I would never displease the Lord like that!" But Jesus said that "anyone who looks at a woman lustfully has already committed adultery with her in his heart" (Matt. 5:28). Also He compared "anyone who is angry with his brother" with "anyone who murders" (vv. 21-22). Let's avoid sins of the heart as well as sins of the hand because, as David learned, all sin is against God (Ps. 51:4) and displeases Him.

THE FATHER'S FORGIVENESS

After David sinned, Nathan the prophet told him about a wealthy herdsman and a poor man who had only a pet lamb. When the rich man wanted to serve a guest, he "refrained from taking one of his own sheep . . . Instead, he took the ewe lamb that belonged to the poor man" (2 Sam. 12:4).

David walked right into Nathan's net and said, "The man who did this deserves to die!" (v. 5) Nathan must have pointed his finger at David as he said, "You are the man!" (v. 7) David was the rich man whom God had blessed. But he took the "ewe lamb" of Uriah the Hittite. After Nathan pronounced God's judgment on him, David confessed, "I have sinned against the Lord" (v. 13; cf. Ps. 51). Then Nathan informed David of God's gracious forgiveness: "The Lord has taken away your sin. You are not going to die" (v. 13; cf. Ps. 32). But Nathan indicated that David's sin would have consequences—"the son born to you will die" (v. 14).

When the child became ill, David prayed and fasted for the child. When the child died, David's servants feared to tell him lest he might "do something desperate" (v. 18). David saw through their cloak of secrecy and learned the child was dead.

Surprisingly, instead of mourning further, he bathed, dressed, worshiped God, and went home and ate. His servants inquired why "while the child was alive, you fasted and wept, but now that the child is dead, you get up and eat!" (v. 21) David said he fasted and wept because the Lord might let the child live. "But now that he was dead, why should I fast? Can I bring him back again? I will go to him [in death], but he will not return to me" (v. 23).

Remember: The Apostle John wrote to believers, "If we confess our sins, He is faithful and just and will forgive us our sins and purify us from all unrighteousness" (1 John 1:9). As in the case of David, confession of sin will lead us into the experience of forgiveness that stems from God's grace.

AVOIDING THE SOW-AND-REAP CYCLE

Nathan told David that because he killed "Uriah the Hittite with the sword . . . the sword will never depart from your house" (2 Sam. 12:9-10). One example of that occurred between David's sons Amnon and Absalom.

Amnon "fell in love with Tamar, the beautiful sister of Absalom" (2 Sam. 13:1). He pretended illness to get her to bring some food to his bedroom, where "he raped her" (v. 14). Then "he hated her more than he had loved her" (v. 15), and locked her out of his quarters. Tamar mourned in disgrace, her brother Absalom sought to comfort her, and David "was furious" (v. 21). But neither David nor Absalom spoke to Amnon about the matter.

Two years later Absalom succeeded in having Amnon murdered. He then fled into exile in Geshur for three years. But David longed to be reconciled with his son Absalom.

So Joab hired a wise woman from Tekoa to tell David a story that one of her sons had killed the other, but now the relatives wanted the first son put to death, leaving her without an heir. She gained David's sympathy and his oath to deliver the remaining son. Then she said, "When the king says this, does he not convict himself, for the king has not brought back his banished son?" (14:13)

David realized that Joab had "put words in her mouth" (v. 3), and gave in, instructing Joab, "Go, bring back the young man Absalom" (v. 21) to Jerusalem. But David did not allow Absalom to see him until after two more years.

A sobering thought: Forgiveness does not necessarily change the principle that "a man reaps what he sows" (Gal. 6:7). The drunkard may be converted but may still die of liver disease. The careless drug user may be converted but may still die of AIDS. The perjurer may be repentant but may not be able to undo the harm he caused in the lives of others. Let's live in obedience to God's Word so that we will not begin the "sow-and-reap" cycle of sin.

LEAVE VENGEANCE TO GOD

Absalom's five-year absence from David's presence did not help their relationship. Absalom eventually launched a conspiracy against David's rule. He "stole the hearts of the men of Israel" (2 Sam. 15:6) by affectionate behavior and promised that if he judged the land, everyone would receive justice. Then he sent secret messengers throughout Israel to say, "As soon as you hear the sound of the trumpets, then say, 'Absalom is king in Hebron' " (v. 10).

David heard of the conspiracy and fled Jerusalem to avoid bloodshed in the city. His household and personal army marched eastward across the Kidron Valley and up the Mount of Olives. He sent Zadok the priest back into the city with the ark of God. He commissioned his friend Hushai to return to the city as a false counselor to Absalom and a spy for David. Just beyond the summit David met Ziba, the steward of Mephibosheth, who provided donkeys and supplies for his journey into the wilderness. He deceitfully informed David that Mephibosheth stayed in the city because he hoped Israel would restore to him the kingdom of his grandfather Saul.

David ignored the curses of Shimei against him, and said, "It may be that the Lord will see my distress and repay me with good for the cursing I am receiving today" (16:12).

David had demonstrated grace toward many people. Some of those remained faithful to him, but many of them betrayed him in his moment of need. Yet David was willing to accept from the Lord "whatever seems good to Him" (15:26).

A question: How do we respond when friends seem to reject us? We may have gone out of our way on many occasions to aid someone, only to have the person treat us as enemies in the end. Let's follow David's example of leaving matters in the hands of God, knowing that He will ultimately cause His will to prevail in our situation.

A MAN AFTER GOD'S HEART

Hushai convinced Absalom that he wanted to serve him instead of David. So Absalom consulted both him and his own counselor Ahithophel for advice. Ahithophel recommended immediate pursuit of David to "attack him when he is weary and weak" (2 Sam. 17:2). Hushai suggested that David would be hiding in a cave somewhere and that it would be better for Absalom to gather more troops from all Israel, "from Dan to Beersheba" (v. 11), to achieve sure victory over David and his men.

Absalom chose Hushai's advice, "for the Lord had determined to frustrate the good advice of Ahithophel in order to bring disaster on Absalom" (v. 14). Hushai sent messengers to David, so that David pressed on and by daybreak had crossed the Jordan River with all his people, finally arriving at Mahanaim, in Gilead. So Hushai's help allowed David to escape from Absalom. Meanwhile Ahithophel, whose advice had been rejected, "put his house in order and then hanged himself" (v. 23).

After Absalom's army reached Gilead and engaged David's men in battle in a wooded area, David's men defeated the army of Israel. As Absalom fled on a mule, his long hair got caught in an oak tree. "He was left hanging in midair, while the mule he was riding kept on going" (18:9). When Joab learned that Absalom was caught in a tree, he plunged three javelins into Absalom and he died.

David was shaken by the news of Absalom's death, and he wept, crying, "O my son Absalom! My son, my son Absalom! If only I had died instead of you—O Absalom, my son, my son!" (v. 33).

Reflect on this: David was merciful and compassionate toward his wayward son. God is merciful and compassionate toward His wayward children. No wonder David was known as a man after God's own heart. Let us thank God for His mercy and love to us even when we wander from Him.

BLESSED ARE THE PEACEMAKERS

After the defeat and death of Absalom, David "won over the hearts of all the men of Judah as though they were one man" (2 Sam. 19:14). He forgave repentant Shimei for cursing him. He was reconciled to Mephibosheth whom he learned had been slandered by Ziba. "All the troops of Judah and half the troops of Israel" (v. 40) accompanied him back across the Jordan River.

However, "a troublemaker named Sheba ... a Benjamite" (20:1) stirred up the Israelites to follow him instead of David. Sheba's effort to gather followers took him far north in Israel to Abel Beth Maacah, just west of Dan. Troops under Joab besieged that city until a wise woman of the city bargained with Joab to spare the city in exchange for the head of Sheba. She said, "We are the peaceful and faithful in Israel. You are trying to destroy a city that is a mother in Israel. Why do you want to swallow up the Lord's inheritance?" (v. 19) When Joab agreed to spare the city for the head of Sheba, "they cut off the head of Sheba ... and threw it to Joab" (v. 22), who then returned to Jerusalem.

The land of Israel in David's time seemed to be populated with women characterized by wisdom and courage to turn potentially tragic situations into peaceful solutions. Abigail, the wife of Nabal, turned David from taking vengeance on her foolish husband (1 Sam. 25:14-35). The wise woman of Tekoa convinced David to take steps toward reconciliation with Absalom (2 Sam. 14:2-20). The wise woman of Abel Beth Maacah took the initiative to negotiate with Joab to spare her entire city (20:16-22).

Consider this: Similar women have played an important role in New Testament times and during the history of the Christian church ever since. Let's give thanks to God for the wise and godly women through whom He has worked to bring physical and spiritual peace in the world.

GIVING GOD THE BEST

David sent Joab throughout all Israel to take a census of the fighting men. Afterward Joab reported that there were 500,000 fighting men in Judah and 800,000 in the rest of Israel.

David suddenly realized his military census reflected a confidence that instead should have been placed in the Lord to fight Israel's battles. He prayed, "I have sinned greatly in what I have done. Now, O Lord, I beg you, take away the guilt of your servant. I have done a very foolish thing" (2 Sam. 24:10).

Through Gad the prophet, the Lord gave David three options for retribution on his sin—"three years of famine . . . three months of fleeing from your enemies . . . or three days of plague in your land?" (v. 13). David chose the third option, believing it was better to "fall into the hands of the Lord, for His mercy is great" (v. 14). After the plague took the lives of 70,000 people from Dan to Beersheba, David said, "I am the one who has sinned. . . . These are but sheep. What have they done? Let your hand fall upon me and my family" (v. 17).

Gad told David, "Go up and build an altar to the Lord on the threshing floor of Araunah the Jebusite" (v. 18). Araunah offered to give all he had to David, even "oxen for the burnt offering" (v. 22). But David insisted on paying for it: "I will not sacrifice to the Lord my God burnt offerings that cost me nothing" (v. 24).

After David "sacrificed burnt offerings and fellowship offerings . . . the Lord answered prayer in behalf of the land, and the plague on Israel was stopped" (v. 25).

Think about it: We do not sacrifice oxen on altars to the Lord. But we do have a stewardship to give the Lord the best of our time, talent, and treasures. Instead, do we give Him the leftovers, or even what costs us nothing? Our service and gifts to the Lord should be sacrificial, beginning with giving Him ourselves.

INFLUENCING THE NEXT GENERATION

David's son Adonijah was much like his half-brother Absalom. He was handsome, spoiled (like many of David's children), and he wanted to be king. He invited many people to a sacrificial meal near En Rogel, a spring just south of Jerusalem, where he planned to be crowned as king.

Nathan the prophet informed Bathsheba of Adonijah's plans. After she informed the aged king of Adonijah's actions, Nathan entered to confirm the crisis.

David told Bathsheba, "As surely as the Lord lives . . . Solomon your son shall be king after me, and he will sit on my throne in my place" (1 Kings 1:29-30). David instructed Zadok the priest and Nathan the prophet to take Solomon on the king's mule down to the Gihon Spring to be anointed king over Israel. They obeyed David, and all the people shouted, "Long live King Solomon!" (v. 39). They rejoiced so loudly that "the ground shook with the sound" (v. 40).

A short distance away Adonijah heard the sound, and soon learned that David had made Solomon king. Adonijah's guests then dispersed in alarm. Adonijah was fearful and he "took hold of the horns of the altar" (as a place of sanctuary from Solomon's potential anger, v. 50). Solomon said Adonijah would live "if he shows himself to be a worthy man" (v. 52), and he sent him home.

On his deathbed David charged Solomon, "Be strong, show yourself a man, and observe what the Lord your God requires: Walk in His ways, and keep His decrees and commands, His laws and requirements" (2:2-3). David died and was "buried in the City of David" (v. 10), and "Solomon sat on the throne of his father David, and his rule was firmly established" (v. 12).

Worth noting: David closed his life with a desire to see God glorified and His promises fulfilled in the lives of his descendants. We should have similar goals as we serve the Lord today.

April

Devotional readings in the Psalms
by Robert P. Lightner

ACRES OF DIAMONDS

The Psalms are filled with spiritual gems. They are an inexhaustible mine. Though we will not be able to plumb the depths of this spiritual treasure house, we can certainly find many precious jewels here.

In the Psalms, God's Person and power are portrayed. We can see Him and His work throughout the Psalms. The Psalms also give us examples of the faith and failures of God's people.

The Psalms are hymns of prayer and praise to be used in worshiping God. The Colossian Christians were exhorted to use the Psalms in this way (Col. 3:16). James told the Christians he addressed to sing psalms in times of sorrow and of joy (James 5:13).

Someone has called the Psalms "the experience book of the saint in the world." Every psalm expresses worship of the true God. Each psalm is like a mirror of reality from life and for life, showing how God's people responded to the opportunities and conflicts of life. The writers of the Psalms expressed their innermost thoughts in what they wrote. These diamonds in God's Word tell us about God and His ways with man and are also a mirror of man's walk before God.

From the emphasis in the Psalms on the need for consistent prayer, praise, and genuine and exclusive worship of God, you will be challenged to live for Him and His glory. In the Psalms the weary pilgrim will find encouragement and the fainthearted traveler will gain new strength to climb spiritual heights for God.

The problems believers face in this computer age as they seek to live for the Lord are not too dissimilar to those the psalmists faced. The writers of the psalms were brutally honest with themselves and with God, and so must we be.

Remember: The solutions to the problems that beset us will be found in God, just as the psalmists' problems were. We too must learn to commit ourselves and our ways to Him. True happiness and contentment can be ours when we find our delight not in our successes or our bank accounts but in God and His Word (Ps. 1:1-2).

THE HOLINESS AND GOODNESS OF GOD

Have you ever felt mistreated? Maybe you were passed over for a promotion where you work. Do you sometimes feel taken for granted at home? Has it been a long time since someone at home thanked you for carrying out your daily duties?

We are often treated unfairly by others. However, God does not show favorites. He is always just in all His dealings with us. He imposes no judgment arbitrarily and He tolerates no injustices. God is good. The basis for His many goodnesses to His creatures is His holiness. Psalm 99 illustrates this beautifully. First the psalmist spoke of the Lord's universal reign (vv. 1-3). Then he described His unqualified righteousness (vv. 4-5) and His unfailing remembrance (vv. 6-9).

The psalmist felt that God's position above all else and all others required a universal submission to Him and His ways. God's reign is displayed in heaven. "He sits enthroned between the cherubim," the angelic beings. On earth God is sovereign also. He is "great . . . in Zion." Because God is holy, all creatures are obligated to honor and worship Him.

Everything God does is good from His perspective and is according to truth. This includes all He permits us to experience as well as what He directly brings our way. Moses, Aaron, and Samuel were all men of prayer and of faith. God in His faithfulness heard and answered their prayers and honored their faith. He will do the same for you. Believe Him.

Psalm 99 concludes with a call to worship this holy God. He alone is to be exalted and praised. He is holy and because He is, He is also good and faithful to His Word.

Reflect on this: Since everything around us has been tainted by sin, it is difficult for us to comprehend God's absolute holiness, His ineffable purity. Today as you are reminded of something affected by sin, think about the sinlessness of God, about His holiness. Think too about His injunction to His people to be holy as He is holy (Lev. 11:44; 1 Peter 1:15).

GOD'S MERCY FOREVER

"Mercy!" screamed Mary, the mother of two-year-old Johnny as she found him hanging by his britches from his big toy horse he had been riding. This was Mary's way of expressing shock and horror at the little boy's plight.

The psalmist had no such thing in mind when twenty-six times in Psalm 136 he referred to God's mercy (KJV; NIV has "love"). He was not expressing surprise; he was proclaiming a precious and profound truth about his God. As we learned yesterday from Psalm 99, God's goodness is established in His holiness. Also God's mercy manifests His goodness.

Perhaps a choir of priests and Levites sang the first line of each verse in Psalm 136, and the congregated people responded in worship with the second line. "Forever His mercy" was their repeated response. In the first three verses there is a description of the Person to be praised and an invitation to praise Him. Various reasons for giving thanks to God and praising Him are then given in the rest of the psalm.

God's mercy is displayed through His creative power (vv. 4-9), through the preservation of His world (vv. 10-22), and through His bountiful provision (vv. 23-26). Truly God is rich in mercy. His mercy is abundant. Because of His mercy toward us, we are not consumed (Lam. 3:22).

Ponder this: As children of such a wonderful God, we should also show mercy. Why do we demand full recompense when we have been wronged? Why do we insist on full payment for every offense toward us? Mercy withholds deserved punishment. Where would we be if God had not been and would not be merciful toward us? The next time you map out in your mind the strategy on how you plan to get even with someone so you can get what you think you deserve, remember that God is merciful and so should His people be.

HE KNOWS IT ALL

At least three great characteristics of God are revealed in Psalm 139, and each one relates to our human experience. In verses 1-6, He is seen as the all-knowing God. That very thought is mind-boggling. Man often spends a lifetime learning all he can about one particular thing. Even then he can know only a small part of a given subject. We learn about a subject line upon line, precept upon precept—that is, little by little, step by step. God does not.

Even the most educated and intelligent people know only an infinitely small portion of all that is to be known. How different it is with God. He really does know it all. In fact, He knows the possible as well as the actual.

God's complete knowledge might be illustrated by the view of a parade from the perspective of a tall building. From that vantage point one might see the whole parade. By contrast, from the sidewalk only a small part of the parade can be observed as it passes.

The psalmist found great delight in the truth that God not only knew *about* him but also knew him personally (v. 1). God knew all about his body (v. 2), his mind (v. 2), and all his activities (v. 3). Even the psalmist's tongue was known by God (v. 4). God knew *everything* about him (v. 5). This all-inclusive knowledge of God was not gained by experience. It was not something God learned gradually about the psalmist.

Think it over: What was true of God's knowledge of the psalmist is also true of us. God knows us in the same way and to the same extent. His knowledge of us and all things about us is both comforting and convicting. It is comforting to know He knows our true motives and intentions even when we fail. It is convicting to know He knows our deepest thoughts which we share with no one. He does know it all and He also understands. He is a God of grace as well as of knowledge.

NO PLACE TO HIDE

In many ways the world seems to be getting smaller. With all the modern means of transportation, it is easy to go from one corner of the globe to another in a short time. It is now possible to visit the moon and also while there to communicate with people on earth. There is no place to hide anymore.

The Credit Card Service Bureau tells its customers that they as bureau members are never alone in times of emergency. The bureau will always be there to give the service card holders need. It is almost as though the bureau is claiming omnipresence. However, only God is omnipresent. He is always present everywhere at the same time in all His fullness. There is no place to hide from Him.

The God of the Bible, our Heavenly Father through faith in Christ, transcends all spatial limitations. He does not possess a physical body; He is a spirit. The psalmist affirmed God's presence everywhere (v. 7). The Lord is present in heaven (v. 8), hell (v. 8), the sea (vv. 9-10), and even in the most secret places (vv. 11-12).

What a comfort to know this truth. When we find ourselves alone, away from friends and family, we are really not alone after all. God has promised never to leave or forsake His own (Heb. 13:5).

A matter to ponder: The truth that there is no place to hide from God is also convicting. This means it is impossible to escape His all-seeing eye. Even our dearest and closest friends and family may not know what we do or say when we are not around them, yet God does. We cannot hide from Him. We are always like an open book to His constant gaze. May this truth of God's omnipresence give you comfort—and, if necessary, conviction—today as you walk with Him.

ALL HAIL THE POWER

We live in a power-conscious age. The United States is referred to as a superpower. We are all aware of the frightening competition among the superpower countries to outdo each other in technology, military strength, education, and so on. On the immaterial level we often speak of things such as word power and the power of this and the power of that, all of which demonstrates our consciousness of power.

"Absolute power belongs to God," wrote the psalmist (Ps. 62:11, NASB). He is all-powerful. It is difficult for us even to imagine this. Satan and the demons of hell are certainly powerful. They do stupendous things. But they are not all-powerful. Their evil power has definite divine restrictions. Only God is omnipotent. In Psalm 139:13-18 the psalmist described how God's power is displayed in the creation of man. "I am fearfully and wonderfully made," he wrote (v. 14).

God, our Heavenly Father, has bequeathed His power to His people. David wrote, "The Lord gives strength to His people" (Ps. 29:11). He fulfills this promise as we trust and obey Him. Strength for the day comes as we cast ourselves on Him. God does not force His power or His strength on us. He will give it as we need it and when we need it, as we come to Him and meet His conditions.

Emotional and spiritual strength are available for God's people. All too often we live like paupers when, in fact, we are children of the King. Jesus reminded His disciples of His divine power just before He returned to His Father. He said, "All authority in heaven and on earth has been given to Me. Therefore go . . ." (Matt. 28:18-19). The people of God are to live and serve in the power or authority of God Himself.

Don't forget: As you face temptation and discouragement, remember whose you are. In all your difficulties remember that the very power of God is yours to draw on. As Jesus said, in our own strength we can do nothing (John 15:5). In God's power we can do all things through Christ who strengthens us (Phil. 4:13).

GOD'S MESSAGE IN HIS WORLD

When we listen to a great musical rendition, it is helpful to know the words associated with the tune. Knowing the words makes the music more meaningful. Then the music is interpreted by the words as they pass through our minds.

That is somewhat the way it is with God's grand revelation in nature. One who has a personal relationship with the Creator through Jesus Christ sees much more in nature than what merely passes before the eye. Such a person sees what the psalmist saw—God's glory and handiwork.

The significance of God's message in His world is far-reaching. It means all humans are accountable to God and likewise all are without excuse before Him. David did not have access to a sanctuary built by a man, but he perceived truth about God's glory based on what he saw with his eyes in the world around him (Ps. 19:1). The glory of God speaks of revelation about God. Here it refers to God's might and power displayed in His creation.

David also saw God's handiwork in the world. God's glory speaks of His Person, and His handiwork points to what He has done. The sun, moon, and stars bore testimony to David of God's infinite skill and wisdom.

God's message in His world does not bring eternal life to people. It was never intended to do that. Only God's message in His Word concerning His Son can do that.

A challenge: Think of ways you can use God's message in His world today to speak to someone about His message in His Word. The Apostle Paul used this approach as he addressed the people of Athens on Mars Hill (Acts 17:22-34). And rejoice in all He has made.

GOD'S MESSAGE IN HIS WORD

God's message in His *world* reveals His existence and His infinite power. His message in His *Word* exposes man's need and reveals God's bountiful provisions.

Psalm 19:7-9 includes six titles for God's written revelation, with six characteristics describing them and six effects produced by the written Word of God. In these verses some wonderful things are said about God's message in His Word. The Word of God does all that is claimed for it in this psalm. Of course the Bible is not a good-luck charm. The message it gives must be believed and appropriated before its promises will be realized.

The results produced by the Word of God are stated in verses 10-14. All of these are true because Scripture is divine and it reveals the character of God. The more David thought on God's holy character, the more he became aware of his own depravity. The Word of God has a way of penetrating and piercing the deepest recesses of our hearts (v. 12a). Knowledge of God's cleansing power also came as the psalmist contemplated God's truth (v. 12b). Meditating on God's message in His Word created within him the desire to please the God who gave it. It will do the same for you.

Meditation on God's Word and obedience to it produce holy living. David concluded Psalm 19 by referring to God as his "Rock" and his "Redeemer." The more he contemplated the message of God, the more he realized his need for a firm foundation and a Redeemer. He found both in God.

Your assignment: Today make a point of thinking about God's written Word during your idle moments. What it did for David so long ago, it will do for you too.

GOD'S KING RAISED FROM THE DEAD

The Savior's prayer while He was on the cross (Ps. 22:21) was answered as were, of course, all His prayers. This prayer was answered not by His being delivered from the cross and all its shame, but through His being resurrected from the grave (Acts 2:24).

Psalm 16 is the resurrection psalm. In it we have a description of the meditations of Christ, God's King, as He faced Calvary. The key to understanding the psalm and seeing Christ in it is in Peter's and Paul's appeals to it (Acts 2:25-31; 13:35-37). Both used Psalm 16 to prove the resurrection of Christ from the grave. To be sure, the psalm is a prayer of David for his own needs, but it is also a prophecy of the Messiah's complete trust in God the Father and Christ's triumph through resurrection.

God is faithful and we can trust Him just as David and Christ did (Ps. 16:1). The Saviour was despised and rejected by those He came to redeem. Yet God the Father raised Him from the dead and exalted Him (vv. 9-11). Christ faced the future with great confidence in His Father's care for Him. He always kept the Lord before Him (v. 8). He came to earth only to do His Father's will. The relationship Christ sustained with His Father meant He was safe and secure. He could face the future with confidence and hope. He knew that after His death He would be raised triumphantly.

The power that raised Christ from the dead is also the believer's power. It has been bequeathed to every child of God (Eph. 1:19-20; Col. 3:1-3). This means, of course, that we too can face the future with certainty even though we may not know what it holds. What is really important is that we know the One who holds the future. We can be victorious over all Satan's power by appropriating the power of God in our lives.

Remember: As a child of God you have died with Christ and have been raised with Him. All the power of heaven is at your disposal. You need not live like a spiritual pauper. You are rich in Christ Jesus!

GOD'S KING REJECTED

The nation Israel begged God for a king to rule over them. The people wanted to be like the nations around them. In time God gave them a king. Saul was the first, and many others followed. When Christ came, He came not only as the Saviour of the world (Matt. 1:21) but also as Israel's King, the nation's Messiah (Matt. 2:1-2). But the nation refused to make Him king (John 1:11). They made their rejection very clear: "We have no king but Caesar" (John 19:15). Soon after that He was crucified.

Israel's rejection of her Messiah did not surprise God. The Psalms refer to His rejection by the very people He came to die for and rule over. Psalm 22 is most pointed in its depicting the Messiah-Saviour's rejection. When David wrote this psalm, he no doubt referred to his own sufferings. And yet as we see in the New Testament, several portions of the Psalm relate to Christ.

The first words of the psalm are among the last Christ uttered as He died (cf. Matt. 27:46). In the first ten verses of Psalm 22, the suffering of God's King is depicted. Christ died alone as He was made a curse for us (Gal. 3:13). He was forsaken by God and was deserted by His own in that awful hour. Why? Because He was being made sin for us (2 Cor. 5:21) as He took our punishment (1 Peter 3:18), and God cannot look on sin. The Saviour paid an incalculable price for our redemption. To the unregenerate, the cross is an offense and foolishness (Ps. 22:7-8; cf. Matt. 27:39-44).

Psalm 22:11-21 speaks of the animal-like treatment David received at the hand of His enemies. This in turn speaks of the way God's King, the Messiah, was treated by those who put Him to death, acting like bulls, lions, dogs, and oxen (vv. 12-13, 16, 20-21) in treating Him viciously.

The indescribably cruel treatment left Him completely exhausted (vv. 14-15). The excruciating torture Christ endured on the cross is detailed in verses 16-21. Piercing His hands and feet (v. 16) and dividing His garments (v. 18) refer in some way initially to David but ultimately to Christ (Mark 15:24).

Act now: Thank the Lord for His death for you on the cross. Then don't keep silent about Him when God gives you opportunity to tell someone about His marvelous love and saving grace.

WHO IS THE KING OF GLORY?

A future time of unprecedented trouble and tribulation is coming. The Prophet Jeremiah wrote of it as so great that "none will be like it" (Jer. 30:7). Daniel described it as "a time of distress such as has not happened from the beginning of nations" (Dan. 12:1). Jesus spoke of this future outpouring of God's wrath on the earth as "great distress unequaled from the beginning of the world until now—and never to be equaled again" (Matt. 24:21). Believers of this Church Age will be delivered from this terrifying time, since they are not appointed to wrath (1 Thes. 1:9-10; 5:9).

Psalm 24 anticipates the coming again of Christ after this future Great Tribulation. The writer saw Him marching triumphantly with His own to Jerusalem, where He will reign as King of kings and Lord of lords over the whole world. This will be a great, grand triumphal procession. Everything belongs to Him and now He claims it all (v. 1). Only those who are rightly related to Christ will enter the kingdom He has come to establish on earth (vv. 2-5). The one who heads the procession calls out to the watchmen at Jerusalem's gates. They are told to make room for "the King of glory" to come in (v. 7). The question comes back, "Who is this King of glory?" (v. 8) The answer is, "The Lord strong and mighty, the Lord mighty in battle" (v. 8). The Lord Jesus affirmed that He is God (John 10:33), and Thomas (John 20:28) and Paul (Col. 2:9) indicated His deity, that is, His identity with Yahweh. Jesus' association with the city of Jerusalem and His Second Advent (Rev. 19:11-16) make the identification certain.

But all this is yet future. What about now? Christ the coming King wants first place in our lives today and every day. He is the sovereign Lord of all.

Consider these questions: Are we submissive to Him as subjects of the heavenly kingdom? Is He Lord of our lives? Does He reign supreme in our choices and our conduct?

PEACE ON EARTH

Two artists set out to paint their concept of peace. The one put on his canvas a beautiful mountain lake protected on all sides by overhanging boulders. The water was placid and gave no indication of the breeze blowing high over it. This was his view of peace. The other artist sketched on his canvas a thundering waterfall. At the base of it there was a small birch tree. In one of the tiny branches he put a bird's nest. A mother bird was there singing sweetly to her young, unaffected by all the commotion going on around her.

Psalm 72 was written by David probably about his son Solomon, but Christ, the Messiah, is the ultimate and final fulfillment. Someone has well said, this psalm was penned by a king for a king and concerns the King of kings. Psalm 72 certainly had a connection with Solomon's reign of peace and prosperity, but it is also apparent that it refers to the Messiah and His righteous reign on earth. The king's reign is described in verses 1-17. A doxology of praise concludes the psalm (vv. 18-20). When Christ returns to the earth, His reign will be righteous (vv. 1-7) and universal (vv. 8-11). His rule will be a most benevolent reign (vv. 12-14) and an everlasting one (vv. 15-17).

What a day that will be! From the beginning of time man has been searching for peace on earth. That great, grand, glorious day will come only when Christ, the Prince of peace, comes.

A wondrous truth: Christ brings peace when He is allowed entrance into the human heart. He makes possible peace *with* God (Rom. 5:1) and the peace *of* God (Phil. 4:7). He *is* our peace! Allow the peace you have with God to be reflected to those around you who do not have it.

LONELINESS

Some people like to be alone most of the time. They seem to be happiest when they are by themselves. Others enjoy companionship so much that they dread being alone, even for short periods of time. Of course, it is possible to be lonely even when you are around others. This is the worst kind of loneliness. It is also possible to be alone and yet not be lonely.

The psalmist found himself surrounded by enemies. While in enemy territory he longed for the sanctuary, the place of public worship of God. His thirsty soul craved fellowship with God and God's people. Though not alone—enemies were all around him, mocking him—he became very lonely, lonely for the house of God (vv. 1-5). And he longed for help from God (vv. 6-11).

Are you bothered when you miss attending a church service you normally attend? Has going to church become commonplace for you? It seems the psalmist missed the public worship of God and it brought him to tears. Instead of eating, he wept (v. 3). He found relief for his loneliness as he engaged in self-examination. This turned his discouragement into encouragement. The psalmist talked to himself. He asked himself questions and then he determined the action he needed to take (v. 5).

Reflection on God and His many past goodnesses to him greatly encouraged the psalmist. The more he thought about God and His past blessings, the less lonely he became. His enemies were still all around him, but he had a whole new perspective on them and on life.

Consider this: This may be a lonely day for you. God knows all about it. He wants you to find intimate fellowship with Him. Remember His promise, "Never will I leave you; never will I forsake you" (Heb. 13:5).

WHY ARE YOU CAST DOWN?

Most likely you have heard of someone who has died in seeming poverty with thousands and thousands of dollars hoarded in some obscure secret place. These people died like beggars because they did not use the means they had.

Many of us today have trouble living within our income. Our plastic-money culture makes it easy to spend more than we have or can even get when we need it. In spiritual matters things seem to be the other way around—much like the hoarders who live in poverty. It is common for Christians to live on a low plane, far below their real means. We often live like spiritual paupers when, in fact, all the wealth of heaven is at our disposal. The human author of Psalm 43 was guilty of this for a while. He always had God's power available to him, but in affliction and dark times he lost sight of it and failed to rely on it.

Then the psalmist began to draw on the divine resources available to him. First, he communed with God about his problems (vv. 1-4), and then he counseled with himself (v. 5).

The psalmist prayed for deliverance from his enemies (vv. 1-3). This was the right place to start. Prayer does change things, including the attitude of the one praying. He had no doubt that he would eventually experience victory (v. 4).

Consider this: This man was the way we often are—unnecessarily sad. He rebuked himself for this, as he should have (v. 5). The advice he gave himself is thoroughly biblical—"hope in God." This is the cure for being cast down. As God's child you can know He is on your side. Hope in Him!

AN EXPERIENCE OF GRACE

We ought to look back occasionally to the time before we were Christians just to remind us of God's wonderful grace and salvation. It is helpful also to review and remember how God has manifested Himself to us since our salvation experience.

Many Bible scholars view Psalm 40 as messianic. We can be assured that some of it speaks of the Messiah because of quotations from it in the New Testament. Note for example how verses 6-9 are quoted in Hebrews 10:5-9. We must always keep in mind though that the psalmist wrote out of experiences he had and which most believers have in one form or another.

The first half of Psalm 40 no doubt describes David's fleeing from Saul. Was David to blame for these awful conditions? No. Sometimes the Lord allows His own to pass through experiences that are terribly difficult and these are not always the result of the individual's sin.

David had just been delivered from great danger (v. 2). On this occasion he had great patience. He waited patiently for God to help him (v. 1). In other words David did not give up. He had stick-to-itiveness. His hope was in God. Everything around him was like miry clay until God set his feet on a "rock."

Because of the deliverance the psalmist experienced, he praised the Lord in music (v. 3). He experienced God in new ways. The person who places and keeps his confidence in God, not turning "aside to false gods," will be a blessed or happy person (v. 4). Does your confidence lie in the Lord?

What you can do: The grace of God was so abundant to David that he could not begin to number His many blessings (v. 5). They were so numerous David couldn't count that high! Think today of how the Lord has blessed you; think of the many "wonders" He has done on your behalf. Can you count your blessings? No doubt you too will say with David, they are "too many to declare!"

TROUBLE AND MORE TROUBLE

Have you ever wished you could start your Christian life over? Most Christians would probably do a lot of things differently if they could. It can't be done, of course. What we can do, though, is learn from the past and therefore change the present and the future. We do not need to repeat the failures of the past or be overcome by our problems.

It is common to wish for the so-called "good old days" of the past. And yet it is possible to spend too much time thinking about how God blessed us yesterday and last year. To be sure, it is good to remember God's past blessings on us. We must never forget these. But we must not live in the past either. We must keep looking ahead if we are to make progress in our spiritual growth. The Apostle Paul said he pressed on "toward the goal to win the prize" for which God had called him "heavenward in Christ Jesus" (Phil. 3:14). The writer of the Epistle to the Hebrews urged his readers to "go on to maturity" (Heb. 6:1).

The psalmist's problems reminded him of his constant need of God. From everywhere "innumerable evils" (Ps. 40:12) surrounded him. Some of these were caused by the sins of others, but David's own sins caused many of these difficulties. He was so overtaken with problems that he could not even look up. He was physically, emotionally, and spiritually weak because of his problems. Have you ever felt that way?

David did not give up. He placed his confidence in the Lord and in His ultimate triumph and victory. He certainly knew he had problems, but he also knew and believed in the strength of his God. He knew the Lord had not forgotten or forsaken him (v. 17). God was David's stronghold.

Worth pondering: When it looks as though the whole world is caving in on you, remember the Lord has not forgotten you. Cling to Him. Whatever He allows in your life He will also make it possible for you to bear it.

ENJOYING GOD'S PROTECTION

Nations, our own included, are trying to gain military might and even superiority. Each one engaged in the race insists on the same reason for doing it—protection from its foes.

God Himself provides protection for all His children which all the military might in the world cannot begin to equal. Psalm 46 assures us that God is with us no matter what happens. This psalm led Martin Luther to write his great hymn "A Mighty Fortress Is Our God." When times were darkest for him, his friends, and associates, he would say to them, "Come, let us sing Psalm 46."

John Wesley's last words were from Psalm 46. And verse 10 was the basis for Katharina von Schlegel's hymn, "Be Still, My Soul." Here is one stanza from that great hymn:

> Be still, my soul; thy God doth undertake
> To guide the future as He has the past.
> Thy hope, thy confidence let nothing shake;
> All now mysterious shall be bright at last.
> Be still, my soul; the winds and waves still know
> His voice who ruled them while He dwelt below.

In the first three verses of Psalm 46 the psalmist considered God Himself as his security and strength. He fled to God in times of danger and despair. "Refuge" (v. 1) comes from a verb that means "to flee" or "to flee to."

We too can be assured that God is ready to be our refuge. He is always ready to be a "present help" to the weakest and most weary saint. The word *ever* (v. 1) conveys the idea that God helps exceedingly; He provides much help.

The figures used in verses 2-3 graphically illustrate that no matter how troublesome conditions may be, the believer may still trust in his God. He has no cause to fear.

Consider this: By faith we must lay hold of God and His promises. He indeed is our refuge and strength, but we must appropriate all He provides if it is to benefit us. The promise is not that our troubles will go away, but that God will see us through them as we entwine ourselves around Him.

SAFE IN THE SECRET PLACE

The feeling of safety is assuring. Nothing is quite like security. We think about protection when we need it the most. When we are in a storm, we look frantically for shelter. If the building we are in were on fire, we would do our best to get out. This is a normal, natural reaction to physical danger and harm.

Spiritual security and safety are much more important than physical safety. The human author of Psalm 91 was led of the Holy Spirit to write about the believer's security in God Himself.

Four names are used of God in verses 1-2. "The Most High" speaks of His power and might and His supremacy over all else and all others. "The Almighty" presents God as tender and gracious even though the English translation "Almighty" does not convey that. "LORD" (*Yahweh*) is the title the Jews refused to pronounce audibly. They felt it was so filled with respect and honor that to verbalize it would be to defile the One it described. This name speaks of God as the self-existing One. "God" (*Elohim*), the name used in Genesis 1:1, describes God as the One possessing eternal power.

Nine things in verses 1-4 speak of the safety and security only God can give: "shelter," "the shadow of the Almighty," a "refuge," "fortress," "save you," "cover [protect] you," "under His wings," "shield," and "rampart."

For you: The first few verses of Psalm 91 raise the question, How does one dwell in this secret place and experience these blessings? Our Lord gave the answer in His parting words to His disciples. "Abide in Me," He told them (John 15:4). When you abide in Christ, it is to be in fellowship with Him. It is to keep His commandments (v. 10). In other words you abide in the Lord as you live according to His Word. This is how the Christian may "dwell in the shelter of the Most High" (Ps. 91:1). Here is safety from Satan and his evil angels. This is the secret place reserved for God's children.

FAITH ON TRIAL

Have you wondered why so many wicked people seem to prosper while many of the godly seem to suffer? Why is it that so many unbelievers seem to enjoy a prosperous and care-free life? Why do they die without even experiencing any apparent judgment from God?

Our faith is often put on trial. Sometimes it is tested severely. Suppose your doctor says you will lose your sight or hearing. Can you imagine how you would react to such tragic news? After the initial shock of it all, most of us would probably ask: "Why is this happening to me? Why is it that so many wicked people we know seem to have no trouble at all with their sight or hearing?"

God is good. The psalmist acknowledged this (v. 1). What disturbed him was the prosperity of the wicked around him. He could not square this with God's goodness (vv. 4-12). He had a threefold problem. He had a hard time reconciling three facts — God is good, the righteous suffer, and the unrighteous prosper. It seems that the devil's logic appealed to the psalmist for the moment. The devil's logic goes something like this: A good God blesses you; your God afflicts you; therefore your God is not good.

Life's shocking inequalities perturbed the psalmist. In this psalm he stated that his faith in God was at low ebb. He had serious doubts about God's mercy, love, and goodness. As he analyzed his situation, he came to the conclusion that he felt this way when he took his eyes off the Lord and contemplated the prosperity of the wicked.

Think about this: True, we do not know the mind of God. His ways are surely above ours, but He is good and nothing ever comes to one of His children without His permitting it. The wicked will be punished in God's time and way. Every trial He allows us to pass through is intended to strengthen us. Don't allow Satan to make you bitter because of life's trials. Instead, become better because of them.

FAITH REASSURED

Yes, silence *is* golden at times. Once words are spoken they cannot be recalled. No amount of apologizing can completely undo the damage caused by harsh, unkind words.

The psalmist knew this and avoided putting God in poor light before others. The things he thought about in Psalm 73:4-12 were not blurted out publicly. The man of God knew if he uttered them he would offend not only God's people (v. 15) but God as well. Instead of doing this, the psalmist triumphed in faith. He got the victory over his doubts and complaints. His faith was reassured.

The prosperity of the wicked had shaken this man's faith. With God's help he came to see that the answers to his questions were to be found in God Himself. Even though the psalmist never did fully understand the ways of God, he knew he could still trust God. When the troubled man went into the presence of God (v. 17), he began to think clearly once again. The wicked will be judged in God's way and time and that was really God's business and not his. The position and prosperity of the wicked is as short-lived as a dream.

Reassurance came to the psalmist's heart after he met with God (vv. 21-28). The problems he complained about were still real, but he was different. Instead of taking the close-up, short-sighted view of things, he took the long view and rested his faith in God.

The psalmist concluded as he began, with an awareness of God's strength. Nothing will ever change that. He learned the lesson well: His faith must rest in the Lord, not in people.

A question: Have you learned that lesson? The next time questions and doubts come your way tell God about them and reassure your heart that He is good and knows best.

I HAVE SINNED

In this psalm David, the sweet singer and great king of Israel, tells how he confessed his sins and found God's forgiveness. Saints do sin.

David found forgiveness and restoration when he turned to God for help. But after he committed adultery and arranged for Uriah to be killed (2 Sam. 11:15), the man of God was tormented with guilt for almost a year before he confessed. Fearless and faithful Nathan confronted David with his sin.

David's penitent prayer is recorded in Psalm 51:1-12. The first thing he did was acknowledge and appeal to God's mercy and lovingkindness. Then he bared his soul before God. He was guilty of transgressions, iniquity, and sin. These he wanted blotted out from God's record. The desire of his heart was that he might be clean once again. The leprosy of sin had defiled him and he was a sick man.

When Nathan said to David, "You are the man" (2 Sam. 12:7), the king made no attempt to hide his sin or deny his guilt. True, David had sinned against people; but even more importantly he had sinned against God, and he knew it. The joy he once knew in serving God was gone. Sin had taken it away. His entire being had been affected by sin. Only a thorough cleansing could restore David to fellowship with God. So serious was his offense that David feared being cast from God's presence (v. 11). Later Christ, David's greater Son, promised this would not happen to a believer who sins (cf. John 14:16).

David then wrote of God's promise and praise in Psalm 51:13-19. Here he made a resolution. He lifted up his voice in praise to God for forgiveness. Instead of allowing his sin to be a hindrance to others, he resolved to teach others God's ways. Once again he was able to praise God. No longer need he be silent because he was laden with guilt. The psalm ends with David desiring for others the forgiveness and cleansing he had experienced.

Remember: The next time you sin, confess it and forsake it immediately (1 John 1:9). Don't let Satan rob you of the joy of your salvation.

I'M FORGIVEN

Nothing brings greater joy than forgiveness. The forgiven person is the happiest person in the world. David promised God that he would praise Him the rest of his life and tell others of His great salvation if only God would forgive his sins (Ps. 51). Psalm 32 bears testimony to the psalmist's attempt to live up to his promise.

In this psalm we hear David rejoicing in his forgiveness. First, he wrote about the blessedness of forgiveness (vv. 1-5). The forgiven saint is truly happy. He is blessed. The three words used in Psalm 51:1-2 to describe David's wrongdoing are also used here — transgressions, sin, and iniquity (32:5). God responded to David's prayer. He was merciful to him. Transgression was lifted; it was taken away. Sin was covered; it was hidden from God's sight. Iniquity was canceled; it was no longer charged to his account. The hand of God was heavy on David until he confessed his sin (vv. 3-5). Then and only then was his burden of sin rolled away.

Forgiveness results in a blessed or happy state, and it also brings benefits to the one forgiven (vv. 6-11). Two special benefits are stated: God becomes the hiding place for the forgiven sinner (vv. 6-7) and becomes his guide as well (vv. 8-11).

Consider this: When we sin, we can turn to the Lord knowing He will forgive us. Like David we may make the truth of God very personal. God is our hiding place. He will preserve us. When we acknowledge our sin and seek God's forgiveness, He will be our guide (v. 8).

God wants His children to love, serve, and obey Him willingly. His desire is also that we be glad and rejoice in Him (vv. 10-11). Sin destroys the believer's joy, but God's forgiveness brings rejoicing and gladness. When you sin, confess it and experience His forgiveness and joy.

THE LORD, MY SHEPHERD

Oriental shepherds provided for their sheep in every way. Sheep need a shepherd; they cannot survive without one, though they don't know it. Being a shepherd was and still is a lowly and lonely occupation.

David, the human author of Psalm 23, was familiar with shepherd life. He was well suited to write of the Lord as the true Shepherd of His people. David presented Him as the Shepherd who loves and provides for His own.

This psalm is probably the most familiar portion of the Bible. It has been called "the pearl of the Psalms." From it we, as God's sheep, can be assured of divine provision.

The Lord Himself is our Provider. He has an intimate relationship with each of His sheep. "I shall not want" or "I shall have no lack" (v. 1b) expresses the basic idea of the whole psalm. The provisions of God for His people include everything of legitimate desire. He has the ability to supply all we really need.

The "green pastures" and "still waters" (v. 2) speak of contentment and complete satisfaction. Our Shepherd provides restoration to our troubled spirits and guidance for us too as He leads us (v. 3). The Lord's presence is with His own even in the hard places like "the valley of the shadow of death" (v. 4). Just as the shepherd of David's day would be sure the area where his sheep were to graze was free of snakes, so the Lord as our Shepherd provides for us and protects us in the presence of our enemies (v. 5).

A reminder: Those who belong to the Lord are promised the supply of all their needs. We sometimes confuse our needs and our wants. The Shepherd knows what we really need and He has promised to supply everything essential.

David found great assurance as he reflected on the Lord as His Shepherd. He needed the reminder of just who the Lord is. We need the same. A good way to start each day is to remind yourself, "The Lord is my Shepherd."

NEAR TO THE HEART OF GOD

"Don't get caught dead sitting on your seatbelt," said the sign on the car's dash. Safety devices like seatbelts are designed to protect us. We often disregard such warnings and advice for safety and decide we'll take our chances.

The Bible gives us many warnings and much advice for safety in spiritual things. However, we often disregard them. All God's children from the weakest to the strongest are promised divine protection. God would have us appropriate His promised protection and live according to Scripture.

While Psalm 23 stresses the assurance of divine provision, Psalm 27 speaks of divine protection. In this psalm David confirmed in his own heart the place of protection for the believer (vv. 1-6). David had no reason to fear anyone, though he certainly had enemies. God was his light and his truth, and therefore He dispels darkness or evil. The Lord was David's strength, so he had no reason to be afraid. These assurances brought him courage, hope, and confidence. As he thought about his God, spiritual fortitude and a supernatural calm came over him. Reflection on God's protective goodness led David to praise his God (v. 6). It will do the same for you.

The danger David faced did not go away. God had protected him in the past and he was grateful, but he needed help again. In his prayer for protection (vv. 7-12), the psalmist presented his needs to God and asked for guidance. His prayer was specific and urgent. Even though David was assured of God's protection, he still requested it. This man had complete trust in God. His testimony is clean and forthright. Apart from God's good hand on him he would have fainted.

Pause and think about it: David's words to his readers are as true today as when he penned them. Patient trust and persistent confidence in God will be rewarded by strength from Him. "Your strength will equal your days" (Deut. 33:25). Our place of protection from any and all danger is where David's was—near to the heart of God.

WHEN YOU FAIL

David wrote Psalm 60 to teach others lessons he had learned. He experienced failure and defeat, and he wanted others to know how to avoid them. In the first five verses of Psalm 60, David lamented about a failure he and his warriors had experienced.

The enemies of God and His people had invaded the land. There was a crisis. As soon as David heard about it, he went to God in prayer. That was the right thing to do, and what a beautiful example it is for all God's people who face crises and failures in their lives. The psalmist was terribly confused and bewildered over what had happened. He knew that for some reason God was dealing with him and His people. Was this the chastening hand of God? Apparently so, though that is not always the case when failure strikes.

David used descriptive language in his confession and cry for help. "You have rejected us . . . You have been angry" (v. 1). Something had greatly displeased God; He had turned His back and allowed His people to experience failure. Apparently something had taken David's eyes off the Lord. The face of God was turned away from David and he knew it. He also knew victory was impossible without God's favor.

David likened the calamity that had fallen on the people of God to an earthquake and to a person who staggers aimlessly, not knowing where he is going (vv. 2-3). David prayed that God would restore His favor to His people. Quickly God assured David that He had heard his cry. God was still Israel's banner. He had pledged Himself and He would not go back on His promise. David was assured of victory at the very time he prayed for forgiveness. Prayer provided a beautiful balm for his troubled soul. It brought assurance and hope.

A good idea: When you fail, when you experience defeat, do what David did. First, try to determine why God allowed you to fail. Second, remember that God has pledged Himself to you. All He allows to come into the lives of His children is for our good and from His loving hand. Through prayer the failure can be turned into a fortress against future failure.

VICTORY

Israel had experienced defeat from her enemies. Because of her sin God had not been with the armies of Israel (Ps. 60:1-3). He allowed them to be defeated. But David was willing now to trust God for victory even over the best protected and most impregnable city of that day. "The fortified city" (v. 9) most likely refers to Petra, the capital of Edom. The city, located in a mountain, was accessible only by a very narrow passageway. This certainly reveals David's simple trust in God to bring the victory over this city which was filled with Baal worshipers.

In the earlier battles God apparently did not have the complete confidence of His people. The clue to the cause of defeat is in verses 11 and 12. David and the people had been trusting in their own strength. But now there was complete trust and confidence in God to bring the victory to His people.

We, of course, will not be marshaling an army to go up against the capital of Edom. But each of us is engaged constantly in a spiritual warfare. Our foe is the devil himself and all the demons of hell. In our own strength we cannot win over Satan and his hosts. The Bible exhorts each believer to put forth effort to live for God. But all these efforts must be motivated and performed in the power of the Holy Spirit. God has called on us to do battle with Satan in the armor He has provided (Eph. 6:11-18). As we fight we must ever keep in mind, however, we can do nothing without Him (John 15:5).

Remember this: All of us have problems over which we need to be victorious. Whether pride, a sharp tongue, lust, greed, or other sin, victory is available to those who fight in God's strength. Today and each day you can do "valiantly" (v. 12) through God. He longs to give you victory.

WHEN IT RAINS, IT POURS

We've all had days when everything seems to go wrong. Maybe yesterday was a day like that for you. Today? How ought believers respond at such times? In this psalm we can find encouragement from David's example. In the strength of the Lord, he triumphed over his troubles. His experiences recorded in Psalm 56 remind us that living for the Lord is to be done "not somehow but triumphantly."

David, like Christ, was anointed by God as king, but before ascending the throne both were rejected and opposed. Patience and complete confidence in God were surely being put to the test. For both, troubles rolled like sea billows, as they often do for us too.

David was fearful as Saul pursued him. He turned to God for help. It is natural for a believer to pray in times of dangers and desperation. But David knew God intimately and communed with Him regularly, not only when he was in trouble. This man stayed, for the most part, on praying ground. How important that is. David's faith was put to the test. It was time for him to trust and not be afraid. And he did just that. He thrust himself on the mercy of God to protect him from his enemies.

The psalmist viewed his enemies as vicious and devouring beasts (56:1-2); but he had great confidence in God (v. 3), a confidence that removed his fear of man (v. 4). David knew only too well his own weaknesses. That is why he asked God for victory over his enemies (vv. 5-7). The psalmist wanted God to remember his sorrows during all his wanderings. Speaking figuratively, he asked God to put his tears in a container so they would not be forgotten (v. 8), as a reminder of his sorrows.

Then David rejoiced in God (vv. 10-13). The enemy still pursued him, but strength came as David concentrated on God. The Lord had delivered David's soul from death and would also keep his feet from falling.

Note this: Many bad things happen to God's people in this life. When it rains, it really pours for us too. But our confidence can be in the Lord during such times. His "grace is sufficient" and His "power is made perfect in weakness" (2 Cor. 12:9).

WHO CARES?

The historical background for this psalm was most likely David's flight from Gath to the Cave of Adullam (1 Sam. 22:1). Many of his family members and friends came to live with him in the area while he was in hiding there. But he still felt alone and cried out to the Lord, "No one is concerned for me" (Ps. 142:4). It is possible to feel alone even when you're not alone.

Surely we have all experienced feelings similar to those David had. In fact, we may even have wondered at times whether God cares. Yet we can be sure He does.

Psalm 142 records the forsaken David's prayer. The already divinely appointed, though yet-to-be-crowned, king of Israel cried out in complaint to God (vv. 1-4).

Like water poured out of a pitcher, David poured out his trouble in detail to His God. Since God knows everything, He certainly already knew all David told Him. Have you ever wondered why you should pray since God knows all about you anyway? Why pray? It helps to remember that Jesus, the Son of God, prayed. Spurgeon has well said, "We do not show our trouble before the Lord that He may see it but that we may see Him. It is for our relief, and not for His information that we make plain statements concerning our woes."

After the supplication there came to David simple trust in God (v. 5). The cave, his friends and family, and his sword gave protection, but David still needed God's help. He turned to Him for refuge. He knew "in the land of the living" God would cause him to triumph once again. David was not alone after all. Trouble surrounded him but triumph was sure. God would manifest Himself to him. Who cared? God did and would help him through the storm.

Then David enumerated some specific needs: relief from discouragement, deliverance from his enemies, and spiritual peace. He wanted these things so he could praise God's name. Triumph over trouble came through prayer.

A question: Why not take your troubles to the Lord in prayer? Even if they are not removed, you can learn to triumph over them and to praise God through them.

PRAISE GOD FOR WHO HE IS

Have you praised the Lord yet today? Not a day should pass, even the busiest or saddest, without your blessing or praising God. Psalm 145, written by David near the end of his life, is without doubt his greatest ascription of praise to God. God had led him every step of his journey. There were times of joy and delight but also many times of sadness and disappointment. He did not understand why many things had happened as they did. But looking back over his life, he was reminded how God had led him all the way and he praised Him.

In the first nine verses of Psalm 145, David praised God Himself. In the remainder of the psalm, which we will look at tomorrow, he praised God for His bountiful provisions, for His works.

Just as we have special times and occasions for praise and thanksgiving so did David and the people of his times. But whether in sacred seasons or common conversation, God is to be praised. Not a day passes without His blessing us. David had plenty of trials and troubles, but none are even hinted at, as this child of God exalted Him.

David had a plan to praise God always (vv. 1-2). We need such a plan too. Satan has his strategy to defeat us and we should be specific and on schedule in our praise of God. Praise to God helps protect us from the pitfalls of the prince of the power of the air.

God is great and good. His greatness is unsearchable; it has no limits. Neither is His greatness diminished through the exercise of His power. David seemed to have all the attributes or perfections of God in mind when he said, "Great is the Lord" (v. 3).

The Lord is also good and gracious (vv. 7-9). Everything He does is the result of His unmerited favor, His grace. We deserve nothing and yet we benefit from all God's bounties.

Try this: Praise the Lord every time you go to Him in prayer. When you awaken in the night, praise Him for who He is. Do the same during the day when you are doing well and even when you're not doing so well. Praise the Lord for who He is.

PRAISE GOD FOR WHAT HE HAS DONE

There is a difference between praising God for Himself and praising Him for what He does. David did both in Psalm 145. We need to do the same. To praise God is to worship Him. Whether or not we understand His ways with us, we can praise Him, knowing He is the sovereign God of the universe.

God's mighty and wonderful works to the children of men find their origin in His attributes. David's God was full of compassion. He was withholding deserved punishment. Of great mercy, He is good to *all,* and His tender mercies are over *all* his works. The repeated reference to the word *all* reveals the universal scope of the Lord's blessings. This same God is our Heavenly Father through faith in Jesus Christ.

As the divine King (v. 13), God rules over heaven and earth. He has always exercised His sovereign control over the affairs of man, and over holy and evil angels. In a future day His universal rule will come to earth in visible form. Little wonder we should praise Him. Then His kingdom will have come and His will be done.

The Lord also supports those who sink low under oppression and affliction. He gently lifts those who are weighed down by the toils of life (v. 14). This same God provides food for the creatures of the earth (vv. 15-16). The temporal blessings of God on His creation are enjoyed by the saved and the unsaved. He cares for all. God's children, however, are the special objects of His preserving love and care (vv. 19-20).

Reach for a pencil: The next time you feel unblessed by God make a list of specific things for which you are thankful, and praise Him for these specifics. The list may surprise you. There is no better way to chase away discouragement and depression than by praising the Lord for His many blessings to you.

May

Devotional readings in Ecclesiastes
by Roy B. Zuck

SEARCHING FOR SIGNIFICANCE

According to a Russian legend, a peasant was to receive a portion of land by inheritance. But the will had an unusual stipulation: He was to inherit all the land he could encompass by running on a designated day. Excited about this prospect for sudden wealth, the peasant prepared himself physically by running long distances each day for several weeks.

Then the eventful day arrived. He began at sunrise and ran for hours, taking in vast stretches of land. It would all be his! Toward sunset he returned to his starting point. But then he realized that a few minutes remained before the sun would be down. So he darted off in another direction to take in another small tract of land. Just as the sun was dropping below the horizon, he returned to the beginning spot, exhausted but elated. But at the very moment of his arrival, he dropped dead!

The peasant attained the land, but couldn't enjoy it. What seeming futility.

Ever feel like that? You gain something but can't enjoy it. You work for something only to lose it. You acquire wealth, education, experience, but you become only more miserable than before. So you wonder, What's the point of living? What's the purpose of existing?

Solomon faced the same dilemma thousands of years ago. The Book of Ecclesiastes records his search for significance, his pursuit of purpose, his race for reality. This book tells how he longed to fill the vacuum in his life, to occupy his void.

Point of action: Let's follow Solomon in his hunt for happiness. Since he had everything, and tried everything, we are wise to learn from him, to gain from his experiences. Why repeat all he did when we can benefit from his foibles and failures, his experiences and experiments? Don't learn the hard way—from your own experimenting. Learn the secret to the meaning of life here in this extremely practical and surprisingly up-to-date book.

IS THAT ALL THERE IS?

A few years ago a popular song "Is That All There Is?" told of a woman whose round of parties, fun, and excitement was unfulfilling. "Busy but empty" summarized her life.

Maybe the words "busy but empty" describe you too. You're in a frantic whirlpool of responsibilities, a round of activities that get you nowhere. You exert energy but you gain no ground. Your motor is running, but your odometer mileage reading stays at zero.

Despair abounds. Life is a bore. People are gloomy, despondent, bewildered, hopeless. The pursuit of happiness only makes them more unhappy! People are expending their efforts and energies on *everything* to try to determine why they should expend their efforts and energies on *anything*.

So it was with Solomon. In his intense look at life, he stated that, in a sense at least, all is vanity. "Vanity," as the Hebrew word is rendered in the King James Version, means futile, empty, transient, fleeting, valueless, meaningless. For Solomon, the wealthiest, wisest king of Israel, every box he opened was empty. Nothing truly satisfied. The key to unlock the meaning of life was lost. Lost, that is, as long as he looked "under the sun" (a phrase he used twenty-nine times). *The point of the Book of Ecclesiastes is that you'll never find the key while you're looking in the wrong boxes. But look in the right place—and the key is there!*

Consider: Ecclesiastes is thus not a negative, pessimistic book, a misfit in the Bible. Instead, it's a positive, optimistic work with wonderful news for modern man. Solomon said, "Don't look there, or there, or there. Look over here. I know. I found it!"

And so can you.

WHERE'S THE KEY?

One time my wife stepped from our utility room into the attached garage, and unknowingly locked the door behind her. As soon as she closed the door, she realized her mistake. But she didn't panic. Why? Because we keep a house key in a secret place in the garage. So she simply got the key and she was back in the house.

No panic, no franticness, no confusion—because she knew where to find the key.

Ecclesiastes takes us to the key to life. And that key hangs at the back door of the book, in the last two verses: "Here is the conclusion . . . Fear God and keep His commandments. . . . For God will bring every deed into judgment . . ." (Ecc. 12:13-14).

Only a right relationship to God—and a realization that He is in control and will correct every iniquity in life—can give meaning to life. That's the key! And Solomon doesn't leave you dangling till the end of the book. He gives you the key throughout the book; four other times he states that man is to fear God (3:14; 5:7; 7:18; 8:12).

Does "fearing God" mean being afraid of Him? Sometimes. But not here. Here it means to respect Him, to be in loving allegiance to Him, to revere Him, to hold Him in awe. The person who respects God as God, and commits himself to Him will willingly worship, serve, and obey Him. And as the New Testament points out, that relationship begins by trusting Jesus Christ as your Saviour from sin.

Want the key to life? Then look to the Creator, not to creation. The secret is not found in life itself and all it offers. Look there and you'll conclude that "all is meaningless." Life without Christ is pitifully empty, but life with Christ is wonderfully fulfilling.

ENJOY LIFE

Many people, on reading the Book of Ecclesiastes, have come away wondering why it's even in the Bible. A number of verses seem to point to hopelessness and gloom. Pessimism seems to pervade the book. "Everything is meaningless" occurs six times; "this too is meaningless" is stated twenty-three times. Life is said to be fleeting (6:12; 7:15; 9:9; 11:10), and several times death is viewed with despair. Injustices seem evident, as mentioned in at least six of the chapters (4, 6, 7, 8, 9, 10).

But is Ecclesiastes really a book of pessimism? Other statements in the book seem to say no. For instance, six times the writer states that life is a gift from God (2:24; 3:13; 5:18-20; 8:15; 9:7, 9). And seven times he enjoins us to enjoy life by eating, drinking, and working. Injustices are present, it is true; but these will be corrected (3:17; 8:12-13; 11:9; 12:14). And God is in control (3:14; 5:2; 7:14; 9:1). Those thoughts hardly seem appropriate for a man of pessimistic despair!

What, then, is the answer? Simply this: Pessimism is the starting point, but not the stopping point.

Yes, admit that life seems in vain, that you can't figure it all out, that life is fleeting and death is coming. But don't stay there! Move on to the truth that, in spite of these enigmas, life *is* worth living.

Solomon's advice to eat, drink, and enjoy life is not a "live-it-up-and-forget-God" approach. Instead, it is sound advice that begins with God. He has given life to us as a gift, and only through Him can we enjoy it.

Remember: Only the one who fears and trusts in the Lord can fully enjoy the simple blessings of life, such as eating and working, because he recognizes these are from the hand of God. That's Solomon's message: Fear the Lord—and enjoy life!

WHAT'S THE USE?

The alarm clock goes off. You reach over from your sleep to turn it off. You drag yourself out of bed. You get dressed and wash your face. You eat breakfast. You go to work. You come home and go to bed tired. You do the same thing the next day.

Why that routine? Where does it get you? With your salary you buy food so you can eat in order to have strength to go to work!

The seeming uselessness of work troubled Solomon. "What does man gain from all his labor at which he toils under the sun?" (1:3). Man works but gets no gain from it. The word _gain,_ an accounting term, refers to the excess of income over expense, the profit on the bottom line. What is "on the bottom line" for man? What _lasting_ benefit, profit, or surplus comes from work? None, actually.

Not that Solomon was opposed to work. But he came to realize that work _of itself_ doesn't really solve the riddle of life. Work has its advantages, obviously. But toil also has its drawbacks.

An entire generation comes on the earth and works, but then dies off, while the earth itself—inanimate and less valuable than man—remains. The sun rises and sets, the wind constantly moves in cycles, and the rivers flow into the sea and return to their sources (vv. 5-7). Though repetitious in motion, these aspects of inanimate nature do continue on and outlast man. By strange contrast, man in his activity never finds total fulfillment or completion (v. 8), nothing for man is ever completely new (vv. 9-10), and nothing and no one is remembered for long (v. 11). Meaninglessness in nature is exceeded by meaninglessness in humanity.

Work hard? Yes. But remember Jesus' words: "For what shall it profit a man if he shall gain the whole world, and lose his own soul?" (Mark 8:26)

CHASING AFTER WIND

"All the things that are done under the sun . . . are meaningless, a chasing after the wind" (1:14).

"Chasing the wind" was Solomon's striking way of picturing utter uselessness. The words *futility* and *chasing after wind* occur eight times in Ecclesiastes—each time in connection with some effort of man. And they are all in the first half of the book (1:14; 2:11, 17, 26; 4:4, 6, 16; 6:9). His subject in 1:12–6:6 is on the wind-chasing *futility of human effort.*

Solomon the Sage then repeated a different refrain in the second half of the book. The question "Who knows what is good for a man?" and the related statement "Man cannot discover" occur in various forms in 6:12; 7:14, 24, 28; 8:7 and 17. And the thought "No one knows what is ahead" is repeated in 9:1, 12; 10:14; 11:2, 5, and 6. These themes in the second half of the book (6:10–11:6) underscore the *inability of man's understanding.*

In Solomon's exploration of "all that is done under heaven" (1:13), he concluded that man's unaided attempts to uncover the key to life are wind-chasing (v. 14). The reason is simple: Much of life's twists cannot be straightened by man's efforts nor can life's deficiencies be made up by human activity (v. 15).

Then he concluded that acquiring wisdom—human understanding—is also a wind-chasing futility (vv. 16-17). The reason: Increased knowledge often brings increased sorrow and distress (v. 18).

And that's where humanism leads us. Life viewed "under the sun"—that is, "down here" on earth apart from God—is a breathless pursuit after air. You can't catch the wind by your hand. And neither can you figure out life by your own doings and deliberations. Without God, your life is a marathon without meaning, a sprint with no significance.

Dashing after wind? Only in Christ can you find true satisfaction.

PROFIT IN PLEASURE?

Many people approach life as if it's a daily Disney World, a continual bustle of fun and games. Their goal is pleasure, amusement, entertainment. Every weekend is a Mardi Gras, an escapade in revelry and festivity. "If it feels good, do it." That's the hedonist's happy-go-lucky approach to life.

For others, life consists of accomplishments, achievements, acquisitions. They long for recognition, for public fame and acclaim. They work for money—to make it, to invest it, to save it, to spend it. "Things" become their companions—posh houses, plush gardens, plump bank accounts.

What these pleasure-maddened people do not know is that a man of great ability and wealth tried all these things 3,000 years ago. And Solomon found that they do *not* satisfy. Ecclesiastes 2:1-11 tells of his hunt for happiness in which he tried the very things people are still trying today.

In his experimentations he checked out laughter; he tried drinking; he undertook numerous building projects; he accumulated slaves and flocks; he had wealth, musical entertainment, and even illicit sex.

He enjoyed great fame and acquired everything he desired (vv. 1-10). Yet he concluded, "everything was meaningless' (v. 11).

Judging by today's entertainment-drugged society, you would think the quest for fulfillment is found in music and money, in buying and building, in levity and lust, in servants and sex. But Solomon shouts, "Not so!"

A question: Why waste your time, money, and energy on things Solomon has already told us don't satisfy? Don't hunt for happiness in the wrong haystacks.

YOU CAN'T TAKE IT WITH YOU

At the age of 97, Bertrand Russell, the humanist philosopher concluded his three-volume autobiography by stating that much of what he had done in life had been useless.

Sounds like Solomon, doesn't it? Solomon considered useless much of what he had done in life. And yet he believed in God and Russell didn't. Even wisdom, Solomon wrote, seems to have only relative merit (2:12-16). True, it is preferable to folly "just as light is better than darkness" (v. 13). But since both the wise man and the fool die and are forgotten (vv. 14-16), wisdom is not the ultimate answer. It can't preserve a person from his final enemy, death.

Many people today fall into the same trap, thinking man's wisdom is the answer to life. So they pursue knowledge—taking more courses, reading more books, earning more degrees. Yet they discover knowledge has its limitations; even the wise die and are forgotten.

What's more, Solomon realized that his possessions, painfully acquired, could not be taken with him after death. They would be left to someone else, and he had no way of knowing if that person would be wise or foolish, industrious or lazy (vv. 18-21). Even in life all he got for his hard work was pain, grief, and restless nights (vv. 22-23). How like so many people today!

Therefore the best thing one can do, the Sage advised, is to enjoy one's life and work, for they are gifts from God (v. 24). Only God can provide genuine enjoyment and He gives it not to sinners but only to those who please Him (vv. 25-26).

Solomon's counsel was not a call to hedonism. He was not saying, "Live it up because you go around only once." No. He was saying, "Enjoy the simple things in life. Food and work are not to be despised. They are to be accepted as God's gifts to those who please Him."

What about you? Are you looking to your education and your job for ultimate satisfaction apart from God? Focus your life on *Him;* seek to please *Him.* For without Him you'll never find true enjoyment.

MAN IN A BOX

In 1974 my daughter Barb, then seventeen, was seriously injured in a car accident. She had two brain surgeries within eight days after the accident, and she remained unconscious for two and a half months. What a painful time for our family! That event—like any hospital experience—was a traumatic time which disrupted and altered our schedule for many months. Life is like that. Events overtake us; circumstances interrupt our plans. Many events are totally beyond our control. But they *are* under God's control.

In Ecclesiastes 3:1-8 the whole range of life is cited in fourteen pairs of opposites. In God's hand "there is a time for everything" (v. 1). God has a planned time for every activity and man's efforts, no matter how strong and persistent, cannot alter them.

When King Solomon wrote, "A time to be born and a time to die" (v. 2), he meant that the day of our birth and the day of our death are beyond our control; they are timed by God. When Solomon wrote that there is "a time to plant and a time to uproot" (v. 2), he meant the farmer's activities are already calendarized for him by God's seasons. Man's seemingly opposite experiences of killing and healing, of breaking down and building up, of casting away stones and gathering stones, of seeking and losing, of keeping and tossing away, of tearing and sewing, of being silent and speaking, of war and peace—the timing of these is not determined by man. Even the situations that move us to various emotions such as weeping or laughing and loving or hating elude our ability to govern them. This confronts us with the startling fact that we are finite, limited, and in a box.

Think about it: Solomon wasn't saying all these activities are acceptable. He wasn't arguing that it is okay for us to do all twenty-eight things he mentioned. Instead, his point was that there are times when these things *do* happen—and their timing is beyond the control of any individual. So be wise and join with the psalmist today in saying to the Lord, "My times are in Your hands" (Ps. 31:15). Keep your eyes on Him who controls all things.

ALL THINGS BEAUTIFUL

"What does the worker gain from his toil?" (3:9). The answer is "nothing"—nothing, that is, of lasting permanent value that can alter God's events and their timing. The experiences of life—though they appear to be controlled by us—are in reality beyond our grasp.

Yet these events are not without a meaningful pattern. God "has made everything beautiful in its time" (v. 11). And yet that pattern often evades us. We have a longing to see some meaningful order ("He has set eternity in the hearts of men"). We want to see the big picture as God does. We have a deep-seated desire to discern the purpose and destiny of life—to sense how it all fits together. Yet we are ignorant of God's ways. He has a plan, but He hasn't revealed all its details to us.

What then can we do? Solomon again pointed to his twofold solution: enjoy life (vv. 12-13) and fear God (v. 14). We can't add to what God has done. What He does will endure forever, and His plans are unchangeable (vv. 14-15). Though boxed in by our human frailties, we *can* submit to His plans and enjoy the gift of life.

Consider the answer: Why has God placed this unquenchable hunger in the hearts of humans, this deep desire for perspective on the eternity of things? His purpose is to get us to sense our inadequacies and turn to Him. You may not understand all the facets of His beautiful plan, but you can bow in submissive worship to Him, recognizing that He is the sovereign God of the universe.

IT'S NOT FAIR

Ron E. Eaton spent sixteen years in prison for a crime he did not commit. Sometimes juries are swayed by strong arguments by prosecuting attorneys who twist facts, or the defense presents a weak case. Other times judges and lawyers are bribed to favor a rich guilty person and punish a poor innocent person.

Injustice in the halls of justice — wickedness where there should be righteousness — is a strange twist of irony. In fact, it's a terrible, hard-to-understand crime. Solomon wrote, "I saw something else under the sun: In the place of judgment, wickedness was there" (3:16).

Is there no answer to this deplorable situation in our courts? Must we continue to see evil men get away with crime and the innocent unfairly punished?

There *is* an answer. Man in his efforts is unable to correct many wrongs. But Solomon points us to the One who has the solution. "God will bring to judgment both the righteous and the wicked, for there will be a time for every activity, a time for every deed" (v. 17).

Not only is there a time to be born, a time to die, a time to plant, and a time to harvest, etc. (vv. 1-8), but there will also come a time when God will right all wrongs.

How about you? Do you feel wronged at times? Do you at times sense that you are not getting a "fair shake" in life? Are you the object of mistreatment, of unfair actions by your spouse, friends, or people at work? Take heart. God is the Chief Judge and in the end He will correct all wrongs and dispense absolute justice. What a comfort!

DEAD LIKE A DOG?

Why should you and I die like animals? Even death seems unfair.

Solomon spoke to this anomaly in Ecclesiastes 3:18-22. Both men and beasts expire, and their corpses are buried and decompose. Humans and animals go to the same place—the grave.

Not that man *is* an animal, but that he is like an animal in physical death. Why is this? Because God is showing people their frailty and their creatureliness, in order to get them to return to Him. Realizing that death comes to humans just as it comes to animals should make us realize we are finite.

Some people say verses 18-22 teach that at death humans, like animals, become annihilated and have no conscious existence after this life. But that misses the point. The passage is teaching that all living creatures die. Like animals, humans die and their corpses are buried. But unlike animals, humans live on in conscious existence in heaven or hell.

We observe the lifeless carcass of our pet dog or the cold corpse of a close relative, but we can't observe the destiny of the life of the animal or the person. "Who knows if the spirit of man rises upward and if the spirit of the animal goes down into the earth?" (v. 21). Some say this verse expresses uncertainty about life after death. However, the verse is affirming that we cannot *observe* what happens after death. We can see what happens to the body of our dog and of our dad, but we can't see with our eyes what happens to either spirit. But God does tell us!

The animal's life goes "down"—he no longer exists. And the spirit of a person goes "upward"—he goes on living. Does this verse claim that all go to heaven? No, it simply affirms that man's spirit lives beyond death, that whereas he dies physically like animals, he lives on spiritually and thus differs from animals. Man's spirit goes upward to God—some people go to Him to face conscious, eternal judgment under His wrath, and others go to Him to enjoy the blessings of heaven forever.

A happy thought: Trust Christ as your Saviour, and you need not fear death. As the writer to the Hebrews wrote, Jesus' death frees "those who all their lives were in slavery by their fear of death" (Heb. 2:15).

MORE DEAD-END STREETS

Oppression has always been with us. Powerful rulers forcing hundreds of slaves to work long hard hours. Whites keeping blacks from getting meaningful jobs. Hucksters taking advantage of the elderly. The wealthy wielding power over the poor.

These slaves, blacks, elderly, and poor sit trapped, with no way of escape. And no comfort. Only unhappiness—and tears. Solomon said that such oppression is an "evil . . . under the sun" (4:1-3). He said that being dead seems preferable to being mistreated and maligned, oppressed and harassed (v. 2). Or not having been born at all seems more desirable, he wrote, than facing harsh treatment at the hands of others.

Cruelty of the powerful and rich over the weak and poor is matched by the cruelty of equals who seek to outdo, outlie, and outstrip each other. Such ruthless rivalry sprouts from envy, a cancerous disease of the soul. Keeping up with the Joneses is not enough. They want to keep *ahead* of the Joneses. "This too," according to Solomon the Sage, is "chasing after wind" (v. 4). It's useless—a waste of time and energy.

What motive compels you in your work? *Why* do you work hard, seeking to achieve? Is it because you envy what others have and you want those things too? Is it because you want to get ahead of other people? Envy-driven labor is seldom enjoyed. It becomes burdensome, with little genuine satisfaction. As Billy Graham said, "Envy takes the joy, happiness, and contentment out of living." Work to serve, to help others, not to ride roughshod over people.

Does Solomon mean we shouldn't be ambitious and industrious? No, because laziness (folding one's hands) leads to self-destruction (v. 5). The point is that a few possessions ("one handful") with peace are much better than much wealth ("two handfuls") with strife and toil (v. 6).

Good questions: Why pursue greedy ambition when it gets you only trouble? Why chase after wealth if it means more strife? Why work from envy if it fails to satisfy?

TWO ARE BETTER

Many people die intestate, that is, without having made a will. It's then difficult to be sure their heirs receive their possessions. But suppose they have no heirs. What then? A lonely person of greed with no heir accumulates goods that cannot be passed on, and this makes his work seem in vain (4:7-8). Never "content with his wealth," always wanting more, he toils endlessly, only to find no enjoyment in life and no one to whom he can pass on what he has acquired.

Solomon advised that in such cases it's wise to stick with a companion, to share one's work and wealth: "Two are better than one." A shared relationship gives better profits, help, comfort, and protection. And three people make an even stronger bond of friendship and help (vv. 9-12).

Even rising from a disadvantaged nobody ("a poor but wise youth") or from being an incarcerated prisoner to a prestigious king is wind-chasing. Why? Because such a person will soon be forgotten, and another ruler will take his place (vv. 13-16).

It's a fact: Human activity has its limitations in providing the key to life. Trying to escape economic or social oppression, ambitiously seeking to advance beyond one's neighbors or coworkers, working alone without an heir, achieving without advancing—where do these get you? Nowhere. Therefore to trust in fleeting things is unwise. To trust in the eternal God is wise.

DON'T FAKE IT

It's Sunday morning. You go to church. But your mind is miles away. You sing the hymns without any thought of the words. You toss a tip in the offering plate. You repeat some memorized formulas. Your mind wanders during the sermon. You're there only because it's expected of you. You mouth some promises to God while only casually aware of what you are saying.

Such worship is actually no worship at all. External motions; pretended religion; thoughtless singing, praying, and giving are repulsive to the heart of God. Fake religion can undo the fruits of your labor.

Solomon explained that genuine worship means going to the house of God with an unpretentious attitude ("guard your steps"), a readiness to listen (5:1), and a hesitation to speak (vv. 2-3). The more the words, the more the possibility of saying something wrong. This is parallel to having problems—the more the cares, the greater the possibility of dreaming about them. Since "God is in heaven" and we "are on earth," that is, since He is infinite and we are finite, we ought not be hasty in speaking (to make a vow) before Him.

True worship means being genuine before God, and promptly fulfilling the promises (vows) you make to Him (vv. 4-6). Trying to get out of keeping a vow to God is worse than making no vow at all. Trying to renege on a promise you made to God may make Him angry.

What God wants in worship is "unconditional seriousness," as one writer put it. Only one thing can transpose stale, empty religiosity into significant worship, and that is fearing God (v. 7). Once again Solomon directed us to the key to life—reverential awe and loving allegiance to God.

Give thought to this: Fail to take God seriously and you undo all the results of your efforts—and you stir the anger of God (v. 7). But maintain an expectant, quiet, heartfelt worshipful attitude toward God—and you'll enjoy His blessings.

KEEP THAT VOW

Richard W. DeHaan and Herbert Vander Lugt of Radio Bible Class coauthored an excellent paperback on Ecclesiastes called *The Art of Staying Off Dead-End Streets* (Victor Books, 1974). In commenting on Ecclesiastes 5:1-7, they offer this advice: "Stop for a moment and take a look at your own life. Perhaps you have made a promise to God in a time of difficulty, and forgotten it now that the crisis is over. Maybe you have sung words of tremendous devotion to the Lord, telling Him that you will give Him your time, your service, your earthly goods, and even yourself. If you have not given serious thought to the words that flowed so glibly from your lips, heed the warning of Solomon."

Have you made a promise to God which is yet unfulfilled (vv. 4-6)? If so, plan now to carry it out. Set a date for keeping that promise—and stick to it. God will honor you for it.

In verses 8-9 Solomon returned to the subject of oppression which he addressed earlier in 4:1-3. Here (in 5:8-9) he said we ought "not be surprised" when the poor are oppressed or when justice is not carried out. Tolerate it? No. Be surprised by it? No. Even officials are oppressed by those above them. In other words oppression occurs at all levels of society. Even kings or other heads of government practice extortion.

So some people ask, Why work if my money is to be taken by someone else? Why be concerned about my rights when justice is not often executed? Again a point made several times in the Book of Ecclesiastes is that we can't correct all the ills and evils of the world. Yes, we should do what we can to alleviate suffering and ease the pains of poverty, oppression, and injustice.

Good advice: Don't be agitated if sin doesn't go away. Rest in the Lord.

MONEY FLIES

A retiree from New Jersey moved to Florida with his life savings of $11,300. When he went to deposit it in a Florida bank, the envelope with the money was missing. Then he remembered putting out some trash that morning. Before he could recover the envelope, it was buried under fifty truckloads of garbage being dumped into a huge pit at the city dump. The loss of his savings put him into deep depression. That's the way with money: easy come, easy go.

Ecclesiastes 5:10-17 tells us seven problems caused by money.
1. Money doesn't satisfy. "Whoever loves money never has enough" (v. 10).
2. Money is consumed by others. "As goods increase, so do those who consume them" (v. 11).
3. Money robs sleep. "The abundance of a rich man permits him no sleep" (v. 12).
4. Money brings trouble. "Wealth is hoarded to the harm of its owner" (v. 13).
5. Money is easily lost. "Wealth [is] lost through some misfortune" (v. 14).
6. Money can't be taken with you at death. "He takes nothing from his labor" (v. 15).
7. Money brings grief. "All his days he sits in darkness with great frustration, affliction, and anger" (v. 17).

Our money-crazed civilization tries to drown out these truths. But that doesn't alter the fact that money increases anxieties.

So don't be continually scrambling for more and more money. Wealth is not the key to life. Instead of reducing your problems, riches often increase them. Remember that Jesus said, "A man's life does not consist in the abundance of his possessions" (Luke 12:15).

Therefore: We should be content with what we have and enjoy life. No need to brood over the brevity of life; instead take life as it comes—as a gift from God (Ecc. 5:18-20).

NEVER SATISFIED

Back in Ecclesiastes 3 and 4 Solomon spoke about several injustices—injustices in courts, dying like an animal, and oppression, greed, and envy. Then in chapter 6 he wrote about another "evil under the sun": Man's work may not even be enjoyed.

A man lies machine-supported in a hospital intensive care unit. His erratic heartbeat is monitored on a computer screen. Tubes stab his body in numerous places. As a wealthy executive, he has lacked nothing his heart has desired. He has money and is honored by others. "But God does not enable him to enjoy them" (6:1). If he dies, his wealth may pass to a stranger (v. 2). Ironically the stranger enjoys the possessions of the wealthy man—a stranger who did nothing to earn or deserve them.

Or suppose a person does live on, and has many children and a long life. Is he better off? Not necessarily. If he can't "enjoy his prosperity," he's worse off alive than being born dead (vv. 3-6).

A man works hard in order to eat, but "his appetite is never satisfied" (v. 7). Work then seems futile. Even wisdom and wise conduct don't seem to have all the answers (v. 8). So a man is better off with what he can see than what he can only imagine. As we would say, "A bird in the hand is worth two in the bush."

All of which says the same thing Solomon underscored before. If God has given you life, be content with what you have, and enjoy life.

Don't forget: "Godliness with contentment is great gain. . . . But if we have food and clothing, we will be content with that. . . . For the love of money is a root of all kinds of evil" (1 Tim. 6:6, 8, 10).

WHAT'S AHEAD?

What do Jeane Dixon and Hal Lindsey have in common? One thing: They both are interested in the future. Jeane Dixon predicts the future by feeling the "vibrations" in someone's hands or looking into a client's eyes. Hal Lindsey, on the other hand, uses the Scriptures as his telescope on what's ahead.

Astrology's prognostications include a lot of guesses—and thus a lot of misses. But prophecy in the Bible is God's firm declaration not of what *might* happen but of what *will* happen. God has programmed the future with numerous details regarding Israel, the church, the second coming of Christ, the millennium, the destiny of the saved and of the unsaved, etc.

Even so, many events in our lives are *not* foretold. We are in the dark regarding tomorrow's occurrences, next year's happenings, next decade's episodes. The future lies beyond our grasp. Our inability to know with certitude what lies ahead in our lives demonstrates that we are finite. That we are limited. That man is not God.

And that's the point of the second half of Ecclesiastes: the inability of human understanding (6:10–11:6). Repeatedly, Solomon wrote, "Man does not know what awaits him." And since we are ignorant of the future, we often cannot know what is best to do now. "Who knows what is good for a man?" is another recurring question in this portion of Ecclesiastes.

Remember this: Since God has the future in *His* hands, it's useless to wrestle with Him who is stronger than you (6:10). The more you argue with God, the more empty your words become (v. 11). You may as well give in and recognize that you alone cannot say which actions may be better than others (v. 12). As Paul asked, "Who are you, O man, to talk back to God?" (Rom. 9:20)

GOOD GRIEF

Joseph was sold to Egypt by his brothers. But years later, when Joseph had become elevated to prime minister of Egypt and had saved many people's lives during a long famine, he told his brothers, "You intended to harm me, but God intended it for good" (Gen. 50:20).

That reversal—from seeming adversity to evident blessing—has been experienced by many Christians. That's the point of Ecclesiastes 7:1-10. *Adversity isn't always a sign of God's disfavor.* This is the other side of the coin that Solomon looked at in the previous chapter. There he had observed that *prosperity is not always a sign of God's favor.*

Hard times *are* hard; but they can *also* be helpful. Why did Solomon say, "The day of death [is] better than the day of birth" and that it's "better to go to a house of mourning than to go to a house of feasting" (7:1b-2a)? Why did he declare that "sorrow is better than laughter" (v. 3)? Answer: More spiritual lessons can be learned in a funeral home than in a banquet hall. Viewing death in the face can cause us to reflect seriously on the grim realities of life's brevity and death's certainty.

How about you? Are all your parties, jokes, and fun times merely a facade, an attempted cover-up to escape thinking seriously about what will happen to you after death? If so, it's time to stop your three-ring circus and to think seriously—to remember that "man is destined to die once, and after that to face judgment" (Heb. 9:27).

WHO WANTS PRESSURE?

No one naturally welcomes or requests pressure. We tend to shun the excessive demands of life, to look for easy ways out. But as we saw in yesterday's reading, adversity—even death—can be deeply beneficial.

In the next verses in Ecclesiastes, Solomon discussed two other kinds of seeming adversity: the pressure of criticism and the pressure of bribery.

Ever been criticized by a person you know is wise? It hurts, doesn't it? And yet you know that heeding the rebuke can have beneficial effects (7:5). By contrast, the empty frivolity of fools is as temporary and useless as dried thornbushes that burn quickly but soon die out (v. 6).

Pressure to favor one person over another—by oppression or bribery—is another problem (v. 7). Such pressure can show up your true colors. It can give you opportunity to exercise patience, rather than to explode in anger (vv. 8-9). It can lead you to accept God's timing rather than to long unrealistically for the "good ole days" (v. 10). True wisdom is beneficial; it can shelter you from problems and even preserve your life (vv. 11-12). Wisdom can also help us see that both prosperity and adversity are from God (vv. 13-14).

Questions: Are you experiencing good times? Then rejoice in God's blessing. Are you experiencing hard times? Then learn from God's lessons. Are you facing pressure today—the pressure of rebuke or of favoritism or of other difficult circumstances? Most people respond to those difficulties with impatience, pride, or anger. What good does anger do? After all, "anger resides in the lap of fools" (7:9). For the child of God suffering may be considered beneficial because it "produces perseverance" (Rom. 5:3).

BALANCED LIVING

We tend toward extremes. We overreact when we see injustices. For example, we see a godly person who dies relatively young or a sinner who lives to old age (7:15), and we conclude that we too may as well be ungodly. Or we react in the opposite way and decide that the godly person wasn't godly enough, and so we decide to become more righteous than he was.

When Solomon wrote, "Do not be overrighteous" (v. 16), he meant, "Don't go to the excess of a pious, holier-than-thou attitude. Avoid extreme legalism, ascetic practices, a sanctimonious hypocrisy." You can't avoid a premature death (v. 15) by working up your own self-righteousness.

When Solomon wrote, "Do not be overwicked" (v. 17), he was *not* suggesting it's okay to sin so long as you aren't excessive. Instead, he meant that if you see a wicked person prospering, don't give in to unbridled sin, hoping *you* will prosper.

The one "who fears God will avoid all extremes" (v. 18). He won't respond to injustices by an overzealous self-righteousness nor by an unchecked, overindulgent sensualism. Fearing God, that is, revering Him, keeps us balanced. It helps us avoid both extremes.

Self-imposed righteousness can never cover the reality of sin. "There is not a righteous man on earth who does what is right and never sins" (v. 20). And man's own wisdom is definitely inadequate compared to God's (vv. 23-25). Some men escape the temptation of the seductress (v. 26), but many don't. Even though "God made mankind upright," people have turned to sin (v. 29).

To consider: Don't trust in your outward piety. That won't eliminate your sin. The only solution is to turn to Christ for salvation. That is wise—and balanced—living.

WILL JUSTICE COME?

Increased taxes. Runaway inflation. Rising national debts. People tend to blame their governments for these and other problems which make it difficult for Mr. Joe Average to make ends meet.

But government is not all bad. Human government was established by God to serve, for one thing, as an agent of justice (Rom. 13:1-5; 1 Peter 2:13-18). This truth led Solomon to point out that justice will be executed even though we do not always know when. Therefore it's sensible to submit to those in authority.

"Obey the king's command," Solomon advised (Ecc. 8:2). Don't try to get out of your oath of loyalty, nor be an accomplice in crime, nor question the king's authority (vv. 2-4). Submission is wise (v. 1), for it will keep you from trouble (v. 5).

You may be in misery now, suffering injustice, but in God's time justice will be carried out (v. 6). Just as we can't control the wind nor determine the day of our death (vv. 7-8), we are also unable to predict when those who are taking advantage of others (v. 9) will be judged. But it is certain that sinners will not "get away with it" forever. "Wickedness will not release those who practice it" (v. 8).

Other evidences of injustice are cited in verses 10-14: (1) Wicked people hypocritically go to the temple and are even praised. (2) Sentences against the accused are delayed, thus encouraging others to get away with it too. (3) Wicked people keep on sinning and living on. (4) Sinners are blessed and the godly suffer.

Though retribution seems missing, Solomon went back again to his double theme: fear God ("I know it will go better with God-fearing men," v. 12) and enjoy life ("nothing is better . . . than to eat and drink and be glad," v. 15).

So take heart: Though "no one can comprehend" God's workings (v. 17), we can enjoy life which is from Him.

HOW THEN SHOULD WE LIVE?

Puny man. We are so ignorant! We don't know whether God will bring prosperity or adversity (Ecc. 6:10–7:14). We often forget that sin can't be covered by self-righteousness (7:15-27). And we don't know when the wicked will be judged by government leaders (8:1-17). Nor do we know what lies ahead. But we do know we all face the inevitable event, death. And yet we are ignorant of *when* it will take place (9:1-12).

We know that death comes to everyone—whether righteous or wicked, good or bad (v. 2). And that's the rub. It doesn't seem right that "the same destiny" (v. 3) should overtake us all. This leads many people to sin, while they reason, "What difference does it make? I'll die anyway."

Yet there is hope so long as there is life. "Even a live dog is better off than a dead lion!" (v. 4) Being despised (in Bible times the dog was considered the lowest animal) and alive is far better than being highly honored (the lion was considered the greatest animal) and dead.

While alive, we have hope But when we're dead, all opportunities for learning, for loving, for achieving are gone (vv. 5-6). In death you can no longer work, plan, and gain knowledge (v. 10). This doesn't mean that we are unconscious and cease to exist, but that in the grave the body has no more share in the activities of earth.

How then should we live? By enjoying the life God has given us (vv. 7-10). Enjoy food, clothes, cleanliness, joy (in Solomon's time wearing white clothes and anointing oneself with oils were done on festive occasions), marriage, and work—"for this is your lot in life."

FLIES IN YOUR CHANEL NO. 5

In and following the days of the Great Depression, my father worked for a company in Phoenix that barely gave him a living wage. When he quit to take a better-paying job, his former boss hired an inexperienced worker and had to pay him much more than he paid my dad.

Maybe you've had a similar kind of injustice. You work hard, but then someone less experienced than you is hired for a position higher than yours.

You expect the swift runner to win the race, but sometimes he loses. You expect the strong person to win the battle, but occasionally he doesn't. You expect brilliant people to gain wealth, but sometimes they don't (9:11). People's efforts seem the objects of mere chance, rather than the result of genuine work and ability. Like fish caught in a net, tragedy suddenly falls on the unsuspecting (v. 12).

Solomon illustrated this strange turn of events by a story (vv. 13-16). A powerful king attacked a small city but couldn't conquer it. Surprisingly the city was saved by the counsel of a poor man who was wise. And yet there was another ironic twist: People in the city forgot the poor wise man. The point Solomon underlined is that even wisdom, though preferable to folly, may be nullified by forgetfulness.

It can also be nullified by a little foolishness. Put dead insects, totally worthless, in your bottle of Chanel No. 5, and the expensive perfume will smell from the rotting. Foolish leaders reveal their stupidity (10:2-7) and often undo the work of their wise predecessors.

Wisdom can also be nullified if you are careless (by falling into a pit you dig, being bitten by a snake, being injured by stones you've quarried, or getting hurt by logs you split, 10:8-9), or if your timing is off (e.g., sharpening an ax after you have cut down a tree, or charming a snake after it has bitten, vv. 10-11).

All of which billboards this truth: Man does not know what lies ahead. So keep your eyes on the One who does.

WISE WORDS

Words can get you in trouble. Ever been in a social gathering where one person talks on and on? Eventually, he says something that reveals his ignorance, words which show that his pretense for knowing something about everything is just that—pretense.

In Ecclesiastes, Solomon called such a person a fool. "A fool is consumed by his own lips," "his words are folly," "the fool multiplies words" (10:12-14).

Even though a talkative fool may weary himself by hard work, he is still so ignorant that he doesn't even know the way to town! (v. 14)

Sometimes such fools even get to top positions in government. And that's why Solomon resumed in 10:16-20 the subject of rulers which he had discussed in 9:13–10:7. A nation with such a ruler— one who is so self-indulgent that he spends mornings feasting—is unfortunate (10:16). Self-focused rulers continue in their levity and drunkenness, thinking that with money they can buy themselves out of any problem (vv. 18-19). But fortunate is the nation with a noble, self-controlled king (v. 17).

Our tendency in such situations is to criticize the ruler (or even our boss), to malign and deride him for his sin. Such criticism, however, is dangerous, Solomon stated. The word may get around by gossip ("a bird . . . may carry your words") and we may be in trouble because of our own words (vv. 20-21).

The lesson: Be wise with your words no matter what your circumstances. "Words from a wise man's mouth are gracious" (v. 12).

STOCK MARKET BLUES

No fortune-teller can affirm well in advance which direction certain investments will take. In fact no business executive can predict with certainty the ups and downs of the stock market. These are unknowns. Weathermen attempt to forecast the weather days ahead, but they are often wrong. Even farmers are incapable of foretelling which crops will succeed and which ones won't.

Solomon wrote that since these uncertainties of investments, weather, and farming are with us, we should be diligent in our work (11:1-6).

The advice "Cast your bread upon the waters, for after many days you will find it again" (v. 1) is probably referring to involvement in foreign commerce in which ships would finally return with a gain in one's trade investments. Some ventures succeed, others fail; therefore, don't put all your eggs in one basket (v. 2). God controls the outcome apart from our knowledge, just as He controls the downpour of rain from the clouds or the falling of a tree apart from our knowledge (v. 3).

If you watch the wind or the clock—that is, if you wait for the perfect time and circumstances before you act—you'll never get anywhere (v. 4). In fact all your wind-watching will never enable you to predict the weather with exactitude. Nor can anyone understand all God's doings (v. 5).

What it all means: Our responsibility is to act, to work hard day and night, and to leave the results to Him (v. 6). Don't sit around trying to outguess God. Invest wisely, work hard, and leave the results with Him.

YOU GO AROUND ONLY ONCE

"Christians are killjoys." So say many people. But they are wrong! Repeatedly Solomon urged believers to enjoy life—and especially when we are young. "Be happy, young man, while you are young, and let your heart give you joy in the days of your youth" (11:9). Since death ("the days of darkness," v. 8) is coming, youth are to "follow the ways of [their] heart and whatever [their] eyes see" (v. 9). But that's no open season on sin! Solomon wasn't approving *sinful* impulses, for he immediately added, "but know that for all these things God will bring you to judgment" (v. 9).

In other words our pleasures are to be pure, our happiness is to be holy. Yes, have fun, but do so within the boundaries of God's laws, and in view of eternity. Life is compared to light and death to darkness. Seeing the sun (v. 7) is a way of saying that being alive is sweet and you enjoy the life-giving benefits of the sun.

A word especially for Christian young people: Don't be sad ("banish anxiety from your heart"), but don't abuse your body either ("cast off the troubles of your body," v. 10). Be balanced emotionally and physically. Since your days of exuberant, carefree youth are soon gone, make the most of them. You go around only once, but don't forget: After that you'll face the sovereign Judge!

> Only one life;
> 'Twill soon be past.
> Only what's done
> For Christ will last.

REMEMBER YOUR CREATOR

"I'll wait till I'm old and then I'll turn to Christ." Such a delay tactic is foolhardy. Only the youth who reflect on the fact that God is their sovereign Creator, and live accordingly, have their lives in proper perspective. As DeHaan and Vander Lugt explain, "When a young person combines the enthusiasm, idealism, and energy of youth with a deep devotion to the Lord, he has all the ingredients for a wonderful life" (*The Art of Staying Off Dead-end Streets*, Victor, 1974).

Wait till you're old and your energy for serving the Lord will be gone. Older years are "days of trouble" when much of life's fun is missing (12:1). Solomon compared old age to the cloudy, depressing days of winter, when the sun, moon, and stars are covered by clouds (v. 2). Then he wrote in figurative language of the many physical ailments and mental fears that come in our sunset years. Our legs and arms become weak, our teeth few, our eyes dim, our ears deaf, our nerves jagged, our fears and apprehensions greater, our pace slower, our physical desires weakened (vv. 3-5). Others believe Solomon was comparing death to an abandoned house in which the keepers of the house are afraid, the strong men are weak, the grinders (of corn) leave ("the sound of grinding fades"), men have no joy in singing, people are afraid of dangers, and in winter ("when the almond tree blossoms") people have no desires.

After the body slowly disintegrates in old age, the person is gone, and loved ones bemoan their loss. Death comes with finality like the cutting of a cord that holds a lamp or like the shattering of a water pitcher (v. 6). Made of dust from the ground (Gen. 2:7), we return to the ground where our physical bodies decay. But our spirits live on throughout eternity.

Don't wait: Serve Him now while you are young. Or if you are already in your later years and have never made Christ your Saviour, turn to Him before it's too late.

THE QUEST FOR THE BEST

As Solomon concluded his book, he repeated in 12:8 his words in 1:2, "Everything is meaningless." Yes, all is futile and without meaning if you have lived out your life and are approaching death and have not found the key! Apart from being content with our lot in life and living in the fear of God, life is in fact meaningless. How sad to see an elderly, depressed person whose life has been dissipated with sin and whose energies have been wasted trying to discover what life is all about. How tragic to face the imminency of death realizing that life will soon be over, and the world in itself has offered nothing permanent.

Under the inspiration of the Holy Spirit, Solomon pointed out in his epilogue (12:9-14) that as a wise man looking back on life, he carefully selected what he wrote in this book; he "searched to find just the right words." Those words, which he said were "upright" (sincere) and true, were written in order to "goad" us into action and to "nail" the truth in our minds. Perhaps you have been prompted into some proper action by Solomon's words in Ecclesiastes.

These words—"given by one Shepherd," the Lord Himself—are hardly the words of a cynic or a pessimist. No need then to keep searching tiringly in numerous other new books, for the answer to life won't be found there (v. 12). The quest for the best in life is answered in his conclusion: "Fear God and keep His commandments." This is everyone's duty: it "applies to every person" (v. 13, NASB), not just some people. Every action, hidden or obvious, will be tested in the judgment (vv. 13-14).

Remember: We are all accountable to God for everything we have done. We may hide our actions from some people, but we can't hide them from God. Since "nothing in all creation is hidden from God's sight" (Heb. 4:13), "there is nothing concealed that will not be disclosed" (Matt. 10:26). Think about this fact and let it prod you to be faithful in fearing God and obeying His commands.

UPSTAIRS, DOWNSTAIRS

The British television series "Upstairs, Downstairs" portrays a bi-level society in an English estate, in which the servants live and work in the downstairs basement below the household members. Ecclesiastes too portrays two levels of living: those who view life apart from God reside "downstairs," they are "under the sun"; but those who take God into account are living "upstairs," above the clouds, in the light of God's truth.

The choice is clear. Pursue life on your own, attempt to uncover its meaning unaided, and you'll end up empty-handed. As Solomon has explained, human efforts are futile (1:12–6:9), and human understanding is inadequate (6:10–11:6). But look to God, trusting and loving Him and enjoying life while it lasts, and you have the key.

Apart from God, every human attempt to solve life's deepest puzzles is futile. Toil, pleasures, fame, and wealth are blind alleys, dead-end streets. Pursuing them is like "chasing after the wind." They have no lasting value. And life is filled with inequities and injustices. The Christian, on the other hand, realizing he can't unravel all of life's enigmas, looks to his Creator, who controls all things and who gives zest for living.

Without the Lord, we are in despair, with no hope, no purpose, no joy, no answer. With the Lord, we have reason for living.

Ecclesiastes gives us two keys: enjoy life, and fear God. Repeatedly, Solomon advised his readers to be content, accept their lot, and enjoy life given by God (2:24; 3:12-13, 22; 5:18; 8:15; 9:7-9; 11:8-9). And repeatedly the writer prompted us to fear God (3:14; 5:7; 7:18; 8:12; 12:13-14). That is, to recognize God's greatness and to respond in love, worship, service, and obedience.

Ask yourself: Am I trusting in the Lord with all my heart? (Prov. 3:5) If so, you can enjoy an above-the-clouds kind of life!

June

Devotional readings in the Minor Prophets
by J. Ronald Blue

OUT OF THE MINOR LEAGUE

They call them "farm camps," not the farms filled with migrant workers, but minor league camps filled with aspiring athletes. Most of the future baseball stars of the major league teams pass through the carefully scrutinized test of the minor league clubs. Some players never make it out of the minor league.

Twelve key players in ancient history were chosen by God to write His prophetic utterances. They are called the Minor Prophets. You will find their writings in the clean part of your Bible. In a way it is unfortunate that they have been labeled the "minor" prophets. In stark contrast to the value distinction made between the more valuable major league players over the lesser "minors," the minor prophets merit the same attention given to the "majors." *"All* Scripture is God-breathed" (2 Tim. 3:16).

The twelve minor prophets are not lesser prophets but briefer prophets. Today we would say the major prophets (Isaiah, Jeremiah, Ezekiel, Daniel) were "long-winded." The minor prophets were more condensed, more concise. In our TV generation of quick quotes and thirty-second news stories, the minor prophets should have instant appeal.

But brief though they may be, the minor prophets are bombastic. They are loaded with vivid illustrations, passionate appeals, direct confrontation, and bright hope. Furthermore their messages relate to our contemporary world. As Western civilization comes unglued under the pressures of drugs, abortion, divorce, AIDS, and pornography, the powerful message of judgment and repentance sounded by the ancient prophets suddenly becomes even more relevant.

Action: It is time to bring the minor prophets out of the minor league. Look to these twelve Old Testament books for spiritual direction and blessing.

A HUSBAND'S HEARTBREAK

I wish I could have been of greater consolation. His tears were visible evidence of the tangled mixture of emotions that gripped his soul. He felt rejection, anger, sorrow, frustration, confusion, hopelessness. His wife had left him. She was attracted to another man. I remembered the joy and the warmth of love that characterized their wedding, and now, after all these years, the marriage was a mangled memory.

My friend was by no means the first to experience the heartbreak of an unfaithful wife. The Prophet Hosea went through the same pain by God's design so that he might understand more fully what God feels when His children forsake Him and lust after the world.

Hosea and Gomer were no doubt happy newlyweds. God soon blessed them with three children, two boys and a girl. In time, however, Gomer became disenchanted with the routine of preparing the meals, changing diapers, and cleaning house. Hosea was so busy in the ministry he just didn't give her the attention she felt she deserved. Gomer was lonely and frustrated. So, when the kids were old enough to be in school, it seemed only fair that she should be able to visit some of her old friends. But the seemingly innocent visits somehow turned into an illicit affair. Love toward her husband was destroyed by lust for a lover.

Be reminded: Oh, the heartbreak God must feel when we turn from Him to the lure of fleshly desires and worldly pursuits. Our flirtation with earthly pleasure, public acclaim, or financial gain may seem natural and innocent, but if they are turning us from an intimate relationship with the Lord, they will lead us to what Hosea calls "the vilest adultery" (Hos. 1:2). Let's not "love the world" (1 John 2:15).

A MARRIAGE RESTORED

Of all the marriage ceremonies I have officiated, none could match this one. It was not held in an ornate cathedral or romantic chapel. Decorations were minimal and the participants few. But the joy was overwhelming, especially for the youngest of the participants. Mommy and Daddy were finally getting back together. The three children were ecstatic when I pronounced the handsome couple standing before me husband and wife. The two had hardly a chance to kiss when the children rushed to join in the hugs and tears of this joyous moment. I even got swept into the act. Two years after a trying divorce, there was a triumphant reunion. A reunion of a couple *and* a family.

Such is the case of Hosea and Gomer. The horror of harlotry in the Book of Hosea is lost in the glory of restoration. However, the restoration in which the prophet was engaged was much more radical than the one I witnessed. Hosea's wife was not merely separated from him. She had skidded to the pit of immorality. When Hosea finally found her, Gomer was a discarded piece of humanity, a prostitute slave on the auction block to be purchased by anyone willing to pay the bargain price. Hosea joined in the bidding. He bought her back! He restored her. He cared for her. He loved her (Hos. 3:1).

Contemplate God's amazing love: Hosea experienced in a small way the wonder of God's love for the wayward nation of Israel in which the prophet lived. And so is the Lord's love toward us. We merit eternal separation. We deserve His wrath. Instead, He bought us with the sacrifice of the Cross so that we might be His bride, without "spot or blemish." And even though we may be prone to wander, prone to leave the God we love, He is quick to restore us when we return to Him in humility and confession. What love!

RUINED CROPS

I grew up in Russell, Iowa, and if you know where Russell is, you must be *from* there. This small farming community in the southern part of the state afforded me with some distinct advantages. One great advantage was the work ethic and the strong dependence on God demonstrated by farmers. One hailstorm, one tornado, one season of excessive rain, or *no* rain, and all the hard work of planting and cultivation was destroyed. Most farmers have a high respect for God.

Before the advent of insecticides, interminable varieties of little creatures could swarm the fields and destroy the crops, as well. Such was the devastation outlined by the Prophet Joel. Four successive waves of locusts left the fields desolate (Joel 1:4). What a picture of the coming judgment of God that will sweep across the world. The "day of the Lord" that "will come like destruction from the Almighty" as Joel describes it (v. 15) is outlined in greater detail in the Book of Revelation. We who trust in Christ can continually rejoice that we will not suffer the unprecedented destruction of the Tribulation.

More than rejoice, we ought to bow in reverence before Almighty God. We need to capture the awe and respect farmers have toward their Creator. Perhaps we need to heed the summons of the Prophet Joel when he called the clerics of his country to "spend the night in sackcloth," to "consecrate a fast," to "proclaim a solemn assembly," to gather "all who live in the land to the house of the Lord," and "cry out to the Lord" (vv. 13-14).

Consider: I well remember the occasions in Russell, Iowa, when we gathered at the church to cry out to the Lord for rain. While God will not put His redeemed children through the Great Tribulation, He may allow a trial of "ruined crops." Bow right now in sincere reverence and renew your declaration of dependence on Him.

BLOW A TRUMPET

On the smaller ships the boatswain's pipe is used. The shrill sound that issues from this little whistle is enough to gain anyone's attention. On the larger vessels the more melodious bugle is used. In either case they serve as a summons. The sounds they issue command the attention of everyone on board and relay a message that a mere human voice cannot match.

No wonder the Prophet Joel recorded God's command, "Blow the trumpet in Zion; and sound the alarm on My holy hill! Let all who live in the land tremble, for the day of the Lord is coming. It is close at hand" (Joel 2:1). The desolation described in Joel chapter 1 brings the decree for repentance in chapter 2 that will result in the deliverance of chapter 3. In a land and age of decadence and decay that parallels that of the land of Judah, we are in desperate need of more buglers. In fact every Christian needs to blow the trumpet and sound the alarm.

Our message to contemporary society is that of Joel: "Return to the Lord your God, for He is gracious and compassionate, slow to anger and abounding in love" (2:13). To the atheists and agnostics, the materialists and humanists, to the hedonists and New-Agers who spurn His love and scoffingly ask, "Where is their God?" (v. 17), we must reply with confidence and clarity, "He is here and He is not silent!"

Oh, that more in our secular society could see Him in all His majesty, power, mercy, and grace. Oh, that they could experience the joy of His deliverance (vv. 18-20), the abundance of His provision (vv. 21-27), the power of His Spirit (vv. 28-32), the security of His protection (3:1-17), and the refreshment of His presence (vv. 18-21).

What you can do: For multitudes yet in "the valley of decision" (v. 14), blow a trumpet and sound the alarm. Point them to the Saviour, the Lord Jesus Christ.

RIGHT ON TARGET

My assignment for "battle stations" was in the forward mount of the five-inch guns. I was called a "safety observer," which meant I was to be certain the gunners were fixed on the right target during practice. It may not sound very significant, but it was exceedingly important to the pilots who pulled the giant canvas "sleeve" that served as our target. Gunners have been known to "lock in" on the plane rather than the "sleeve." For some reason pilots did not appreciate their slight mistake.

Without a good Bible atlas, the reader of Amos, chapters 1 and 2, would miss the significance of his prophecy. It sounds as if he were firing God's judgments indiscriminately on unsuspecting targets like Damascus, Gaza, Tyre, Edom, and other strange-sounding places.

Lay out a map of Old Testament lands and you discover a pattern that brings each shot fired by Amos from God's judgment cannon one step closer to the ultimate target, Israel. From distant Damascus, each shot moved in a clockwise spiral pattern until one reached the all-too-close neighboring sister nation of Judah before the final round was fired to land right on target: Israel, the land in which the Prophet Amos resided.

This would be like hearing that God is going to judge China. Many would declare, "Great! They deserve it!" The next target is India. Not a few might say, "Why, of course, look at the evils of Hinduism." South Africa appears on the list. "Certainly, God will not tolerate apartheid." Then Colombia is cited. "Yea! The drug lords are going to get their due." Canada now appears on the list. "Strange," many would say, "it must be their socialism." God's final target is the USA. Suddenly, there is stunned silence.

An awesome thought: Could this invincible land become God's target for judgment?

I WARNED YOU

I had absolutely no regrets about spanking her. I had issued a clear warning, "Don't touch! If you touch that again, Daddy will have to spank you!" Coffee tables are always laden with those tempting breakable objects within easy reach of little hands. Some contend that the answer is to remove all temptation. I believe it is better to learn to resist temptation. A firm word should do it. In this case the warning was not heeded. So a firm hand followed. For the rest of the evening our little daughter found no interest in the objects on the coffee table.

I could only wish that we as adults were as quick to learn. So many of our Heavenly Father's warnings go unheeded. Amos shared the frustration. "The lion has roared—who will not fear? The Sovereign Lord God has spoken—who can but prophesy?" (Amos 3:8)

The layman sheepherder Amos faithfully proclaimed God's warning, but no one seemed to take heed. They continued to oppress the poor and needy, to enjoy their abundance of wine, and to look as religious as they could (4:1-5).

So God put His hand to work. The people suffered drought, disease, death, and destruction, but even these calamities did not seem to catch their attention (vv. 6-11). Four times God declared, "Yet you have not returned to Me" (vv. 6, 8, 10-11). It is little wonder God finally allowed the nation to be taken captive by enemy forces. It seems He had to go beyond "spanking" and permit "time in jail" to get the people to see their need.

Amos cried out, "Prepare to meet your God, O Israel" (v. 12), and in a beautiful way he described the greatness and majesty of the Lord God Almighty (v. 13).

An assignment: Today, try to be alert to God's voice and responsive to His warnings. Just a word should do.

NOISY SONGS

I would much rather sit in a pew next to a monotone who makes every attempt to sing with meaning and enthusiasm than with a trained vocalist who seems totally oblivious to the words being sung. I am usually more blessed by hearing a brand new believer talk to the Lord in a broken, honest way than I am by the high-sounding phrases of a professional cleric. Why does so much of what we do in church today seem routine and unrelated to life? I do not favor mediocrity, but I would plead for more reality.

Amos had some shocking words from God to those engaged in a religious routine. "I hate, I despise your religious feasts; I cannot stand your assemblies. Even though you bring Me burnt offerings . . . , I will not accept them. . . . Away with the noise of your songs! I will not listen to the music of your harps" (Amos 5:21-23). These people seemed to be doing all the right things. They prayed. They gave. They sang. But to no avail. They were not rightly related to the One to whom they were praying, giving, and singing.

The religious exercise was all a show. Real life centered in the ease and security of vacation resorts, banquets, and soothing music at home, plus arrogant activity at work (Amos 6). All their "God talk" was reserved for the ritual carried on in their religious gatherings.

Could we be guilty of the same error? Do we simply give God dominion for an hour on Sundays? Are we involved in evangelical ritual that soothes the conscience? Has church turned into some kind of "Protestant mass" to fulfill an obligation instilled in us by our parents? Are our hymns only noisy songs in God's ears?

Act on this: Vow right now to make your worship real. Turn from religious routine to a vibrant, meaningful relationship with the living Lord.

A PERENNIAL PLANT

I am impressed with the ability my wife has with African violets. They are delicate plants. They must be watered with care at measured intervals. Light is a necessity, but too much direct sunlight can destroy the fragile plant. At least this is what Libby tells me. I try to enjoy their beauty from a distance. Somewhere I have gotten the notion that if I touch them they will die.

The destructive forces declared on Israel by the Prophet Amos might lead you to believe that here is a plant doomed to everlasting oblivion. Reading the prophets can be discouraging unless you read to the end. The gloom is turned to glory. The destruction ends in delight. The rebuke is followed by restoration.

In the concluding chapters of Amos, the visions of devouring locusts (7:1-3), consuming fire (vv. 4-6), measuring plumbline (vv. 7-9), rotting fruit (8:1-14), and the all-powerful Lord of hosts (9:1-10) is followed by a vision of future blessing (vv. 11-15). In this final paragraph, Amos wrote these encouraging words, "'In that day I will restore David's fallen tent. I will repair its broken places, restore its ruins, and build it as it used to be . . . I will plant Israel in their own land, never again to be rooted up from the land I have given them' says the Lord your God" (vv. 11-12, 15).

The destruction is not irreparable. From the dry leaves, torn stems, and parched roots, God will bring forth a perennial plant of beauty and blessing. One that can never again be uprooted. Israel will be restored.

Think about it: These encouraging words apply to us as well. Though we are like frail blades of grass that will wither, we have been born again by an imperishable seed—the living, abiding Word of God (1 Peter 1:23-25). We too are perennial plants to show forth His beauty.

HUMPTY DUMPTY

It is a clever little rhyme: "Humpty Dumpty sat on a wall; Humpty Dumpty had a great fall. All the king's horses and all the king's men couldn't put Humpty together again." Behind this little ditty is a potent political message. Humpty Dumpty was no egg. This was a jibe at King John from whom the thirteenth-century populace forced the Magna Charta, their charter of liberty.

Obadiah wrote of another Humpty Dumpty that had a great fall. In this case not just a leader but an entire nation fell. In constant conflict with Israel, Edom finally ran head-on into God and fell.

The Edomites were filled with *arrogance*. They felt secure (Obad. 1:1-4). But the seemingly impregnable fortress of Petra hidden in the "clefts of the rock" was no match before Almighty God.

These descendants of Esau, Jacob's twin reveled in *affluence*. But their prosperity made them a ready target. Edom was ransacked. Even their carefully hidden treasures were taken (vv. 5-10).

Worst of all, the Edomites were noted for their *aloofness*. They watched as Jerusalem was invaded, and they actually gloated over the tragic defeat of their neighbor. But Edom's presumption led to her own destruction (vv. 11-14).

So great was Edom's fall that not one survivor was left. The surrounding neighbors quickly possessed the lands, and to this day Edom is but a distant memory (vv. 15-21).

What of other nations caught up in pride, prosperity, and presumption? Obadiah warned, "The day of the Lord is near for all nations. As you have done, it will be done to you; your deeds will return upon your own head" (v. 15).

Be careful: What happens to nations can happen to individuals. Don't become a Humpty Dumpty statistic. The fall can be fatal.

NO PLACE TO HIDE

I had always played hide-and-seek in the streets and alleys of Milwaukee, Wisconsin. It was easy to find places to hide.

When my parents moved to Iowa, I encountered a greater challenge, especially when the corn was not yet knee-high. When we visited my cousins in Nebraska, I found the game next to impossible. There was no place to hide. Seemingly, you could look farther and see less out there than any place else in the world.

Just try to play hide-and-seek with God. The game is over before it begins. Jonah should have known this. He was a prophet, a full-time minister (2 Kings 14:25). Yet, when given very specific instructions by the Lord, Jonah tried to escape. This prophet was willing to go to a distant land. He was even willing to pay his own way. But he did not want to go in God's direction. Jonah tried to play hide-and-seek.

It was an easy contest for God. The Lord hurled a storm at the little ship in which Jonah hid. The sailors discovered that Jonah was the reason for their hopeless battle against the elements. They finally threw the prophetic pest overboard, and the sea was suddenly calm.

Through Jonah's miserable testimony and the amazing intervention of God, the sailors turned from their pagan gods to Yahweh (Jonah 1:14-16).

Jonah tried to hide but God found him. The sailors too found Jonah, but far more important, they found the Lord. Meanwhile, God tucked Jonah away in a new hiding place where he might not so easily escape. It was a bit damp but nonetheless quite secure (v. 17).

Face it: Have you ever tried to hide from God? There is really no point to it. Be honest and open with God today. Be quick to obey Him and serve Him. It is the only reasonable option. There is simply no place to hide from Him

DEAD OR ALIVE

An early graduate of Dallas Seminary and well-known Bible teacher, the late Dr. J. Vernon McGee, once wrote a clever little booklet entitled *Jonah: Dead or Alive?* This is a valid question. Was Jonah alive in the stomach of the fish three days and three nights or did he die and rise again?

There is some strong evidence in the text that Jonah died. He cried for help "from the depth of the grave" (Jonah 2:2). "Grave" is literally Sheol, the Hebrew word for the place of the dead. Water encompassed him to the point of death, wrote Jonah (v. 5). "When my life was ebbing away, I remembered You, Lord" (2:5, 7). If indeed Jonah died, the parallel between Christ's burial and Jonah's experience becomes even more striking (Matt. 12:40).

Whether Jonah died or not, one thing is very certain. Jonah prayed from the depths of the sea and it reached heaven's door. When the prophet acknowledged his need, cried out to the Lord, and vowed to serve Him, God brought him up "from the pit."

For you: You may be going through a Jonah crisis right now. You may feel distant from God, trapped in a pit of despair and discouragement, wishing you were dead rather than alive. If so, there is good news for you. There is no need to panic. It is time to pray.

Jonah prayed and suddenly he found himself on dry land. Whatever your situation, pray right now. Confess your sins to Him and He will cleanse you. Express your thanksgiving for Him and He will encourage you. Commit your way to Him and He will restore you and guide you. "Salvation comes from the Lord" (Jonah 2:9).

WHO CARES?

The attractive folder slipped from the bundle I pulled from the mail box. I reached down to pick it up. It was a missions conference brochure. In big bold letters the cover read, "Who Cares?" *Now that is a good question,* I thought to myself. *Who cares?*

Who cares about the billions of this world who have no knowledge of our Lord? Who cares about the kid in tattered rags on the streets of Bombay? Who cares about the drug addict curled up in a dark alley of Caracas?

The Book of Jonah gives the answer. This is not a "tale of a whale" or a "whale of a tale." The main point of the book is found in the concluding chapters.

God gave Jonah a second chance and this time he obeyed. Jonah preached in the wicked city of Nineveh. The entire city repented and God spared them from the judgment they deserved. But instead of rejoicing, Jonah was angry. In the heat of his anger, Jonah was blessed with the shade of a plant that all too quickly was removed. Jonah was furious.

The key point of the book is found in the Lord's closing comments to Jonah, "You had compassion on the plant. Should I not have compassion on Nineveh?" (See 4:10.) God cares!

A question: Do you have greater concern about your own welfare than you do for the needs of lost people? It is so easy to lose perspective. Pray right now that God will give you more of His compassion. Be one who cares.

HEAR YE! HEAR YE!

They called them town criers. While they paced through the streets, their voices pierced the silence. "Hear ye! Hear ye!" they cried. People stopped their activities, filed out their doors, or rushed to their balconies to hear the news. It was like a newspaper boy shouting, "Extra! Extra! Read all about it!"

So the prophets cried out, but few stopped to listen. Repeatedly, Micah pleaded, "Hear, O peoples, all of you" (Micah 1:2). "Listen, you leaders of Jacob, you rulers of . . . Israel" (3:1, 9). "Listen to what the Lord says" (6:1).

Micah declared impending destruction to those who "plot evil on their beds" and when morning comes, "they carry it out" (2:1). These covetous people schemed ways to seize the real estate of others through extortion and eviction notices (vv. 2-9). Today it is called "white collar crime." Whatever the collar color, it is crime. Even though it may go unnoticed in the courts of law, sin does not escape God's attention.

"Uncleanness . . . brings on destruction, a painful destruction," declared the Prophet Micah (Micah 2:10, NASB). Someone has said, "Sin does not pay." Wrong. Sin pays, all right. It pays wages. "The wages of sin is death." This bad news, however, is followed by good news: "But the gift of God is eternal life in Christ Jesus our Lord" (Rom. 6:23).

Hear and act: Shun evil. Pursue what is upright and honest. Rejoice in the eternal life granted to everyone who puts his trust in the Lord Jesus Christ. Respond to His leading today. Give heed to His call. "Hear ye! Hear ye!"

PRICE-TAG PREACHERS

It is bad enough when politicians and business tycoons are guilty of extortion and graft, but when preachers are guilty of dishonest gain, it is devastating. The TV evangelist scandals of the '80s have taken their toll. Suddenly every minister looked like Elmer Gantry to the suspicious unbeliever. Graft is a curse to the nation, a blight to the ministry, and above all it breaks the heart of God. It detracts from His purity and His glory.

Little wonder the people of Micah's day were so prone to do evil. The prophet presented a word picture that is nauseating. Merciless leaders were figured as human butchers preparing some kind of cannibalistic stew (Micah 3:1-3). So heinous were their actions that, though they cried to the Lord, He would not answer them (v. 4).

Even more disconcerting, Micah's contemporaries did nothing to stop the violence. The prophets called for "peace" while evil continued unabated (v. 5). How could these preachers allow the injustice and bloodshed to continue? Simple. They were paid off by the evildoers.

Micah minced no words. "Leaders judge for a bribe, her priests teach for a price, and her prophets tell fortunes for money" (v. 11). Furthermore, in the midst of their greedy schemes these ministers gave a false assurance with their clever talk of God's abiding presence.

God's servants must have no price tags. While ministers deserve to be well cared for, they must not be available for purchase.

What you can do: Pray for your pastor and for other spiritual leaders you know. Pray that God will guard them from the attraction of money. Pray that you will not become a price-tag Christian. Be faithful. Be generous. Be free from the love of money (1 Tim. 6:10).

SMALL-TOWN PROMINENCE

They hardly looked like a viable team. Yet this crew of short-statured teenagers scrapped their way to the state championship basketball tournament. What they lacked in height they made up for in speed. These young men showed what a little high school in an unknown Iowa hamlet could do. The Roland Rockets defeated the top-ranked high school in Des Moines and became the 1958 state champions. Their small town rose to national prominence.

Bethlehem was hardly a city of significance. This little sleepy town went unnoticed in the world. Micah wrote that it was "too little to be [counted] among the clans of Judah" (Micah 5:2, NASB). Yet little Bethlehem was skyrocketed to international acclaim.

Micah's prophecy about Bethlehem was doubly fulfilled, "Out of you will come for Me One who will be Ruler over Israel." The town was the birthplace of King David (1 Sam. 16:1), but more than that it was the birthplace of Christ, the Messiah.

It is amazing that God chose a place like Bethlehem to be the point of entry for His visit to this dusty planet. Think of it. He came as a helpless little baby born of a lowly maiden in a town where there was no room in the inn. He, the Creator of the universe, was placed in a manger on that first night on earth.

Micah pointed out that the Babe of Bethlehem "will stand and shepherd His flock in the strength of the Lord, His God" (5:4). He is the King of kings and Lord of lords. He is more than prominent; He is preeminent.

Pause right now: Worship Him, and express anew your love for Him. In a world clamoring for prominence, let Christ have the preeminence.

CROSS-CULTURAL HOPE

It can hardly be said that the world is getting better and better. Violent crime is on the increase; morals are in decline. Prisons are overflowing with inmates, abortion clinics are running a record-breaking business, homes are falling apart at the brisk rate of one every twenty-seven seconds, drug lords hold the world in their grip, sexually transmitted diseases have arrived at epidemic proportions with a sure killer at the top of the list: AIDS. Is there any hope for this messed-up world?

Micah felt his society was doomed. He felt like a migrant worker moving among barren branches (Micah 7:1). The only grapes were the grapes of God's wrath. The prophet lamented the decline in morals. He concluded that "not one upright man remains. All men lie in wait to shed blood" (v. 2).

Deception in government was evident in both the executive and judicial branches (vv. 3-4). Worst of all, the disintegration in the home caused the prophet to exclaim, "man's enemies are the members of his own household" (vv. 5-6). It almost sounds as if Micah wrote this book yesterday.

In spite of the corrupt society in which he lived, Micah wisely declared, "I wait in hope for God my Saviour" (v. 7). The prophet knew that his confession would result in God's gracious restoration and redemption (vv. 9-20). Micah wrote, "Who is a God like You, who pardons sin" (v. 18), who casts our sins "into the depths of the sea?" (v. 19) Micah was definitely different; he was counter-culture.

For today: Pray that you can be noticeably different from those around you who seem to float with the cultural current. Be one who swims upstream. Be one of God's counter-cultural agents of light and blessing.

THE MOUNTAINS QUAKE

Have you ever experienced an earthquake? It is definitely earth-shaking. We were seated together in prayer in a third-floor office in the city of San Salvador when a quake hit. I have to confess I opened my eyes to see what was going on. I was sure my time was up. My friend Arturo continued his prayer but with increased volume and a bit more intensity, "Estamos en las manos de Dios!" ("We are in the hands of God"). He was right—and thankfully, we were spared. The quake suddenly subsided.

Nahum used natural phenomena to describe our "jealous and avenging" Lord (1:2). The prophet wrote, "His way is in the whirl-wind and the storm, and clouds are the dust of His feet" (v. 3). "Mountains quake before Him and the hills melt away" (v. 5).

Those who see God as some doting father to whom we must occasionally pay our respects need to read the Book of Nahum. God is awesome in His power. He is majestic in His presence. He can shake this earth down to mere dust any time He should so desire.

More people need to see Him in His fury so they might seek Him for His forgiveness. Nahum wrote, "Look, there on the mountains, the feet of one who brings good news, who proclaims peace" (v. 15).

A call to action: Be sure to notice the evidence of God's great-ness and glory in His creation. Worship Him as you observe His handiwork. Then ask that you might be His messenger to bring the Good News to those who have missed seeing the Author of all that exists. Tell them how even mountains tremble in God's wrath, and then lead them to His peace.

THE NOISE OF BATTLE

If you have ever watched a documentary on World War II or a Hollywood production centered on the events of Vietnam, you are aware that the sound of battle is deafening. Screaming jets, exploding bombs, the rapid fire of machine guns, wailing sirens, the whistle of flying shrapnel make it all but impossible for the actors to shout their lines above the roar.

The sounds are slightly different, but they are just as terrorizing in the record given by the Prophet Nahum. Though judgment on Nineveh was stayed in the days of Jonah, in 100 years the Ninevites had reverted to their cruel and pagan practices.

Nahum pictured the invading hoards in chapter 2 and then added a sound track in chapter 3. "The crack of whips, the clatter of wheels, galloping horses, and jolting chariots! Charging cavalry, flashing swords, and glittering spears!" (3:2-3) To think some people believe the Bible is dull reading! Nahum concluded, saying that Nineveh would be devoured by fire (v. 15).

The Ninevites should have learned from earlier civilizations. Nahum pointed to the fall of No Amon, better known as Thebes, the capital of Upper Egypt that was sacked by the Assyrians (vv. 8-10). Kingdoms rise and kingdoms fall. The higher they rise, the harder they fall. Usually the fall comes from inner decay rather than external attack. Such was true of Nineveh. Nahum wrote, "Nothing can heal your wound; your injury is fatal" (v. 19).

Be on guard: Watch out for the inner decay. Don't let unconfessed sin fester. Seek God's daily cleansing, and then rely on His strength. In the noise of battle whisper a prayer to the One who hears and answers.

HOMEMADE JUSTICE

I had just never quite thought of it that way. I was relating my concern over the diplomatic difficulties workers for Wycliffe Bible Translators were facing and declared to founder Cameron Townsend, "Some of these governments really give you a hard time, don't they?" Uncle Cam replied, "Well you know, Ron, governments don't make decisions; people do." What an astute observation! Decisions are not made by the government. They are made by people. Congress, the Supreme Court, and the President's Cabinet are simply a group of people very much like us. Little wonder the decisions are not perfect.

Habakkuk complained about faulty decisions in government. He wrote that "justice is perverted" (Hab. 1:4). It was a bad case of homemade justice.

God agreed with His prophet and revealed that He would take care of the problem. He was about to send in the wild barbarians of Babylon to execute judgment (vv. 5-11).

But Habakkuk was confused. How could God use this iniquitous and idolatrous nation to judge Judah? Where was the justice in using a people of injustice to execute justice (vv. 12-17)? It didn't make sense.

Herein is one of the great mysteries of life. God continues to use common ordinary people, sometimes even evil people to accomplish His purposes. We may not understand God's plans, but of one thing we can be sure: His judgments are right. God is just.

Trust God: Take your case to His tribunal. Even if the response to your plea seems unfair, continue to trust Him. God-wrought justice is always better than homemade justice.

IT'S A SAD, SAD SONG

There are some musical numbers that grip the emotions and unstop the tear glands. At a high school graduation banquet, they played Michael W. Smith's "Friends" as candid shots of the graduates flashed across the screen. The music really touched me, "A friend's a friend forever. . . ." They should sell a package of Kleenex with every cassette. It is a sad, sad song.

Written in repetitive rather than rhythmic style, Habakkuk's song may not carry so much emotion. Nonetheless, the prophet's dirge is another sad song. There are five stanzas in Habakkuk's song, each starting with the word *Woe*. The prophetic composer wrote while he stood at his guard post (Hab. 2:1).

God relayed to His prophet the reasons for the pending judgment on Judah (vv. 2-5). Intimidation (vv. 6-8), intemperance (vv. 9-11), iniquity (vv. 12-14), indignity (vv. 15-18), and idolatry (v. 19) gave the Righteous Judge every right to punish the accused.

Habakkuk concluded his song with a majestic finale, "The Lord is in His holy temple; let all the earth be silent before Him" (v. 20). The verdict is final. There is no further appeal. God is just and holy.

Think it over: Is there any charge against you today? Are you making yourself rich with loans, growing weary for nothing, trusting in your own handiwork? These were just a few of the specific charges in Habakkuk's song (vv. 6, 13, 18). Confess sins that you may discover. He will forgive you and cleanse you (1 John 1:9). The sad song can become a glad song.

SUNLIGHT AFTER THE STORM

Like a giant dagger out of heaven, the twister thrust its fury into the heart of the unsuspecting Ohio town. Xenia was literally ripped apart on that fateful day in 1974. So severe was the damage that some predicted the historic community would become a mere ghost town. Those predictions proved wrong. Xenia would not die. Today it is a thriving community. The path of destruction simply cleared the way for a new shopping center, modern homes, and an attractive community park.

After every storm the sun shines brightly. Habakkuk ended his prophetic discourse with a majestic doxology that conveyed both the awesome force of God's storm (Hab. 3:1-16) and the blessing of God's sunlight (vv. 17-19). In fact the prophet's unfailing confidence in the Lord was made strong in the dark hour of the Lord's fury in which "mountains where shattered" and "ancient hills collapsed."

Habakkuk concluded, "Though the fig tree should not blossom, and there be no fruit on the vines . . . the fields produce no food . . . there be no cattle in the stalls, yet I will exult in the Lord, I will rejoice in the God of my salvation" (vv. 17-18, NASB). Even though the storm of God's wrath may obliterate the land, God's child should be able to see the sunlight of His salvation.

Take heart: You may be in the midst of a storm right now. The circumstances may look so bleak you are convinced there is no hope, that the sun will never shine again. Look to God. You need not merely endure. You can exult. God is ready to pick you up in His strength and cause you to walk in high places. Read Habakkuk 3:17-19 and rise above your circumstances. Bask in the sunlight of His wonderful salvation.

THREE BLIND MICE

When the late Queen Mary was approaching her eightieth birthday, she was asked how she would like to celebrate the event. The Queen said she would like an "Agatha Christie play." Mrs. Christie promptly wrote a thirty-minute radio production called "Three Blind Mice," which eventually became "The Mousetrap," the longest-running stage play in history.

Of even greater duration than Agatha Christie's clever mystery play is the prophetic revelation of three blind mice who brought judgment on Judah and surrounding nations.

Zephaniah rebuked the blind religious leaders, idolatrous priests, who turned "back from following the Lord" (Zeph. 1:6), the blind political leaders, insolent princes, "who fill the temple of their gods with violence and deceit" (v. 9), and the blind economic leaders, indifferent peddlers, "who think, 'The Lord will do nothing, either good or bad' " (v. 12).

The "blind mice" leaders of Judah were cause for more than a few "tails cut off." God said He would cut "off man from the face of the earth" (v. 3) and would "bring distress on the people" so that "they will walk like blind men, because they have sinned against the Lord" (v. 17). Their blindness brought judgment on surrounding nations as well (2:1-15).

Beware of leaders who are blind to God's ways. It is important to be a law-abiding citizen, but when man's laws are in conflict with God's laws, those who see must denounce those who are spiritually blind.

A challenge: Use your God-given vision to walk uprightly today. Don't be led astray by humanistic, hedonistic, materialistic blind mice who run wildly in places of leadership.

I'LL TAKE THE LOW ROAD

Apparently there were two ways to get to Scotland. Long before the rush of traffic on interstate highways, someone had figured out which road provided the most rapid route, declaring, "I'll get to Scotland before you."

Like the unknown composer of the little Scottish song "I'll Take the Low Road," Zephaniah provided some helpful rules of the road in the conclusion of his prophetic discourse. He showed that the high road may actually be the low road and the low road may be the high road. What seems like a confusing paradox is nonetheless an eternal principle drawn from God's perfect plan.

The citizens of Jerusalem walked proudly along what they thought was the high road. Zephaniah's self-confident neighbors were moving right into God's vengeance. The "rebellious" inhabitants who accepted "no correction" and did not "trust in the Lord" were about to experience the Lord's "fierce anger" (Zeph. 3:2, 8).

A remnant of "meek and humble" people who trusted "in the name of the Lord" (v. 12) moved on the low road. To them was promised divine blessing, victory, and joy (vv. 14-20). The low road was in reality the high road.

The confusion continues today. Most of life's parades move down Pride Avenue. Cheers and applause fill the air as conceited participants pass by. By contrast, Meek Lane can be a very lonely road. But look at the destinations. Pride Avenue leads to destruction. Meek Lane ends in blessing.

Remember: Don't let the world's bright signs put you on a detour that leads to ultimate failure. Learn from Zephaniah. Learn from the Lord. It is the meek who inherit the earth. The way up is down. Today, take the low road of a humble heart and experience God's joy and blessing.

OPERATION REBUILD

It has taken over sixty years of restoration and preservation to give tourists the unforgettable encounter with America's beginnings in famed Colonial Williamsburg. The rich heritage of a colorful past comes alive in the stately government buildings, elegant colonial homes, and busy craft shops. Over 500 buildings have been either restored or reconstructed in the amazing project that might be called "Operation Rebuild."

While not of the magnitude of Williamsburg, the rebuilding project outlined in the Book of Haggai was of equal or greater importance. The Israelites who had been taken captive were finally permitted to return to Jerusalem. Their priority assignment was to rebuild the temple.

Typical of people today, the Israelites became so consumed with building and improving their own homes they forgot about rebuilding the temple. Haggai called the people to think (Hag. 1:1-6), to plan (vv. 7-13), and to work (vv. 14-15).

The project was by no means an easy one. Perhaps the greatest enemy was discouragement. The new temple in no way compared to the more majestic temple of Solomon. Haggai faced the problem squarely and then turned the eyes of his work force to the One who gives both courage and encouragement (2:1-9).

Ask yourself: Do any of my projects seem to miss my expectations? Do I feel the pain of failure? Listen to the words of the Lord through Haggai: " 'Be strong,' . . . declares the Lord, 'and work. For I am with you,' declares the Lord Almighty" (v. 4). Think of it: the Creator of the universe abides with you to help you, to sustain you, and to bless you in your "operation rebuild."

CERTIFIED LETTER

I was intrigued by the ancient practice performed as I waited to sign the necessary forms for the certified letter I was sending from Guatemala to the United States. The clerk carefully positioned the flame so that the melted wax dropped on the flap of the envelope. He then took a large seal that bore the emblem of the postmaster general and pressed it firmly in the soft wax. The letter was sealed and certified.

The king's signet (or sealing) ring served as an apt illustration for Haggai to show how God wanted to use His servants. After pleading for purity and integrity (2:10-19), Haggai concluded his prophetic discourse by reminding the governor of God's power (vv. 20-22) and His purpose (v. 23). " 'I will take you . . . ' declares the Lord, 'and I will make you like a signet ring, for I have chosen you,' declares the Lord Almighty."

It is God's purpose to take those He chose before the foundation of the world and use them as "sealing rings." We are in His hand to be used by His power to make an impression in this world of sin-cursed wax.

The ring that is not on the hand is totally inanimate and ineffective. It is really not the ring, but the king that counts. It is amazing that God should choose us. It is even more amazing that He should choose to use us as His witnesses. We are valued rings in His hand.

Assignment: Sense your worth as one of God's chosen servants. Yield to His almighty hand as He seeks to use you to make an impression on a neighbor, a friend, or a relative today. By God's grace and power, live in holiness, purity, and integrity. Let Him place His seal of approval on you. Be God's certified letter of love.

GET THE PICTURE?

I soon learned the amazing value of a picture to convey the truth of God's Word. A barrage of words was hardly adequate for people who were illiterate or semi-literate. The people in rural Guatemala appreciated even the simplest chalk drawing or a familiar object to help them remember what was being said.

The old Chinese proverb that a picture is worth a thousand words is twice as true as it is repeated. It seems reasonable that God would provide visions, like so many videos, to impress on Zechariah the importance of His prophetic message.

Zechariah sat through eight strange and diverse scenes. Horses and riders (1:7-17), four horns (vv. 18-21), surveyor (2:1-13), high priest (3:1-10), golden lampstand (4:1-14), flying scroll (5:1-4), woman in a basket (vv. 5-11), and four chariots (6:1-8). Each of the pictures added to the impact of God's message of restoration of Jerusalem to a place of prominence and productivity. The illustrated message of hope was of great encouragement to all those who had returned from captivity to help in rebuilding the city.

Briefly the heavenly video presents an earth patrol of horsemen and an encounter with four "Texas longhorns" of opposing nations. Meanwhile Jerusalem is being surveyed, the high priest and a golden lampstand of the Holy Spirit's power installed, the woman of wickedness removed, and "chariots of fire" preparing the way for the Lord. Will all this actually happen? Zechariah declared, "This will happen if you diligently obey the Lord your God" (6:15).

Trust God: Your dreams may never match Zechariah's visions, but you can be sure God will accomplish His purpose in your life if you obey Him. Obey Him today. Watch His hand at work in your life. Your life may be God's illustration to others, a picture for the world to see. Get the picture?

TRUTH OR CONSEQUENCES

Back in the days when radio was a primary source of home entertainment, an innovative program captured the attention of thousands. It was based on the simple premise "If you haven't told the
truth, you must pay the consequences." The program is but a
distant memory in the history of time, but to this day a community
in New Mexico still bears the name of the program, "Truth or
Consequences."

Zechariah reveals the hypocritical actions of his people. They
pretended to fast in search of God's favor and forgiveness. While
they engaged in this vain ritual, they were guilty of oppressing the
widow, the orphan, the stranger, and the poor. They had not told
the truth so they had to pay the consequences. "So the Lord
Almighty was very angry" (Zech. 7:12). The people were scattered
and the land left desolate (v. 14).

In spite of the deceit and hypocrisy in Jerusalem, the city was
not obliterated forever. The city lives on. "Jerusalem will be called
The City of Truth" (8:3). Zechariah pictured the restoration in
which the elderly will enjoy protection and peace (v. 4) and "the
city streets be filled with boys and girls playing there" (v. 5).

By God's grace the consequences have turned from destruction
to delight. "I will save My people. . . . They will be My people, and
I will be faithful and righteous to them as their God" (vv. 7-8).
Jerusalem will be a city of peace, prosperity, and prominence
(vv. 12-13, 19-23).

Really do it: Make this a day of truth in your life or you could
suffer the consequences. And what about the hypocrisy in your
past? Rejoice, God is ready to forgive you. He longs to renew you.
The consequences deserved are not often delivered. His truth can
cover your consequences.

I SHALL RETURN

In March 1942 President Franklin D. Roosevelt ordered General Douglas MacArthur to leave the Philippines in what seemed a hopeless battle. Before leaving for Australia, MacArthur declared, "I came through and I shall return." Return he did. On December 18, 1944 the determined general waded ashore with his troops and within months MacArthur had recaptured the Philippines.

The Prophet Zechariah foretold the return of the King "endowed with salvation, humble, and mounted on a donkey" (Zech. 9:9, NASB) which, of course, occurred in Christ's first advent precisely as it was prophesied. Even the rise and fall of the opposing Greek Empire was foretold centuries before it occurred (v. 13). It seems only reasonable, therefore, to assume that the prophecy concerning the restoration of Israel will also come true.

In spite of the seemingly irreversible destruction Israel suffered (Zech. 10) and the vain attempts of a helpless shepherd to protect his flock (Zech. 11), Jerusalem will experience the Lord's care and cleansing (Zech. 12–13).

The King who "came through" on a donkey and died for our sins on Calvary has declared, "I shall return." His return is as certain as His Word. When He comes back to the mount from which He ascended, the Mount of Olives will split in two (14:4). And "the Lord will be King over the whole earth" (v. 9).

Pause right now: Express your thanks to the Lord for His sure Word. Rejoice in His first coming as Saviour. Bow in worship in anticipation of His return as Sovereign. He who "came through" "shall return." Count on His promise and live today in His hope.

BOOK OF REMEMBRANCE

There is something gratifying in seeing the name of my mother inscribed in the leather-bound volume that rests on a table in beautiful Collins Lounge of Dallas Seminary's Walvoord Student Center. The gift given in her honor for the ongoing ministry in the lives of young men and women at the seminary seemed a most appropriate tribute to Mom's love and ministry to me and countless others. I'm glad "Wretha Blue" is listed in the Book of Remembrance.

Malachi wrote about God's "scroll [book] of remembrance . . . written in His presence concerning those who feared the Lord and honored His name" (Mal. 3:16).

Israel needed a reminder of God's love (1:1-5). She also needed a reminder of God's anger over her defiled offerings (vv. 6-14), distorted instruction (2:1-9), divorce and deceit (vv. 10-17). Malachi, as all the prophets, wrote a "book of remembrance."

Beyond the written record, Malachi told of a messenger who will prepare the way for the coming Saviour. Clearly referring to John the Baptist, the prophet wrote of the verbal reminder to be given of the need for repentance from self-indulgence and self-confidence (3:1-15).

The greatest reminder, however, is not of God's punishment. It is of His pardon. Malachi concluded, "But for you who revere My name, the Sun of righteousness will rise with healing in its wings" (4:2). None need miss God's healing touch.

Question: Do you "fear the Lord and esteem His name"? Then you can rejoice. Your name is in the "book of remembrance." Remember His Word. Take heed to the message of His prophets. May the reminders of the minor prophets find a major place in your life for your blessing and His glory.

July

Devotional readings in the Gospel of John
by Kenneth O. Gangel

WHO IS JESUS CHRIST?

If there is a God (and there is), and if that God has spoken in history (and He has), then it is vitally important to discover what He has said.

The familiar and beloved Gospel of John was written precisely to provide that information for us. John himself affirmed, "These are written that you may believe that Jesus is the Christ, the Son of God, and that by believing you may have life in His name" (20:31).

In the first eighteen verses of his book John introduced the Lord. He began by proclaiming that Jesus reveals God the Father (1:1-5). When He came to earth, God's Son showed the human race what God the Father is like—eternal, personal, Creator, and the Source of all life.

The word *life* appears fifty times in this Gospel. Along with several other key words such as *light, word,* and *believe,* "life" establishes the central theme for the book.

When Jesus came to show God to the world, He was rejected. The world preferred its own way to the righteousness of the Father. Only "those who believed in His name" (v. 12) received the right to become the spiritual children of God.

The contact had been made and earth became "the visited planet." God Incarnate had come in human flesh, the exclusive explanation of the Father. He came to show us God, to feel our hurts and temptations, and to die for our sins. That's why Christians, those who have received the life He gives, can joyfully sing Charles Wesley's words:

> Christ, by highest heaven adored,
> Christ, the Everlasting Lord.
> Late in time behold Him come,
> Offspring of the virgin's womb;
> Veiled in flesh the Godhead see;
> Hail the incarnate deity.
> Pleased as man with men to dwell,
> Jesus, our Emmanuel.

What are your answers? Who is Jesus Christ to you? Personal Saviour? Living Lord? Coming King? Give Him total control of your mind and heart for this day.

LOOK, THE LAMB OF GOD!

John the Baptist introduced the Lamb of God to the world (John 1:29). But first he explained his own ministry, including a proper identification of his credentials. He was neither Messiah nor the prophet spoken of by Moses in Deuteronomy 18. From Isaiah 40:3 he reminded the gathered crowds that he was merely "the voice of one calling in the desert" (John 1:23). Then John affirmed Jesus' ministry, announcing that He is the promised Messiah, the One who came to take away the sins of the world.

Verses 35-42 report how Andrew and Peter chose to follow the Lamb. These verses remind us that people are won to Christ *through* us, not *by* us nor *to* us. In bringing Peter to Christ, Andrew illustrates what we might call "family evangelism." Some commentators suggest that Andrew might have also been the one who brought Philip to Christ (v. 43). Philip was an "up-front" witness, who boldly proclaimed to his friend that he had personally seen the Messiah. Like Philip, we must witness of who Christ is, what He has done, and how people can find salvation in Him.

Ponder this: How like God to speak of His Son as a lamb. Unimportant by worldly standards, nevertheless gentle and meek, lambs still offer a model for our behavior in a hostile world. Then someday, in the halls of heaven, the slain Lamb will become the symbol of victory. With Christians of all ages we will sing to Him, "Worthy is the Lamb, who was slain, to receive power and wealth and wisdom and strength and honor and glory and praise!" (Rev. 5:12)

THE MASTER OF WEDDINGS AND WORSHIP

The town of Cana lies about ten miles north of Nazareth, so Jesus' first miracle (John 2) occurred not far from home. Weddings are splendid opportunities for families to reflect on spiritual values, and this was no exception. Mary, Jesus' mother, thought the wedding in Cana would be a fine time for Jesus to display His messianic identity publicly. But His answer, "My time has not yet come," shows she was wrong. This phrase appears several times in John's Gospel as our Lord made His way to the cross.

Weddings also are a time for glorifying God and that is precisely what Jesus did in Cana. In seeking to glorify God the Father, Jesus brought glory to Himself, and His disciples put their faith in Him. How has the Lord revealed His glory to you? Have you responded in faith and obedience?

The second half of this chapter reminds us that Jesus also reigns as Master of our worship. The practice of these temple salesmen shows that worship must not be commercial activity, whether in the first century or today. When challenged to prove His authority, Jesus issued the first prophecy of His resurrection: "Destroy this temple, and I will raise it again in three days" (v. 19).

Consider: Worship cannot be relegated to a building like the temple; it centers in the person of Christ Himself. We'll see more of that in John 4; for now let's concentrate on what John said about faith. The disciples focused on the Saviour and believed. Others "believed" only because of the miracles and "Jesus would not entrust Himself to them" (2:24). Not all faith is saving faith; God honors only faith that selects the right object. Today, as in the days of John, He looks at our hearts to examine whether what we say we believe really represents our inner selves.

ETERNAL LIFE

Is there a verse anywhere in the Bible more well known and loved than John 3:16? How poignantly it states that eternal life is not earned by begging, crying, praying, working, or joining! Salvation comes as a free gift when we believe what God has said. For almost 2,000 years men have been adding to the Gospel. But the truth still rings clear today—"whoever believes in Him shall not perish but have eternal life."

Nicodemus was a man with superb religious training but very little spiritual insight. He could not grasp Jesus' statement that one must be born "from above" to experience eternal life. Four times in three verses (vv. 16-18) Jesus used variations of the word *believe,* perhaps the most important key word in John's Gospel. In no uncertain terms the Son of God classified the entire human race into two groups—those who believe and are not condemned, and those who do not believe and are condemned already.

Verses 22-36 of the chapter confirm John's witness. Competition between his disciples and those of Jesus was encouraged by neither leader. Such diversionary activity takes away from the main event—God sent His Son into the world to bring salvation to the lost. Twenty-three times in this book John recorded references by Jesus to the One who "sent" Him.

The chapter ends with another warning (v. 36). This is the only time in his Gospel and Epistles that John mentioned "wrath."

Be reminded: Faith brings eternal life; rejection produces the abiding presence of God's wrath. Which have you chosen?

GOOD NEWS FOR THIRSTY PEOPLE

In 1972 my family and I visited Jacob's well while we toured Israel for two weeks. The water is as refreshing and cold today as when Jesus met the Samaritan woman there almost 2,000 years ago. Noon was an unlikely time for her to come, however. This suggests that this woman may have been an outcast in her town.

Though the conversation began with metaphors about water and drinking, Jesus soon turned directly to the point: "Go, call your husband and come back" (John 4:16). Embarrassed by His penetrating analysis of her moral condition, the woman turned the discussion to religion, notably the proper place of worship.

Our Lord spelled out some "ground rules" for Christian worship which certainly apply today:

(1) Worship must be "in spirit," from within our hearts and not merely external.

(2) Worship is first attitude and then action.

(3) Worship must be "in truth," that is, genuine, not pretentious.

(4) Worship is unrelated to geographical location.

The conclusion? Through one woman's simple testimony, an entire town learned that Jesus "is the Saviour of the world" (v. 42).

In the midst of this Samaritan evangelism, the disciples were confused about Jesus' need for food (vv. 31-38). He pointed them to the immediate opportunity for ministry, fields white and ripe for harvest, a description Christians have always found applicable to their own situations in any age.

The chapter ends back in Cana with the healing of the official's son, Jesus' second recorded miracle (vv. 43-54). Again the focus of this Gospel writer falls on faith. People would not believe without "signs and wonders" (v. 48), yet because this man "took Jesus at His word" (v. 50), his son lived.

Remember: This book calls us to reverse the common motto of the world and embrace instead a motto of faith—"believing is seeing."

LIFE THROUGH THE SON

People in our society are fond of saying, "God helps those who help themselves." But John 5 demonstrates precisely the opposite—God helps those who are incapable of helping themselves. The invalid at Bethsaida had been rejected by other people who took advantage of his pitiful helplessness. Jesus asked just one question, "Do you want to get well?" (v. 6) People need help—and only He can help them.

Jesus performed this miracle on the Sabbath, and that became the point of argument in the next four chapters. Why the fuss over a day? Because people want rules, not grace. They want to boast about what *they* did to earn merit from God and that attitude directly opposes the Gospel. Luke mentioned the Sabbath only nine times in Acts and not once in connection with Christian worship.

The Pharisees could not see over the Sabbath hurdle, however, and began to persecute in earnest. The words *life* or *live* occur eight times in John 5:16-30 as Jesus called on these religious leaders to accept life through the authority of the Father, through faith in the Father, and by the power the Father gives.

The Lord reviewed some of the testimony available to substantiate His claims—John the Baptist, Jesus' own works, the Father, and the Scriptures. Once again, the chapter ends with God's demand for faith: "But since you do not believe what [Moses] wrote, how are you going to believe what I say?" (v. 47).

It's a fact: Salvation comes only through simple and complete faith in the Saviour. How true the words of the old hymn:

> I am not skilled to understand,
> What God has willed, what God has planned;
> I only know at His right hand
> Is One who is my Saviour.

GIVE US THIS BREAD

Starvation poses a stark and unpleasant reality in our modern world. Ten percent of the world's babies die before their first birthday, and one of every four children suffers from malnutrition. Yet the problem of spiritual hunger reaches even more severe dimensions. Like the 5,000 in John 6, millions today need the living bread that only Jesus can provide.

John's beautiful record of this miracle offers so many interesting observations for us. First, notice the failure of human resources as Philip bemoaned, "Eight months' wages would not buy enough bread for each one to have a bite!" (v. 7) Then Andrew found a boy with five small barley loaves; barley—the grain used in the poorest offerings.

But like an ancient rod, the jawbone of a donkey, and a simple sling, this peasant lunch shows again that seemingly useless things can become important in Jesus' hands. *Jesus Christ is all-sufficient.* Everyone was apparently satisfied and each disciple had his own personal basket of leftovers as a reminder of the Master's power.

Jesus' walking on the Sea of Galilee revealed His authority to the disciples and His purposive ministry to the crowds. The requirements for help in their distress were simple enough—recognize their own need and take Jesus into the boat. That hasn't changed much today.

Public discussion of the miraculous feeding displayed a basic materialism which Jesus promptly condemned. The crowds loved Jesus for what they could get out of Him, preferably another free lunch. When He spoke again of the Father, they seemed ready to respond, only to reject Him more vehemently in the latter part of the chapter.

Mark this: How important for us to pray sincerely, "Lord, give us this bread." Jesus' spiritual bread is necessary for living the Christian life. He lovingly prepares it to meet each individual need, and we must eat it daily. Only by feeding on His Word can we experience spiritual life and growth.

I AM THE BREAD OF LIFE

Seven times in his Gospel, John recorded Jesus' announcements about Himself, introduced by the words, "I am." The first of these is Jesus' affirmation, "I am the Bread of life." This discussion about the Bread of life developed from the miraculous feeding of the 5,000. How powerful and how deep this dramatic address which covers the doctrines of election, security, resurrection, and eternal life!

Some believe the Lord referred to partaking of what we call "communion" when he told the people to eat His flesh and drink His blood (John 6:53, 55), but there was no such ordinance before the night of the crucifixion. Furthermore, partaking of the elements in the Lord's Supper in no way provides eternal life. Surely His emphasis centered on spiritual appropriation of the life He alone can offer.

Eating and drinking are used in Scripture as metaphors of faith. But many of His "disciples" misunderstood everything He told them and refused to follow Him further. Nevertheless, when pressed for their decision, the Twelve demonstrated their selection by the Lord. Peter's bold answer offers a model of testimony when folks ask us about our faith in Christ.

Notice: Certainty *follows* faith—"We believe and know." Such courage, however, can come only as we regularly appropriate the resources for godly living which He makes available. These are demanding times for sincere Christians; we must be prepared to live biblically in an alien environment.

JESUS IS THE MESSIAH

Israel's Feast of Tabernacles began on the fifteenth day of the seventh month, five days after Yom Kippur (the Day of Atonement). One of three annual feasts, it served as a memorial of the Lord's care of His people in the wilderness (Lev. 23; Deut. 16). Public opposition to Jesus had reached serious levels now, placing His life in constant jeopardy (John 7). The feast was half finished when Jesus arrived and began to teach. Discussion centered on His person and authority.

How differently we view people when compared with God's assessment! While paying tribute to Moses and the Law, these purveyors of man-made religion sought to destroy the very One who came to fulfill the Law. Their penetrating question remains unanswered to the present hour: "When the Christ comes will He do more miraculous signs than this man?" (v. 31) He had fulfilled Scripture, offered eternal life, and healed broken hearts. Yet they rejected Him.

On the last day of the feast, Jesus issued His generous invitation to all who struggled with spiritual thirst. He offered to give the Holy Spirit in regenerating power to all who would only believe in Him. What happened? Some believed part of what Jesus said (v. 40); others believed, but did nothing (v. 41); some fell into useless religious argument (v. 42); others reacted in hostile indignation (v. 44).

Yes, the temple guards were impressed and, yes, Nicodemus defended a more lenient application of the Law. But we must recognize that when our Lord offered Himself to crowds in Jerusalem, the only positive response came from the Twelve.

Note this: Rejecting the Saviour and His Gospel has been a global pastime for almost 2,000 years. We should not be surprised or discouraged when people respond the same way today.

FORGIVENESS IS A PROMISE

Even people who don't appreciate bumper stickers would have to agree with one some folks like to display: "Christians Aren't Perfect, Just Forgiven." John 8:1-11 records the beautiful story of the woman caught in adultery illustrating the central dilemma of salvation—how justice and mercy can be harmonized without encouraging sin or hopelessly condemning the sinner. The drama unfolds in three scenes.

The sin at issue represents a characteristic behavior of modern Western culture—adultery. Jesus' enemies hoped to use this woman in a trap to catch the Lord in violation of either Jewish or Roman law. The first scene ends in the middle of verse 6 and could be entitled, "The Charges."

Scene two (vv. 6b-9) shows us "The Response." Preachers and commentators waste time guessing what Jesus may have written in the sand; the Bible simply does not tell us. The centerpiece of this scene is the Lord's answer: "If any one of you is without sin, let him be the first to throw a stone at her" (v. 7). Perfect reply, of course. Both Jewish and Roman law were preserved while the Master exposed the wickedness of the accusers.

The final scene describes "The Verdict" (vv. 10-11). The accusers vanished and Jesus offered no condemnation. Her sin was not just set aside, for soon He would pay the penalty for both the woman and her accusers.

But remember: A behavioral change must be implemented, because repentance demands a clean break with sin. This same Jesus offers us forgiveness today, both for initial salvation and for daily cleansing. Will you accept it? Forgiveness is God's promise that He will no longer remember our sin nor use it against us. And that is the model for our forgiveness of others.

THE SHINING LIGHT

The second of the seven "I ams" of John's Gospel appears in John 8:12: "I am the light of the world." Like water (John 4) and bread (John 6), light is absolutely necessary to sustain life. And the Lord wasted no time in explaining that spiritual light comes only to those who willingly follow Him.

As we might suspect, "the Pharisees challenged Him," arguing that His own self-defense was not admissible evidence (8:13). But, of course, it was, since He is the omniscient, impartial, and perfect Son of God. They misunderstood and misconstrued everything He told them. When He spoke of heaven, they thought of Nazareth. When He mentioned the Father, they impugned the legitimacy of His birth. When He spoke of going home, they concluded He was planning suicide!

One inescapable truth jumps at us from these verses: the heresy that everyone will someday be saved denies the clear teaching of the Bible! There will be no escape for Christ-rejectors, not in the first century, and not today. Three times Jesus warned them, "You will die in your sins" (once in v. 21 and twice in v. 24).

Good news: This shining light wants to shine on you. Do you need the light of the Gospel for initial salvation? The light of wisdom for the confusing problems of life? Join those present that wonderful day, of whom John wrote, "Even as He spoke, many put their faith in Him" (v. 30). Faith for eternal life, yes. But also faith for contemporary living. The Light of the world wants to brighten your little world and enable you to reflect His brilliance.

THE TRUTH WILL SET YOU FREE

We have already learned that faith alone does not guarantee salvation (John 2). That faith must center in the Saviour Himself, not just His miracles or some teaching about Him. John 8:31-59 tells us how we can be set free from faith in inadequate but attractive objects that often clamor for our attention—relationships, religion, and righteousness.

Some of the Jews "who believed in Him" claimed that their relationship with Abraham kept them from any bondage. His descendants, they argued, have always been free (conveniently forgetting their bondage to Egypt, Assyria, Babylonia, Persia, Greece, and Rome). True disciples must be set free from such error, from sin, and from the unholy zeal these "disciples" displayed right in this very discussion.

We do well to notice again that these were so-called "believing" people. Yet Jesus chided them by saying, "You are doing the things your own father does" (v. 41). In their ignorance they did not understand that He meant Satan, so the Lord sharpened His condemnation in verses 42-47. Liars, murderers, terrorists, and all rebellious people reflect the attitude of Satan, even when they act in the name of religion.

Jesus turned their own appeal to Abraham against them (vv. 48-59). Such self-righteousness must be debunked and abandoned if people would receive God's grace.

Keep in mind: True disciples keep Jesus' words, and because of that, the world hates them just as Jesus was hated by these people whose ill-placed faith He exposed. Faith in relationship, religion, or righteousness will fail; indeed, faith in faith will fail. Perhaps man's greatest need is to understand and admit man's greatest need— the grace of God revealed in Jesus Christ His Son.

THE DIFFERENCE BETWEEN
LIGHT AND DARKNESS

He was a common sight on the dusty streets of Jerusalem, this blind beggar whose plight evoked no compassion, only curiosity (John 9). Yet his life was about to change, for on that day he became the focal point of the world's endless conflict, the battle between fate and faith, between sin and Christ. This man's hurting served as preparation for God's healing; his sorrow provided occasion for God's joy.

Notice that healing came only when the beggar responded in obedience to Jesus' command, "Go wash in the pool of Siloam" (v. 7). In front of incredulous neighbors this man had to take the first step of faith, accepting the fact of what Christ did for him. As God's light opened his dark world, this poor beggar became a walking model of what Jesus had taught shortly before: "I am the Light of the world. Whoever follows Me will never walk in darkness, but will have the light of life" (8:12).

Prejudice, pressure, and persecution followed as the man and his parents attempted to explain to the critical Pharisees what had happened. With simple peasant impatience, the man soon tired of their religious double-talk and put it as simply as he could: "One thing I do know. I was blind but now I see!" (9:25)

We talk a lot about people "finding Jesus," but here Jesus found this man. Physical healing became spiritual healing; blindness turned to sight; darkness gave way to light; and fate became faith.

Note this: Like this blessed beggar, we too have access to the light that dispels darkness. Our fate also yields to the greater power of faith in the One who is the Light of the world—and who has told us to become lights in our world as well.

THE SHEPHERD AND THE SHEEP

Entering John 10 we come on a period of intense conflict in the life of our Lord. The Pharisees and their cohorts had committed themselves to exterminating this one they considered a "pesky prophet" from Nazareth. The wonderful Parable of the Shepherd and the Sheep (10:1-21) follows immediately after the healing and hatred found in chapter 9.

The first six verses of chapter 10 emphasize *security*. The Shepherd knows His sheep, calls them by name, and leads them. In the ancient Middle East, one sheep pen held several flocks so that shepherd recognition was imperative. Only personal identification with the Shepherd could make the sheep feel safe.

Then our Lord spoke of the *shelter* a shepherd provides (vv. 7-10). He alone determines who may enter the fold. He guards the sheep, provides for them, and cares for them. Genuine care shows the difference between a true shepherd and a hired hand.

But most important, the shepherd *sacrifices* for the sheep (vv. 11-18). He relates to them in trust and intimacy; he joins them with other flocks; and in the case of the Good Shepherd, He died for the sheep. Twice Jesus identified Himself in His parable: "I am the Good Shepherd" (vv. 11, 14). Five times in this passage He spoke of laying down His life for the sheep (vv. 11, 15, 17, 18 [twice]). Our Saviour's substitutionary atonement is the heart of the Gospel.

What a beautiful word picture for us: We are Christ's sheep. He has purchased our salvation with His blood, and now He offers shelter and security to all who follow Him. Trust Him!

THEY SHALL NEVER PERISH

On September 1, 1983, Korean Airlines flight 007 was shot down in Russian-controlled airspace. Various interpretations of fault followed the tragedy, but whatever the correct explanation, 268 passengers died, including 61 Americans. We have come to expect in this confusing world that security and safety are rarely guaranteed.

But Christ's sheep can look to Him for assurance, though the world around them crumbles daily. How can those sheep be recognized? John 10:22-42 makes it clear: they believe in the Shepherd, they listen to the Shepherd, and they follow the Shepherd. Sheep follow because they are sheep; they are not sheep because they follow. Christians obey the Saviour because of their new natures. They behave like sheep because that's what God has made them.

Instead of converting hypocritical hearts, this shepherd promise ignited a new effort to stone Jesus. His enemies understood correctly His claims to be God and they wanted Him dead (vv. 31-33). Since the time of crucifixion had not yet come, He escaped their grasp and went to Perea on the east side of the Jordan River. There many more heard His message and believed.

What lessons does this passage contain for us? Certainly one truth is the joy of security in His promise of eternal life. But another is the surety of biblical authority—"the Scripture cannot be broken" (v. 35).

Think about it: Certainly we must also evaluate our own "sheeply" behavior. How well do we listen to the Shepherd? How familiar is the sound of His voice? How obediently do we follow?

JESUS IS OUR FRIEND

Disciples, brothers, sheep—Jesus used several terms to describe those who choose to follow Him. In chapter 13 He will refer to His disciples as "friends," a warm and loving designation He applied in chapter 11 to Lazarus of Bethany, brother of Mary and Martha.

Christians today as well can know that Jesus is our Friend. He deliberately delayed His return to Bethany because He knew that Lazarus' illness and death would glorify God. The disciples (particularly Thomas) seemed to misunderstand the plan from the start, yet the entire strategy was arranged for their benefit. What a great lesson we find here: If God is glorified in any sickness or death, it is good.

But with the Son of God, death never has the final word. Along with Lazarus' family, the Twelve learned that Jesus was more than their friend; He was their life. When the group arrived in Bethany, they found Lazarus in the tomb for four days already and two grieving sisters who had forgotten to "practice the promises" of resurrection. To Martha, Jesus offered a challenge to faith which has been repeated countless times to grieving loved ones at gravesides: "I am the resurrection and the life. He who believes in Me will live, even though he dies; and whoever lives and believes in Me will never die" (vv. 25-26).

In anger over sin and death, agitated by the heart-wrenching grief of the sister, Jesus called forth His friend from the dead and said to the astounded bystanders, "Did I not tell you that if you believed, you would see the glory of God?" (v. 40)

Worth noting: This glorious chapter closes with a portion that tells us yet again that Jesus is our Substitute. Caiaphas, an unlikely prophet indeed, "prophesied that Jesus would die for" sinners (v. 51). What a promise! What a hope! But only for those who know Jesus as their Friend.

THE CRISES OF THE CHRIST

Published in 1903, G. Campbell Morgan's book *The Crises of the Christ* stands as a classic handbook on Christology almost a century later. He covers events from Jesus' birth to His ascension, emphasizing the effects of the Lord's ministry on all who put their trust in Him.

John 12:1 tells us we have come to the last week of the Lord's life before the cross. John spent nearly half of his Gospel narrative on events of that crisis-filled week.

He began with the account of Mary anointing Jesus' feet with expensive perfume. As she offered this generous gift, Judas spoke his first recorded words in the Gospels: "Why wasn't this perfume sold and the money given to the poor?" (v. 5) At issue here is a contrast of values. Judas spoke not out of concern for the poor, but as a tight-fisted treasurer of the disciples.

Quickly the crisis of *values* gave way to a crisis of *confrontation,* the first truly public presentation of the Messiah to Israel. Jesus initiated the event, probably to stir good people to action, to fulfill Scripture, and to offer Himself as the Passover Lamb. How we could wish the bitter reaction of the Pharisees was true, both then and now: "Look how the whole world has gone after Him!" (v. 19)

Then came a crisis of *timing* as our Lord once again raised the issue of "the hour." But this time, it *had* come; the time of death had arrived. How should we pray in crisis, when our souls are troubled? Look again at verse 28: "Father, glorify Your name." The dying Son of Man "will draw all men" to Himself (v. 32). That is, the true Gospel knows no boundaries of race, color, or culture.

Consider this: Finally, chapter 12 tells of a crisis of *faith.* John called us to faith in the prophets, faith in the Father, and faith in the message of Jesus. Because His command leads to eternal life and that's what this Gospel is all about.

LOVING TO THE FULL EXTENT

The last part of John 13:1 could be translated "to the limit," but the NIV captures well the intent of John's words—Jesus loved His disciples to "the full extent." How interesting that two of this Gospel's key words each appear twice in the first verse of this chapter. *Love* forms one of John's central themes, and *world* appears 185 times in the New Testament, 105 of them in John's writings.

Like us, these disciples lived in a society that had rebelled against God. Like us, they learned more quickly from modeling and demonstration than by being told what was right. So on that final night Jesus exemplified love, explained it, and then exhorted His disciples to follow His example. How patient He was with Judas, how humble with these proud disciples! In contrast, Peter acted too "spiritual" to allow the Lord to wash his feet, but not too spiritual to command the Son of God!

As stated in verse 10, those who have been bathed (cleansed from sin's penalty through repentance) need only to wash (to be cleansed from sin's power through confession). As Peter learned that night, Christ's body holds no place for those who have not been cleansed by the Lord.

Perhaps there exists no act more menial than washing another's feet, but nothing is beneath a disciple. Did the Saviour intend to initiate an ordinance here? Some believe the command to wash the feet of others must be taken literally, but more than likely Jesus called us to acts of humble service for other Christians.

Worth remembering: Harry Ironside used to say: "When washing each other's feet, we should be careful of the temperature of the water." Whose feet should you be washing today?

WHEN YOUR FRIENDS LET YOU DOWN

Each year the football season begins with Charlie Brown charging the football while Lucy holds it. Each year he believes this time she will keep it there till he kicks it. But each year she yanks the ball away at the last second and Charlie falls on his backside, once more let down by his friend. We must learn to cope with such disappointment in life; those whom we most trust will sometimes fail us, and often that failure occurs when we least expect it.

Jesus, however, knew precisely what to expect from His friends. Of the original Twelve He chose, all would turn away in His time of greatest crisis. One would betray Him for money (13:21), and one would deny Him publicly (v. 38).

Though He knew in advance what would happen, Jesus was "troubled in spirit" as He told His disciples about the betrayal (v. 21). So unaware were they of Judas' true nature, they couldn't even grasp his guilt when Jesus clearly pointed it out. We should learn here that we cannot identify Christ's elect by any outward appearance. We should also learn that even someone who seems to be close to the Lord may be lost.

Jesus offered Judas the bread, perhaps a last opportunity for him to repent. But love's appeal became hate's dynamic and Judas, controlled by Satan, went out into the night. Yet God glories in what man often sees as tragedy. Five times in verses 31 and 32 John recorded Jesus' use of the words *glorify* and *glorified* as He now directed the disciples' thinking toward the cross.

Still boastful, Peter could not understand Jesus' statement, "Where I am going, you cannot come" (v. 33). Peter's courage seemed strong enough to handle martyrdom if necessary, but the Lord told him, "You will disown me three times" (v. 38). Such a sad chapter contains one of the greatest verses in John: "All men will know that you are My disciples if you love one another" (v. 35).

Keep this in mind: Unsaved people need more than an example or a sermon; they need to see God's people genuinely loving each other as Jesus loved Peter and, yes, even Judas. How should we react when our friends let us down? With patience, honor, forgiveness, and love. In short, we must react as Jesus did.

ONE WAY TO THE FATHER

In May 1981 writer William Saroyan lay dying of cancer. Picking up the phone next to his hospital bed, he dialed Associated Press and said to the reporter who answered, "Everyone has to die, but I always thought an exception would be made in my case. Now what?"

The thought of death troubles human beings and always has, even when it is not their own. Jesus had just spoken to the disciples about His death (13:33, 36), and they were troubled. Now He said to them in essence, "Stop worrying" (14:1).

The danger with troubled people is not that they will believe nothing, but that they will believe anything! To avert such loss of truth and certainty in His disciples, Jesus turned their minds to the Father. The word *Father* appears twenty-two times in chapter 14, and twelve of those are in the first thirteen verses. Jesus offered the personal touch of a heaven where the Father lives, personally prepared by the Son and containing enough room for all who would follow Him.

These verses teach an exclusive Gospel. No universalism, the hope that everyone will someday be in heaven, but a narrow way—salvation through Jesus alone (v. 6). Still confused, Philip wanted tangible evidence, the privilege of seeing the Father (v. 8). But that is precisely what he had seen for three and a half years; anyone who has seen Jesus has seen the Father, for They are one.

Once again John's Gospel reminds us that believing is seeing. And such faith will be important for these men who would do even greater things than Jesus had accomplished (v. 12). How was that possible? Certainly their ministries were greater in geography, number of converts, and length of time. But the power of those ministries (and of ours as well) centered in the risen Lord and their dependence on Him.

Remember: Jesus' wonderful promise is just as true today as it was that day: "You may ask Me for anything in My name, and I will do it" (v. 14).

ANOTHER COUNSELOR

No illustration can adequately describe the relationship among the members of the Triune Godhead; but think for a moment of a law firm with two partners. One partner handles all cases involving rural real estate while the other specializes in urban real-estate law. In one simplistic sense we could say that Jesus is our Advocate in heaven and the Holy Spirit handles matters on earth. These disciples would not be "orphans" (14:18) when Jesus returned to the Father; the Holy Spirit would be their consistent Comforter (v. 16).

Several important teachings surface in John 14. First, the Holy Spirit *lives permanently in believers.* He identifies them as God's children; He unites the family; and He fosters obedience (vv. 17-21). Family members show that they belong to Christ by the way they behave, not just by what they say.

Second, the Holy Spirit *teaches believers.* He reminds them of truth and of peace, and He strengthens their faith (vv. 26-27). Peace of mind and spirit is surely essential to a healthy life at home, in school, and on the job. To Christians *of* all ages and *in* all ages, Jesus said, "Do not let your hearts be troubled and do not be afraid" (v. 27).

Take note: This glorious chapter ends on a high note of testimony. Jesus affirmed His purpose to glorify the Father, and His words might well become ours: "The world must learn that I love the Father and that I do exactly what My Father has commanded Me" (v. 31). What a testimony! Make that your goal as you serve the Lord today.

REQUIREMENTS FOR A FRUITFUL LIFE

In the Old Testament, God spoke of the vine as a symbol of Israel (Ps 80:8-13; Isa. 5:1-2, 7; Jer. 2:21). Now in John 15 Jesus expanded the analogy. As the fulfillment of the Lord's purpose for Israel, the great Son of David identified Himself as the Vine and His followers as branches. If you like to look for key words in Bible study, note the eleven occurrences of *remain* (abide) in 15:4-10.

What results come from remaining? Joy, and a lasting friendship with Jesus. Up to this point in Scripture only Abraham had been called God's friend; but now the circle widened and the Lord invited eleven disciples in. Notice again the emphasis on love. Described in an earlier chapter as a testimony to the world (13:35), love now becomes an absolute command for believers (15:12). Love is the chief fruit of the Spirit (Gal. 5:22-23), the essential quality for all ministry.

But love among the saints may cause antagonism in the world. Why does the world hate Christians? Because of their link with the Lord. We could say that persecution comes because of *separation* (Christians are not a part of the world), *association* (Christians belong to the Saviour), and *proclamation* (Christians, like their Lord, speak the truth about sin).

Note: One thing stands out in this chapter: We must arrange or rearrange our lives to make room for abiding in Christ, or His will for our lives can never be realized. And that realization will most likely come in small steps, day by day, as we actively abide in Him and in His Word.

THE HOLY SPIRIT'S WORK IN US

John 15:26–16:16 represents a continuation of our study on July 21. In 14:15-31 we learned that the Holy Spirit lives permanently in believers and teaches those believers. Now Jesus adds additional information about the Spirit's role in the world.

This Counselor sent from heaven testifies to the world about Christ through miracles, through witnesses, and through persecution (15:24–16:4). Among His miracles, surely the greatest is the new birth. We are His instruments for witness, and every maturing Christian understands the Holy Spirit's role in forming thoughts and words for testimony.

Persecution comes to those who faithfully stand up for Christ. The Book of Acts barely gets underway as two of these disciples (Peter and John) are arrested for their proclamation of the resurrection (Acts 4:1-3). So the promise of the Spirit also warns that those indwelt by Him will suffer for their faith.

The Spirit also brings conviction to the world (John 16:5-11). In doing so He centers His message on three areas: sin, righteousness, and judgment. Sin reigns because of unbelief, the ultimate sin that closes the door to heaven and opens the door to hell. Righteousness comes only through the risen Son who shares His righteousness with all who believe in Him. Judgment here emphasizes not some coming event but the accomplished condemnation of Satan at the cross.

Grasp this important lesson: The Holy Spirit is not some supernatural "influence" hovering in the clouds above. He comes *to us,* and *through us* He carries out His ministry to the world. May we avoid quenching or grieving Him. May we yield to His control so that Christ's power may be evident in such a needy world.

WHEN JESUS COMMUNICATES TO YOU

In John 16:17-33 Jesus reviewed for the disciples many of the promises and challenges He had already put before them. Verse 20 seems to be the key: "I tell you the truth, you will weep and mourn while the world rejoices. You will grieve, but your grief will turn to joy."

Communication can be defined as "meaningful exchange," two or more people sharing ideas and understanding what is *meant*, not just what was *said*. In verses 17-33 words about communication occur repeatedly, including "ask," "said," "tell," and "mean." Along with the disciples, we can learn much in these verses about what happens when Jesus communicates to us.

First, we learn that *our grief will turn to joy*. This happens when we understand the Lord, when we actualize the hope of seeing Him again, and when we ask in His name (vv. 20-24). The result is not just grief *followed* by joy, but the actual transforming of grief itself into joy.

Second, we learn that *our doubt will turn to faith*. During the forty days between His resurrection and the Ascension, Jesus taught His disciples that the Father loved them and the Son claimed them (vv. 25-28). We too need those important lessons.

Glibly the disciples responded, "Now we can see that You know all things and that You do not even need to have anyone ask You questions. This makes us believe that you came from God" (v. 30). Jesus punctured such deceptive self-assurance with a penetrating question: "Do you now believe?" (v. 31, NIV margin) He reminded them that soon they would scatter and leave Him, and yet His peace would abide with them in their grief and confusion.

We also learn: Faith will turn to sight when Jesus returns. What a splendid ending to chapter 16 and what an encouraging word for this day: "In this world you will have trouble. But take heart! I have overcome the world" (v. 33).

WHAT OUR LORD PRAYS FOR US

My childhood was marked by the traumatic experience of hearing my mother in the next bedroom praying for me while my father hurled insults and hostility at her. I always felt I invaded her privacy by listening; and I've always felt that way about John 17, the real "Lord's Prayer." Four relationships come into view in this chapter, relationships Jesus apparently thought important enough to include in one of His last times of prayer with the Father.

The first relationship is between *the Son and the Father* (vv. 1-5). Jesus, the model "Finisher," asked the Father twice to have His glory returned (vv. 1, 5). Right at the beginning of this prayer we learn that the Father's glory is the foundational purpose in praying.

The second relationship describes contact between *the Son and believers* (vv. 6-12). Words like "them," "those," and "they" dominate this paragraph. Believers are described as those who have obedience, faith, and knowledge. Yet the Lord felt a need to pray for two more gifts of God's grace for us: protection in the world, and unity among ourselves (v. 11).

The third relationship pertains to *believers and the world* (vv. 13-19). In these verses Jesus used twelve prepositional phrases in requesting that the Father watch over Christ's people who must stay *in* the world though they are not *of* the world. He wants us to be kept *from* evil so that we can be witnesses *to* the world. Notice that His prayer, "sanctify them by the truth" (v. 17), includes the means as well as the end.

Fourth, our Lord asked the Father about the relationship of *believers to each other* (vv. 20-26). Mentioned earlier, this now becomes a main theme. Unity in the church is to be patterned after the unity of the Triune Godhead so the world can see how believers dwell in the Lord and He in the Father.

Assignment: Let's concentrate today on showing the world how we can lovingly relate to other believers—including those in our own families.

FOUR WITNESSES—FOUR DECISIONS

In April, about the time Jesus crossed from Jerusalem to Gethsemane, the Kidron became a roaring stream running south into the Valley of Hinnom. At Passover season it was often red with lamb's blood, a striking divide between the city and the wealthy mountain gardens to the east. To an olive grove in one of those gardens, Jesus retired with His disciples to await the arrest that would signal the events of that dark night.

Four people occupy John's report in chapter 18, people who saw Christ the very night of the crucifixion and were forced to draw some conclusion about Him. The first is Malchus, servant to the high priest. Merely a curious bystander during early events, he became actively involved when Peter swung his sword with good courage and poor aim. The Bible records no response by Malchus, but one can certainly imagine some interesting explanations to Mrs. Malchus later that day. Jesus healed the ear and told the disciples to stop their violent behavior (Luke 22:51).

The second person dominating this chapter is Peter, strangely warming himself at the fire built by Jesus' enemies. The predicted denial now took shape as this confused and frightened disciple offered the wrong answers for the wrong reasons.

Then Annas took over the official questioning. No longer high priest himself, this powerful man still controlled Jerusalem politics through his son-in-law, Caiaphas. Any Jew of that day knew about the Bazaars of Annas, where sacrifices were sold for twenty times the honest price.

Then Pilate entered the saga, ready to play the only role which has kept his name notorious for almost 2,000 years. This weak man learned that he confronted a King, and that he had an opportunity to defend truth rather than protect the fragile political peace of Israel. But he failed, caving in to the screaming crowds stirred up by the agents of the high priest.

Four witnesses. Four decisions. Each of these men had opportunity to select righteousness and truth; and at least three of them failed miserably.

Two questions: Which one represents you? Where does your relationship with the Lord stand today?

BEHOLD THE MAN

Like most Roman officials of his day, Pilate functioned according to a single political mandate: protect the *Pax Romana*. The potential for riot in Jerusalem would have frightened even a courageous governor. Throughout his confrontation with Jesus, Pilate must have known that he was not the one in control. Jesus spoke when He wanted to and remained silent when He wished. John 19:11 gives the key to guilt: those who sent Jesus to Pilate (Annas and Caiaphas) held the greater guilt.

Ultimately, Pilate gave in to the "bottom-line" argument: "'If you let this Man go, you are no friend of Caesar'" (v. 12). For this pagan politician, career survival loomed more important than truth, or even life, and so "Pilate handed Him over to them to be crucified" (v. 16).

John gave a detailed account of the crucifixion. Pilate's sign was written in the language of the Jews (Aramaic), the language of the empire (Latin), and the language of culture and commerce (Greek). Only John remained close as the Saviour died. In looking back on that day, the beloved disciple remembered the tender instructions given by Jesus relating to Mary (vv. 26-27).

God's holiness and justice made the Cross an absolute necessity. Events at the crucifixion happened as they did, so that "the Scripture might be fulfilled" (v. 24). No fewer than twenty Old Testament prophecies were fulfilled within twenty-four hours at the time of our Lord's death.

Burial was provided by Nicodemus and Joseph of Arimathea—two prominent men, certainly tender friends of Jesus, and probably secret believers. The price had been paid. The suffering was over. Satan had been defeated at the Cross, but full victory awaited God's power at the open tomb.

A glad truth: We participate in both the Cross and the empty tomb. God's Spirit "baptizes" all believers into Christ's death and resurrection. Awareness of that fact can help us live holy lives today.

SIGHTS OF SUPER SUNDAY

In late twentieth-century North America, "Super Sunday" means that day in January when the annual Super Bowl football game is played. But in much broader historical perspective, there has never been a Sunday like the day of Christ's resurrection. For every Christian this will always be Super Sunday.

Three people occupy John's account of those morning hours (John 20:1-9). When Mary arrived at the tomb, she saw the displaced stone. She came running to Peter, but Luke said her report was largely ignored (Luke 24:11). Apparently, Peter and John (almost all commentators identify John as the "other disciple") believed enough to go see for themselves.

What sights awaited these eager, running men! Looking in, John saw strips of linen and reacted with hesitation and uncertainty. Peter, not known for timidity on any occasion, blustered right in and saw the folded burial cloth. Surely it was obvious that no graverobbers had been in this tomb; the orderly scene evidenced God's hand in delivering His Son from death. When John went in, he "believed," that is, he perceived the reality of the Resurrection for the first time.

This historical event and its meaning became the centerpiece of apostolic preaching in the Book of Acts. Perhaps from impetus provided by Peter and John, New Testament preachers proclaimed that the Saviour is forever alive, a dramatic truth at the heart of the Gospel to this very hour.

Think of it! The living Lord has conquered both sin and death. We can function amid trouble and heartache, knowing the ultimate victory is His, and therefore ours.

WE ARE WITNESSES

Just before His ascension, Jesus challenged His disciples to be witnesses of all they had seen and heard. That challenge, and particularly the word *witnesses,* must have made a significant impact on Peter. In four sermons recorded in Acts, Peter alluded to witness responsibility (Acts 2:32; 3:15; 5:32; 10:39), and in every case he referred specifically to the Lord's crucifixion and resurrection.

John 20:10-31 records Jesus' three appearances immediately after His resurrection. These are not His only appearances, but the apostle built his theme of faith by selecting these particular events. The first was to Mary Magdalene, who had gone to the garden looking for a body, not a risen Lord. Even after He first spoke, she couldn't take her eyes off the tomb to see the Person. How beautiful to learn that though the Cross may have killed faith and hope, it could not destroy love. Jesus told her not to hold on to the past. Now there was a new relationship, and she was to be a witness to the other disciples that Jesus lives.

In Jesus' second appearance, His frightened disciples were hiding behind locked doors. As Jesus brought them the message of peace, the angels' promise to the shepherds was fulfilled (Luke 2:14). You may also remember Jesus' promise to relieve the disciples' grief by replacing it with joy (John 16:20). He gave them a measure of the Holy Spirit, probably to enhance their important learning times between the Resurrection and the Ascension. He also gave them a priestly mission, to bear witness of the living Gospel which can lead to forgiveness and new life.

But not all the Eleven were present that first Sunday night. Thomas' characteristic pessimism had erupted into full-blown skepticism, and he showed no hesitancy in telling his friends how he felt. One week later, however, he did muster the courtesy to attend their little meeting, and there he saw the Master face to face and yielded his doubting to the risen Lord.

Question: Do you have doubts? We all do from time to time. Like Thomas, allow the reality of the living Lord to handle your hesitation today.

JESUS IS LORD

As John brought this wonderful book to a close in John 21, he left his readers with one thought beyond the oft-repeated emphasis on faith. He wanted to show us that these disciples, once mystified and confused, were at last beginning to sense the depth of the commitment they must have to their Master. To make this point, he chose a personal conversation between the Lord and Peter (which John may have heard) and to which Peter probably referred on many subsequent occasions.

The setting was a seaside breakfast at which seven of the disciples were present. Jesus disclosed Himself to them through a miracle, and John announced to Peter, "It is the Lord" (v. 7). After He ate with them, Jesus turned His attention to Peter, probably because of the dominant role that he would play in the early church. Three times Peter had denied the Lord; so three times Jesus asked him, "Do you truly love Me?" (vv. 15-17) Embarrassing as it must have been at the time, this tender exchange genuinely restored Peter to leadership, a role he exercised early in Acts.

Called by his Lord to be a dedicated follower, Peter could not resist comparing how Jesus dealt with John (v. 21). He seemed to be saying, "If I have to be a martyr, why doesn't John receive the same fate?" Then the Lord told Peter something you and I need to recall every day of our lives. Paraphrased, verse 22 sounds like this: "What I choose to do with other people is none of your business; you follow Me."

Remember: Jesus is Lord of our lives; Jesus is Lord of our service; Jesus is Lord of our future. He allows no selfishness to stand in the way of those who would follow Him in full obedience.

NOW WHAT?

This month our studies have led us on a spiritual odyssey through one of the greatest books of the Bible. We have learned about faith from this Spirit-inspired record of the life, ministry, death, and resurrection of Jesus of Nazareth, God's Son.

John's purpose has been clear: to point people to faith in the Saviour by showing both the historical record and the interpretation of His life and ministry. John alone among the Gospel writers recorded his own personal testimony about the Lord, the visit of Nicodemus, the raising of Lazarus, and the detailed prayer of chapter 17. He carefully selected those words and works of the Lord which he calculated would lead his reader to faith.

Let's not miss the emphasis on Jesus' death and resurrection. Scarcely half way through his record John came to the end of the Lord's three-and-a-half year ministry and concentrated in chapters 12–21 on the last week. So central are the crucifixion and the empty tomb that God's Spirit wishes us too to focus clearly on them.

Give this thought: The question now centers not on John's purpose nor even the splendid content of his book. The real issue is what we will do in response. Has God brought us to greater faith through this study? Do we understand more of the Light and Life of which the apostle wrote? Are we prepared to respond to the Lord's command to Peter, to follow without reservation or complaint? Take time right now in prayer, asking God to allow the impact of John's Gospel of belief to make you more like the One of whom he wrote.

August

Devotional readings in Paul's Letter to the Romans
by John A. Witmer

SPREAD THE WORD

The first year it was introduced in the United States the Pentel pen sold almost two million units. This was accomplished without heavy promotion. The secret was word-of-mouth advertising by enthusiastic owners.

So it should be with the Good News of forgiveness of sin and the gift of eternal life through faith in the Lord Jesus Christ. This is the message unregenerate persons desperately need. Without it they are doomed to eternal separation from God. Yet most Christians advertise everything from abalone to zwieback except the Gospel. One estimate is that 95 percent of all church members have never led anyone to Christ.

This was not true of the Apostle Paul. He wrote the Roman Christians that he was "eager to preach the Gospel" (Rom. 1:15) in Rome as well as all the other places he had preached it. Like a town crier, Paul was "eager to herald the good news" (literal translation). When he finally got to Rome, Paul did exactly that. Despite house arrest with a guard (Acts 28:16), he witnessed to "the whole palace guard" (Phil. 1:13). His expressed desire was no idle boast.

Like Paul, every believer has been "set apart for the Gospel of God" (Rom. 1:1). Jesus has called each one who believes in Him to be a witness to Him (Acts 1:8). Like Paul, every believer should serve God wholeheartedly "in preaching the Gospel of His Son" (Rom. 1:9).

Paul's motivation for heralding the Good News of Jesus Christ was twofold. First, he was a debtor to unregenerate humanity (v. 14). This sparked his eagerness. Paul owed every person he met the opportunity to hear the Good News. So do you and I.

Paul's second motivation was the fact that the Gospel "is the power of God for the salvation of everyone who believes" (v. 16). In it "righteousness from God is revealed" (v. 17). For this reason Paul was "not ashamed [embarrassed] of the Gospel" (v. 16). Neither should you and I be.

What you can do: Meditate on the truth of Scripture concerning the Gospel and pray that the indwelling Holy Spirit will spark your eagerness to herald the Good News.

NO THANKS

A biting one-liner says, "If you want to find gratitude, look for it in the dictionary."

The sad fact is that human beings are not naturally thankful. After printing thousands of letters to Santa Claus as a special feature before Christmas, a newspaper editorialized after Christmas that it had received only one "thank you" letter for Santa.

When the Lord Jesus healed ten lepers, only one, a Samaritan, returned to thank Him. Jesus poignantly asked, "Where are the nine?" (Luke 17:12-19).

Unthankfulness is not unique to modern man; it is endemic to humanity since the Fall. In tracing God's judgment on unregenerate mankind, Paul indicted them because "although they knew God, they neither glorified Him as God nor gave thanks to Him" (Rom. 1:21).

This lack of thankfulness was the starting point of a progressive and accelerating degeneration leading to idolatry, immorality, sexual perversion, and "a depraved mind" (v. 28). As a result, before a righteous God unregenerate humanity is "without excuse" (v. 20; 2:1).

If ingratitude is the sin that leads to the whole catalog of iniquities, the reverse is also true. Someone has said, "A thankful heart is not only the greatest virtue, but the parent of all other virtues."

Thankfulness is a distinctive mark of the child of God. We are commanded to "give thanks in all circumstances" as "God's will for you in Christ Jesus" (1 Thes. 5:18). For the Christian, therefore, to be unthankful is disobedience to God, and sin.

Christians are also commanded to give "thanks to God the Father for everything" (Eph. 5:20; cf. Col. 3:15). This includes the unpleasant and injurious, because "in all things God works for the good of those who love Him" (Rom. 8:28).

To develop a thankful heart: Think first about God and His perfections. Then consider the salvation God has provided in Jesus Christ through the indwelling Holy Spirit. Finally, begin to count God's blessings. Your heart will overflow with praise and thanksgiving.

GOD HAS NO FAVORITES

A judge is reported to have opened court with this statement: "I have in hand two checks—a bribe you might call it—one from the defendant for $15,000, the other from the plaintiff for $10,000. My decision is to return $5,000 to the defendant and judge the case strictly on its merits."

Contrary to this judge, God is absolutely and totally impartial. Moses said that God "shows no partiality and accepts no bribes" (Deut. 10:17). Similarly King Jehoshaphat charged his appointees to "judge carefully, for with the Lord our God there is no injustice or partiality or bribery" (2 Chron. 19:7; cf. Job 34:19).

In the house of Cornelius, Peter realized that God's impartiality applied to the offer of salvation (Acts 10:34). Even as believers, our lives are impartially evaluated by God. As Peter stated, our Father "judges each man's work impartially" (1 Peter 1:17; cf. 2 Cor. 5:10) and rewards accordingly (1 Cor. 3:10-15; cf. 4:2-5).

Since God, our Heavenly Father, is perfectly impartial and totally just in all He does, He expects believers as His children to be impartial. This applies to Christian leaders. Paul charged Timothy "to keep these instructions without partiality, and to do nothing out of favoritism" (1 Tim. 5:21).

Impartiality is also expected of all Christians in all the activities of daily life. He closed his instructions to "masters" (i.e., employers, supervisors) concerning their treatment of their "slaves" (i.e., employees, fellow-workers) with the reminder that with the "Master ... in heaven ... there is no favoritism" (Eph.6:9; cf. Col. 3:25). The principle applies to all interpersonal relationships (cf. James 2:1-4).

Note: God's standard of impartiality is impossible to achieve. A measure of achievement is possible, however, as the Holy Spirit controls your life, providing and manifesting "the wisdom that comes from heaven," which among other qualities is "impartial" (James 3:17).

PRACTICE WHAT YOU PREACH

We have all heard the excuse for inconsistency, "Don't do as I do, do as I say." Perhaps we have used it ourselves, because all of us have difficulty in being completely consistent. Inconsistency in incidentals is not only insignificant, it is sometimes refreshing. In moral and ethical issues that impinge on our Christian profession of faith, however, it is important to practice what you preach.

The IRS questioned a minister's $450 deduction for a clerical collar. "It was $4.50," he explained. "I forgot the decimal point." A suspicious agent checked previous returns and found the same type of mistake here and there. The dishonest clergyman had been cheating on his income tax return for years.

This illustrates that inconsistency borders on and merges into hypocrisy. This is what Paul indicted the Jews for. They boasted of being Jews, of having the Mosaic Law, of knowing God, of being spiritual teachers (Rom. 2:17-20). Despite this profession, they dishonored "God by breaking the Law" (v. 23). They were not merely inconsistent; they were hypocrites. They did not practice what they preached.

The Lord Jesus indicted the scribes and Pharisees for their hypocrisy (Matt. 23:3), pronouncing "woe" on them (23:13, 15-16, 23, 25, 27, 29). He also said that they nullified "the Word of God by [their] tradition" (Mark 7:13).

The tragic harm of Christian inconsistency and hypocrisy is its impact on the unsaved. Our failure to practice what we preach gives the unregenerate an excuse to reject faith in the Lord Jesus Christ, a chance to say, "If that's what Christianity produces, I don't want it." Even worse, as Paul told the Jews, "God's name is blasphemed . . . because of you" (Rom. 2:24; cf. 2 Peter 2:2).

Give heed: When we fail to practice what we preach, we should frankly confess it as sin and seek in the power of the indwelling Holy Spirit to be a consistent Christian. This will preserve the impact of our witness to the Lord Jesus Christ. Live without hypocrisy, so others can do as you do, not just do as you say!

NOTHING BUT THE TRUTH

When a person appears as a witness in court, he takes an oath to "tell the truth, the whole truth, and nothing but the truth, so help me God." No one is ever asked to confirm his oath by "so help me Satan." This is because Satan is the antithesis of truth. As the Lord Jesus said, "He is a liar and the father of lies" (John 8:44).

Oaths to tell the truth are vouchsafed by God because God is the God of truth (Ps. 31:5; Isa. 65:16). Through Isaiah God declared, "I, the Lord, speak the truth" (Isa. 45:19). Among the things the Lord Jesus claimed to be is "the truth" (John 14:6).

The truthfulness of God is closely identified with His faithfulness. In fact, some translations frequently translate "truth" instead of "faithfulness." The point is that in all He does and says God does not equivocate; He can be trusted.

Following the statement, "Let God be true," Paul said, "and every man a liar" (Rom. 3:4). Compared to the absolute truthfulness and faithfulness of God, everyone is, to some degree, a liar.

In preparation for the next Sunday's sermon on lying, a pastor asked his congregation to read Romans 17. The next Sunday when he asked how many had read the chapter several hands were raised. "There is no Romans 17," he revealed and launched into his sermon.

Most human beings are like the Cretans, whom "one of their own prophets" described as "always liars" (Titus 1:12). God, however, desires His children to reflect His truthfulness. Through Paul, God said, "Each of you must put off falsehood and speak truthfully" (Eph. 4:25; cf. Col. 3:9). Believers are to "live as children of light . . . the fruit" of which "consists in all goodness, righteousness, and truth" (Eph. 5:8-9).

The secret of being truthful: Saturate your mind with the Word of God, which "is truth" (John 17:17). As Paul wrote, "Whatever is true . . . think about such things" (Phil. 4:8). Then trust the "Spirit of truth" (John 14:17; 15:26; 16:13) to control your speech.

A RIGHTEOUSNESS FROM GOD

A husband was helping his wife rearrange some furnishings in their home. When he picked up a costly crystal vase, he was warned to be careful. Cautiously, he carried it from one end of the room to the other. Just as he was putting the vase down, it slipped and fell to the floor, breaking into pieces. He refrained from reminding his angry wife that he had carried the vase safely across the room, for that would only have irritated her more; the vase was broken nonetheless, and words would not replace it.

So it is with seeking to establish one's righteousness by doing good or keeping the Mosaic Law. As James wrote, "Whoever keeps the whole Law but stumbles at just one point is guilty of breaking all of it" (James 2:10).

This is why Paul wrote, "There is no one righteous, not even one" (Rom. 3:10), and "therefore no one will be declared righteous in His [God's] sight by observing the Law" (v. 20). The fact is that "all have sinned and fall short of the glory of God" (v. 23).

If no one possesses righteousness and no one can earn it, how then can a human being be accepted by a righteous God?

The answer is that there is "a righteousness from God." The "righteous God" (Ps. 7:9; cf. Ps. 11:7; 116:5; 119:137; 145:17) requires righteousness in those He permits to stand in His presence, but He provides it as a gift. Paul wrote, "This righteousness from God comes through faith in Jesus Christ" (Rom. 3:22).

Jesus Christ died "as a sacrifice of atonement" (v. 25) and accomplished "redemption" from sin and Satan (v. 24). As a result, any person who accepts by faith Christ's death for him is "justified [declared righteous] freely [as a gift] by His grace [unmerited favor]" (v. 24).

Consider this: God faced a divine dilemma. How could He, infinitely righteous, accept into His presence eternally sinful people unable to achieve righteousness by their own efforts? The solution is the redemptive death of His incarnate Son, Jesus Christ, accepted by faith. That enabled God "to be just [righteous] and the one who justifies [declares righteous] those who have faith in Jesus" (v. 26). Are you trusting in your own righteousness—or in God's?

IS HE YOUR FATHER?

Liberal Christian theology speaks of "the Fatherhood of God and the brotherhood of man." This is true in the sense that God is the Creator of all men (cf. Mal. 2:10). It is not true in the spiritual sense that every man possesses a spark of divinity, however, as liberal theology insists.

God is also Father of Israel by virtue of His covenant with Abram (Gen. 15:18; 17:2; 7–8), confirmed with Isaac (26:3-5) and Jacob (28:13-15). God instructed Moses to tell Pharaoh, "This is what the Lord says: Israel is My firstborn son" (Ex. 4:22).

The personal spiritual benefits of this filial relationship, however, were dependent on faith. When the Jews who opposed the Lord Jesus boasted, "The only Father we have is God Himself" (John 8:41), Jesus responded, "You belong to your father, the devil" (v. 44). Their rejection of the Lord Jesus showed that they did not have faith in the God of Abraham, who was their physical but not their spiritual father (8:33-40).

Although God is identified in Scripture as Father in several ways, He is Father redemptively and spiritually only of all who believe. Abraham is the model of this saving faith in the promise of God (Rom. 4:3; 18-22). In this age of grace, faith is focused on God's promise of salvation through the death and resurrection of the Lord Jesus Christ (vv. 23-25).

John explained that "to all who received Him, to those who believed in His name, He gave the right to become children of God" (John 1:12). Through the Holy Spirit the believer cries "Abba, Father" (Rom. 8:15; Gal. 4:6).

As a spiritual Father, God supervises our training toward spiritual maturity (Heb. 12:5-13). At the same time, since "He knows how we are formed, He remembers that we are dust. . . . As a father has compassion on his children, so the Lord has compassion on those who fear Him" (Ps. 103:13, 14).

Question: Are you a child of God by faith in Christ? Then thank Him today for His fatherly care for you.

PEACE WITH GOD

Peace on earth is a rare and elusive commodity. It has been figured that in almost 4,000 years of recorded history less than 300
years have been without war. During that time more than 8,000
peace treaties have been made and broken.

For the vast majority of human beings, peace with God also is
elusive, something they do not know. Alienated from God through
sin, unregenerate persons are "powerless" (Rom. 5:6), "ungodly"
(v. 6), "sinners" (v. 8) and "God's enemies" (v. 10). They persist
in their opposition to God, having never heard that "God was
reconciling the world to Himself in Christ, not counting men's sins
against them" (2 Cor. 5:19).

When the treaty was signed with Japan on the USS *Missouri*
ending World War II, units of Japanese soldiers had to be informed
that the war was over and peace had been declared. Similarly,
Christians have the message and ministry of reconciliation (2 Cor.
5:18-19) to the unregenerate. We are to implore them to "be
reconciled to God" (v. 20).

When that message of reconciliation through Jesus Christ—the
Good News of salvation and eternal life—is received by faith, the
individual is "justified" (declared righteous) by God on the basis of
his faith (Rom. 5:1). At that moment he is accepted by God "in the
One He loves" (Eph. 1:6), the Lord Jesus Christ. As a result, at
that moment the individual has "peace with God" (Rom. 5:1).

Some translations prefer the hortatory translation instead of the
declarative statement—"Let us enjoy peace with God." Both
translations are valid. Obviously, we cannot enter into and enjoy
what we do not possess; therefore the declaration "We have peace
with God" is basic. On the other hand God desires that believers
enter into and enjoy all they possess in Jesus Christ (Eph. 1:3; Col.
2:9-10). Therefore "let us enjoy peace with God."

It's a fact: Entering experientially into "peace with God" is the
first step toward knowing "the peace of God" (Phil. 4:7) that
marks the spiritually mature Christian.

GRACE ON THE INCREASE

John Bradford was a leader in the Protestant Reformation in England along with Cranmer, Ridley, and Latimer. He is described by a biographer as having a "singularly gentle character." As he frequently watched criminals led away to execution, he repeatedly commented, "But for the grace of God there goes John Bradford.

Bradford was conscious of the virus of sin that infects every descendant of Adam. He recognized that, apart from the grace of God, that congenital principle of sin within could express its most malignant corruption and wickedness in any individual, even John Bradford.

The grace of God is frequently defined as "God's unmerited favor." While this is true, God's grace is more accurately defined as "God's favor expressed toward those who deserve His wrath." Human beings not only do not merit God's grace; they deserve His judgment.

The grace of God involves two elements. It is first an attitude, a disposition. It is an aspect of the love of God, the heart of God's nature (1 John 4:8, 16). As such it reaches out to all mankind (cf. John 3:16). In addition to an attitude, however, the grace of God is an action, an activity. As such, it is related to God's blessings, which are expressions and manifestations of His matchless grace (cf. John 1:16). As a result, the grace of God continues to be bestowed and can increase (cf. 2 Cor. 9:8).

The grace of God is focused on and centered in the Person and redemptive work of Jesus Christ. As John wrote, "Grace and truth came through Jesus Christ" (John 1:18). As a result, it is sometimes called "the grace of our Lord Jesus Christ" (Acts 15:11; Rom. 16:20) as well as "the grace of God" (1 Cor. 15:10; Eph. 3:7-8).

God's grace is both the source (Titus 2:11) and the means of human salvation (Eph. 2:5, 8) through the agency of faith. This is true of the entire process of divine salvation from its start in justification to its consummation in glorification. All is the result of the "incomparable riches of His grace" (Eph. 2:7; cf. 1:7).

A daily challenge: Allow His infinite grace to increase in your life day by day.

ALIVE TO GOD IN CHRIST

One of the interesting stories in the apocryphal gospels describes Jesus as a small boy playing with His friends in Nazareth. The children were fashioning small birds out of mud. When they finished, Jesus touched the birds. Instantly, they came to life and flew away to the delight of Jesus' playmates.

Such pointless miracles are a mark of the false gospels. This story, however, illustrates a point. In His public ministry to validate His deity and Messiahship, Jesus did restore physical life to dead individuals — Jairus' daughter (Luke 8:41-42, 49-56), the widow of Nain's son (Luke 7:11-16), and Lazarus (John 11:38-44).

Less spectacular but infinitely more important than restoring physical life, the Lord Jesus Christ gives spiritual life, eternal life, to those who believe in Him. This is the result of identification by faith with Jesus, who through His resurrection is alive forevermore (Rev. 1:18).

Each of us before we trusted Jesus Christ was spiritually dead — "dead in . . . transgressions and sins" (Eph. 2:1; cf. v. 5; Col. 2:13). As a result of our faith in Jesus Christ, "God . . . made us alive with Christ" (Eph. 2:5).

As a result of your faith in the Lord Jesus Christ, God sees you as identified with His Son. From God's perspective you died with Jesus Christ on Calvary, were buried with Him in Joseph's tomb, and were resurrected with Him to eternal life.

Paul urges us to adopt God's perspective of our identification with Jesus Christ as our own. By faith we must recognize that we have died to sin with Christ and we have been raised together with Christ. We must write in the ledger of our life and act accordingly that we are "dead to sin but alive to God in Christ Jesus" (Rom. 6:11).

Remember: The next time temptation comes, recognize that you are dead to that sin, that you are to be unresponsive to it, and that you are alive, not to sin but to God.

241

SLAVES TO GOD

Slavery was commonplace in both Old Testament and New Testament times. The great Greek philosopher Plato, for example, was a slave for some years until purchased and freed by his former students. It is estimated that at one point the Roman Empire included 10 million slaves. Frequent references to slavery in Scripture, therefore, are not surprising.

This is true in part because slavery lends itself readily to metaphorical use in the spiritual realm. Unregenerate persons are described as "slaves to sin" (Rom. 6:17) and "slaves to those who by nature are not gods" (Gal. 4:8). Paul spoke of them as "in slavery under the basic principles of the world" (v. 3). Then they offered "the parts of [their] body in slavery to impurity and to ever-increasing wickedness" (Rom. 6:19).

The Gospel of salvation through faith in the Lord Jesus Christ, therefore, is a spiritual Emancipation Proclamation. The redemption (manumission) price has been paid. In response to our faith in Christ, God "has rescued us from the dominion of darkness" (Col. 1:13). As a result the believer is "no longer a slave" (Gal. 4:7) but has been "set free from sin" (Rom. 6:22).

However, as believers, "when you offer yourselves to someone to obey him as slaves you are slaves to the one whom you obey" (v. 16), whether sin or God. Even though as believers identified with Christ by faith, we "died to sin" (v. 2; cf. vv. 6-7), the principle of sin within us has not died to us. It constantly seeks to express itself through our thoughts and our actions and to make us its slave once again.

Don't forget: As a believer, therefore, you have a responsibility to "not let sin reign in your mortal body" (v. 12). As believers we "have become slaves to God" (v. 22). This we must freely acknowledge, allowing God to control and direct us so that "sin shall not be your master" (v. 14).

RELEASED FROM THE LAW

According to the Apostle Paul, marriage is to be for life (Rom. 7:2). The usual marriage vows agree, stating "until death do us part." This biblical principle has never been abrogated despite the laxity of modern divorce laws. Sweden's divorce law, for example, permits couples to divorce almost as soon as the marriage ceremony is completed.

Paul used marriage to illustrate the believer's relationship to the Law of Moses. The marriage is binding as long as both partners are alive. As soon as one partner dies, however, the marriage ends and the surviving partner is free to remarry. Since the Law of Moses encompasses the will of God for the moral and religious life of mankind, every individual, whether Jew or Gentile, is bound by that standard. In a sense, human beings are married to the Law of God.

"Through the body of Christ" sacrificed on Calvary according to the Law, the individual who is identified with Him by faith "died to the Law" (v. 4). The believer, therefore, is free to be married to another. That one is the resurrected Lord Jesus Christ, the one who lives in everlasting newness of life.

Many Christians believe that, even though it is impossible to gain salvation by keeping the Law of Moses, after an individual is saved by grace through faith, the Law is his rule of life; and God enables him to live up to the Law of Moses.

Not so, according to Paul. Through the death of Christ "we have been released from the Law" (v. 6). Joined to Jesus Christ, we now serve God "in the new way of the Spirit, and not in the old way of the written code" (v. 6; cf. Gal. 5:16, 18, 22-23).

For you: Allow the Holy Spirit to enable you to live above the Law.

RESCUED!

Some years ago comedian Flip Wilson played a character named Geraldine on television. No matter what crazy escapade Geraldine got into, when she was faced with the consequences of her actions, her stock response was, "The devil made me do it."

The dilemma the Apostle Paul described in the second half of Romans 7 is somewhat reminiscent of Geraldine. Paul confessed, "What I do is not the good I want to do; no, the evil I do not want to do—this I keep on doing" (7:19). He concluded that "it is no longer I who do it, but it is sin living in me that does it" (v. 20).

The difference between Paul and Geraldine is that Paul was telling the truth while Geraldine was only making an excuse. Like every human being, Paul had a principle of sin within him, a sinful nature inherited from Adam (5:12). This indwelling sin principle constantly sought to express itself in his thoughts and actions.

The question is raised, Was Paul describing his situation (yours and mine as well) before he trusted Jesus Christ as his Saviour or after? The circumstances are true of both the unregenerate and the regenerate person, but I think Paul was describing his situation as a Christian.

The fact of the matter is that the sin principle within is powerful. It reigns uncontrolled in the individual before he trusts Jesus Christ as his Saviour. It is not removed when the individual is saved. It seeks to control the individual after he is saved as it did before. In his own strength as a human being the believer is not able to control the sin principle.

That is what Paul discovered. That is why he cried, "Who will rescue me from this body of death?" (7:24) Then he praised God that the answer is "through Jesus Christ our Lord" (v. 25). At death or the rapture, Christ will deliver us from "this body of death." Meanwhile, He provides the indwelling Holy Spirit to control the principle of sin (Rom. 8:2).

A question: Do you face this struggle, this conflict between the "flesh" (the sin principle) and the Holy Spirit? The answer, Paul wrote, is to "live by the Spirit," that is to live under the control of the Spirit. For only then will you not "gratify the desires of the sinful nature" (Gal. 5:16).

CHRIST IS IN YOU

An enthusiastic person is one who manifests an "intense or eager interest" in a particular subject or in life in general. Some synonyms for enthusiasm are "ardor," "fervor," "zeal." The word, however, comes from the Greek language and basically means "possessed by a god." When the ancient Greeks saw an enthusiastic person, they would say, "He has a god in him."

A Christian, therefore, should be an enthusiastic person because the Lord Jesus Christ lives in him (Rom. 8:10; cf. Gal. 2:20).

The Lord Jesus Himself first stated this amazing truth to His disciples in the metaphor of the vine and the branches (John 15:1-8). He told them, "Remain in Me, and I will remain in you" (v. 4; cf. v. 5). Later in His high priestly prayer (John 17) in praying for the unity of all believers Jesus said, "I in them and you in Me" (v. 23) and "that I Myself may be in them" (v. 26).

At the moment of faith each believer is "baptized into Christ Jesus" (Rom. 6:3). As a result his position is now "in Christ" (8:1; 2 Cor. 5:17; Gal. 3:27-28). Conversely, the Lord Jesus Christ is in the believer (Col. 1:27) and is actually his life principle (3:4).

Astounding as this truth is, it is only the beginning. The believer is also the residence of God the Holy Spirit (Rom. 8:9, 11). From the moment the Holy Spirit regenerates the individual who believes (Titus 3:4-7), He takes up residence within that person as the seal and guarantee of God (2 Cor. 1:21-22; Eph. 1:13-14). The believer is "a temple of the Holy Spirit" (1 Cor. 6:19-20; cf. Eph. 2:22).

That is still not the whole story. God the Father Himself comes to dwell in the Christian. Jesus told His disciples, "My Father will love him, and We will come to him and make Our home with him" (John 14:23).

An amazing fact: You as a believer in Jesus Christ are a dwelling place of the Triune God. What a marvelous privilege! What an awesome responsibility!

IF GOD IS FOR US

Because of his brilliance as a military strategist and tactician, Napoleon was dubbed by his troops "Wee One Hundred Thousand Men." In battle they would ask one another, "Is Wee One Hundred Thousand Men in the army today?" Napoleon was considered worth that many men.

As a Christian in your daily struggles against Satan and his hosts of demons and wicked men, you have better odds than the French army with Napoleon. As the adage states, "You and God are a majority."

The Bible is replete with examples of this fact. God gave David victory over the giant Goliath (1 Sam. 17:32-51). God enabled Jonathan and his armor bearer to rout the camp of the Philistines (14:6-15). The Spirit of the Lord empowered Samson in his victories over the Philistines (Jud. 14:19; 15:3-17). God whittled Gideon's army down from 32,000 to 300 so that the victory over the Midianites would be recognized as the Lord's (7:2-23). Joshua told the Israelites, "One of you routs a thousand, because the Lord your God fights for you" (23:10; cf. Deut. 32:30).

God has a reason for working in this way. Paul explained, "God chose . . . the things that are not—to nullify the things that are, so that no one may boast before Him" (1 Cor. 1:27-29). The purpose is that God should be glorified. As Paul exhorted, "Let him who boasts boast in the Lord" (1:31).

As a Christian you can rejoice and rest in the truth that "you and God are a majority." As Paul wrote, "Since God is for us, who can be against us" (Rom. 8:31, personal translation).

At the same time you must remember Jesus' warning to His disciples, "Apart from Me you can do nothing" (John 15:5). As someone has said, "The important thing is not whether God is on our side, but whether we are on God's side. Then victory is assured."

What about it? Are you on God's side so that He can give you victory?

CHILDREN OF THE PROMISE

In one sense of the phrase, all members of the human family are "children of the promise" (Rom. 9:8). To Noah and his family — progenitors of the entire human family after the Flood — God promised that "never again will there be a flood to destroy the earth" (Gen. 9:11). That promise has been kept to this day.

The Apostle Paul used the phrase, however, with reference to "the people of Israel," for to them belong among many other things "the promises" (Rom. 9:4).

The application of the phrase is restricted still more, however. Paul recognized that "not all who are descended from Israel are Israel" (v. 6; cf. 2:28-29). By God's election the line of promise was through Isaac (9:7-9) and, in turn, through Jacob (vv. 10-13).

Paul continued, "It is not the natural children who are God's children, but it is the children of the promise who are regarded as Abraham's offspring" (v. 8). The promise to Abraham was received "through the righteousness that comes by faith" (4:13; cf. 20-22). As a result, "the promise comes by faith, so that it may be by grace and may be guaranteed to all Abraham's offspring — not only to those who are of the Law but also to those who are of the faith of Abraham" (v. 16).

As believers in the Lord Jesus Christ, Christians are among the "children of the promise" because they have the faith of Abraham. Abraham "did not waver through unbelief regarding the promise of God" (v. 20), but was "fully persuaded that God had power to do what He had promised" (v. 21). This faith "was credited to him as righteousness" (vv. 3, 22).

A reason for joy: That same faith in the promise of God concerning redemption from sin and eternal life through the Lord Jesus Christ has secured our justification by God (vv. 23-25). Take a moment now to praise God for choosing you to be among "the children of the promise."

RIGHTEOUSNESS BY FAITH

Many fine restaurants have a dress code. A sign at the entrance reads: "Coat and tie required." To help patrons who do not meet the code some restaurants provide coats and ties.

A biblical example of this principle is found in the experience of Adam and Eve. When they realized their nakedness after eating the forbidden fruit, "they sewed fig leaves and made coverings for themselves" (Gen. 3:7). These makeshift clothes may have satisfied them, but they were totally unacceptable to God.

In His grace, therefore, after stating the punishment for their sin, God slew animals and "made garments of skin for Adam and his wife and clothed them" (v. 21).

This incident at the beginning of human history illustrates a principle of God's gracious dealing with the human family. On the basis of the redemptive sacrifice of His Son, the Lord Jesus Christ, God will give a garment of righteousness to any individual who acts on the Good News of salvation. It is "a righteousness that is by faith" (Rom. 9:30).

This is the only righteousness that is acceptable to God, the one He provides. Our own human righteousness may appear quite satisfactory when compared with that of other human beings. In fact, like some of the Pharisees in Jesus' day (Luke 18:9-12), we may be quite proud of our moral and ethical attainments.

In the sight of God, however, "all our righteous acts are like filthy rags" (Isa. 64:6). As the Apostle Paul concluded, "There is no one righteous, not even one" (Rom. 3:10; cf. Ecc. 7:20).

Important: The only way to stand before God and be accepted by Him is to cast aside our own righteousness and receive the righteousness He provides through Jesus Christ, "a righteousness that is by faith." If you do not have this righteousness from God, accept Jesus Christ by faith.

THE END OF THE LAW

In wealthy Greek homes of ancient times one of the slaves was called "the pedagogue." He was not the teacher of the children in the family—the meaning of pedagogue in English—but the escort of the children to school and back.

The Apostle Paul stated that this was the ministry of the Law of Moses. He said that "the Law was put in charge [literally 'our pedagogue'] to lead us to Christ that we might be justified by faith" (Gal. 3:24). The Law was provided to show people that they could not meet the righteous standards of God in their own strength so that, when God offered a righteousness by faith in Christ, they would respond and believe.

In this sense "Christ is the end of the Law so that there may be righteousness for everyone who believes" (Rom. 10:4). Jesus Christ as the Object of faith is the goal or final purpose of the Law of Moses.

This was the objective of the famous sermon by D.L. Moody entitled "Weighed in the Balances and Found Wanting." Moody took each of the Ten Commandments and graphically portrayed how mankind failed to live up to its requirement. When he had removed every possibility for anyone to be accepted by God on his own merits, Moody presented the Lord Jesus Christ as the object of faith for salvation.

The Lord Jesus Christ also is the "end of the Law" in the sense that He is the only Person who ever perfectly kept the Law. Jesus challenged His Jewish accusers, "Can any of you prove Me guilty of sin?" (John 8:46) Hebrews says that He was "tempted in every way, just as we are—yet was without sin" (4:15). The Lord Jesus Christ fulfilled the Law for each one who believes in Him.

Just now: As a believer thank God that in Christ you are not judged by the standard of the Law.

DID YOU HEAR ME?

Abraham Lincoln's Gettysburg Address contained only 270 words and took less than three minutes to read. Lincoln had finished before the photographer with the cumbersome equipment of that day was ready to take his picture.

Alexander Woollcott suggested that few of the 15,000 in attendance heard what Lincoln said because the brief speech was over before the "arc of attention" had been fully established. They heard the words but did not really hear because their minds were not focused to understand.

What parent has not said to an inattentive child, "Did you hear what I said?" Perhaps even a wife has had that experience with her husband.

This points up the fact that two kinds of hearing exist. One is hearing the words merely as sounds that make no intelligible impression on the mind because of inattention or some other reason. The other is hearing that communicates a message to the mind and provides information or demands a response.

The soldiers who accompanied Saul of Tarsus on his journey to Damascus "heard the sound" (Acts 9:7) of Jesus speaking to Saul from heaven, but "they did not understand the voice of Him who was speaking" (22:9).

The kind of hearing that produces faith is the second kind, the kind that receives the message of God directed to that person's mind and heart, demanding a response. That kind of hearing is heeding.

Paul indicated that that kind of "hearing the message" comes "through the word of Christ" (Rom. 10:17). It is not enough, therefore, to say that you will live your testimony for Christ before your family, friends, and neighbors. Important as a consistent Christian life is, it must be accompanied sooner or later with the message of the Gospel in the Word of God.

A challenge: Give your witness to Christ in life and word.

A REMNANT CHOSEN BY GRACE

Throughout human history God has worked with "a remnant chosen by grace." When God destroyed the antediluvian world, He rescued and repopulated the earth with one family—eight persons—Noah and his three sons and their wives (Gen. 7:7, 13; 8:18).

When God wanted to develop a chosen people for His own possession, out of the thousands in Ur of the Chaldees, He chose one man and his wife—Abram and Sarai (12:1, 5). Of the adult generation of Israel that left Egypt, only Joshua and Caleb entered Canaan, the Promised Land (Num. 14:26-35). Among the nations of the ancient world Israel, God's chosen, was the smallest (Deut. 7:7-8), a remnant nation.

After the captivity of God's people in Assyria and Babylon, only a remnant returned to Jerusalem and Judah with Zerubbabel and later with Ezra and still later with Nehemiah. Even today, a generation after the establishment of the State of Israel, only a remnant of the Jews have returned to their homeland. Almost twice as many Jews live in the United States as live in Israel. Truly it is a remnant surrounded by 100 million Arab enemies.

Even though God has promised that, after the completion and translation of the church, "all Israel shall be saved" (Rom. 11:26), that will be only a remnant of all the Jews who have lived since the advent of the Lord Jesus Christ.

During the present Church Age, however, a special remnant exists which Paul called a "remnant chosen by grace." It includes him, the eleven apostles, Barnabas, all the other Jews in the Apostolic church, and through the centuries all who have responded by faith to the Gospel of the grace of God in Jesus Christ.

The church of Jesus Christ in its totality—Jew and Gentile—is "a remnant chosen by grace" because it is such a small percentage of the total human family.

Do it now: If you have received Christ as your Saviour, then thank God you are a part of that remnant.

GOD'S GIFTS ARE IRREVOCABLE

Despite repeated efforts to eradicate the people of Israel—from the Pharaoh "who did not know about Joseph" (Ex. 1:8; cf. Acts 7:18) to Adolph Hitler—the Jews survive and prosper. The Jews are indestructible.

A Jewish Christian one time called the Jews "both waterproof and fireproof." He explained that they miraculously passed through the Red Sea while their pursuers were drowned and Daniel's companions were preserved in the fiery furnace while those who threw them in were burned to death.

The explanation is that the Jews are God's chosen earthly people. As a pagan poet said, "How odd that God should choose the Jews." The Bible makes it clear that He did (Deut. 7:7-9), and that "God's gifts and His call are irrevocable" (Rom. 11:29). Though God chose Israel, He disciplined them with captivity and worldwide dispersion. And though He chose Israel, He put Israel aside temporarily so He could carry out another purpose in the church of Jesus Christ. And yet God has not abandoned Israel (vv. 1, 11, 26-27).

God's gifts (literally "grace gifts"—*charismata*) still belong to "the people of Israel" (3:1-2; 9:4-5). God's "call" to Abraham and to his descendants in the line of promise is still valid. We Christians need to pray for the Jews and "for the peace of Jerusalem" (Ps. 122:6).

The fact that "God's gifts and His call are irrevocable" is just as true for you as a believer in Jesus Christ as for the Jews. Nothing "will be able to separate us from the love of God that is in Christ Jesus our Lord" (Rom. 8:39). Concerning His sheep, Jesus said, "No one can snatch them out of My hand" and "no one can snatch them out of My Father's hand" (John 10:28-29).

Day by day: Rest in the assurance from God's Word that you are "safe in the arms of Jesus."

NO MAN IS AN ISLAND

In *Devotions Upon Emergent Occasions,* published in 1624, John Donne wrote, "No man is an island, entire in itself; every man is a piece of the continent . . . any man's death diminishes me, because I am involved in mankind; and, therefore, never send to know for whom the bell tolls; it tolls for thee."

True as that is of the human family, it is even more true of the church of our Lord Jesus Christ. One of the most graphic pictures of the church is a human body. Paul wrote, "Just as each of us has one body with many members . . . so in Christ we who are many form one body" (Rom. 12:4-5). Paul used this metaphor frequently (1 Cor. 10:17; 12:12-31; Eph. 1:23; 3:6; 4:4, 12-13, 15-16; Col. 1:18; 2:19; 3:15; cf. Gal. 6:15; Eph. 2:14-18).

Paul pointed out that "each member belongs to all the others" (Rom. 12:5). As a result "if one part suffers, every part suffers with it; if one part is honored, every part rejoices with it" (1 Cor. 12:26; cf. Heb. 13:3). We need to "rejoice with those who rejoice; mourn with those who mourn" (Rom. 12:15; cf. Job 30:25).

Counterbalancing the fact of our unity and interrelatedness as members of the body of Christ is the distinctive function each believer has in that body. Concerning our physical body, Paul wrote, "These members do not all have the same function" (Rom. 12:4). Similarly, in the body of Christ "we have different gifts, according to the grace given us" (v. 6).

These grace gifts are distributed by the Holy Spirit "just as He determines" (1 Cor. 12:11) and "for the common good" (v. 7).

As a result: We should not envy and jealously desire the spiritual gifts of other believers. Likewise, we should not boast of our gift since it was given by the grace of God. Instead, through varied service we should determine what our grace gift is and then exercise it as fully as God enables us (Rom. 12:6-8).

OVERCOME EVIL WITH GOOD

When a big sergeant in a Highland regiment was asked how he was brought to Christ, he told this story. "A young private in my company was a Christian. The rest of us gave him a hard time. One night he came in wet and tired from sentry duty and kneeled in prayer before turning in. I threw my boots at him and hit him on the side of the head. He just kept on praying. The next morning I found my boots by the side of my bed beautifully polished. I wanted the Saviour that private had."

That Christian private fulfilled the biblical command to "overcome evil with good" (Rom. 12:21). The negative side of this is Paul's command, "Do not repay anyone evil for evil" (v. 17). Revenge for evil is the natural human reaction, but Paul wrote, "Do not take revenge" (v. 19).

Our Lord Jesus Christ gave the pattern for the Christian response. On the cross He prayed, "Father, forgive them, for they do not know what they are doing" (Luke 23:34). Following Jesus' example, the first Christian martyr, Stephen, prayed, "Lord, do not hold this sin against them" (Acts 7:60).

The cynic is always quick to remind us that it is a dog-eat-dog world we live in. He may not endorse the principle, "Do unto others before they do unto you"; but he certainly approves, "Do unto others as they have done unto you." The Lord Jesus, however, said, "So in everything, do to others what you would have them do to you" (Matt. 7:12).

In the same vein Paul wrote, "Bless those who persecute you" (Rom. 12:14), "Live in harmony with one another" (v. 16), and "If it be possible, as far as it depends on you, live at peace with everyone" (v. 18). This is still ultimately God's world, and He says, "It is mine to avenge; I will repay" (v. 19).

Think about this: By acting in this way, we are not "overcome by evil, but [we] overcome evil with good" (v. 21). This is a tall order, a tough assignment. But with God's help you can do it.

SUBMIT TO THE AUTHORITIES

The notorious Nero was the emperor in Rome from A.D. 54 to 68. Philip Schaff, a church historian, called him "one of the basest and vilest of tyrants." Nero's first five years, while advised by Seneca and Burrhus, were good, especially when compared with the rest of his reign.

Nero persecuted Christians after the great fire of Rome in July of A.D. 64, which consumed almost three-fourths of the city. He accused them of starting the conflagration as a means of diverting suspicion from himself. Both Paul and Peter were among the thousands martyred for their faith in Jesus Christ.

This Nero occupied the emperor's throne when Paul wrote the Roman Christians that "everyone must submit himself to the governing authorities" (Rom. 13:1). This was undoubtedly written before Nero's persecution of Christians began, but similar instructions in 1 Timothy 2:1-4; Titus 3:1; and 1 Peter 2:13-17 were given after Nero's reign.

One reason Christians should submit to governmental authorities is because those leaders have been "established by God" (Rom. 13:1) and are "God's servants" (v. 6; cf. v. 4). This is true even of despots like Nero (cf. Dan. 4:17) and of men who seize power by force. To rebel "against the authority," therefore, "is rebelling against what God has instituted" (Rom. 13:2).

Another reason Christians are to submit to the authorities is that of "conscience" (13:5). Peter wrote, "For it is God's will" (1 Peter 2:15). The only exception to this biblical command to submit to the authorities is when they demand that which violates what God requires. Examples are the Hebrew men being asked to worship Nebuchadnezzar's image (Dan. 3:16-18) and Peter and John being ordered to be silent concerning Jesus (Acts 4:18-20).

Pray: Paul urged Christians to pray for "all those in authority" (1 Tim. 2:1-2). We are to do this so we may "live peaceable and quiet lives" and because God "wants all men to be saved" (vv. 2, 4). Take a moment now to pray for your local, state, and federal leaders.

WHO IS MY NEIGHBOR?

One year a farmer on the plains of the Midwest, where wheat is the money crop, was seriously ill during the winter and spring. He was unable to prepare his field and to sow his wheat, so his neighbors got together to help him. With twenty-two sets of plows, harrows, and planters, in one day they planted one hundred acres of wheat. Their wives came with food and served lunch on the lawn.

In that case it was not too hard to decide who was the neighbor who fulfilled the commandment to "love your neighbor as yourself" (Rom. 13:9; cf. Matt. 22:39; Mark 12:31). Many times, however, we must ask the question the lawyer asked Jesus, "Who is my neighbor?" (Luke 10:29)

Jesus' answer was given in the Parable of the Good Samaritan (vv. 30-37). A clue is found in the Greek word translated "neighbor," which literally means "nearby, close." Your neighbor, therefore, is anyone in need who crosses your path to whom you can give love and help.

How can you love that person "as yourself"? By providing for his needs as carefully and as completely as you would for your own. As Paul said in another context, "No one ever hated his own body, but he feeds and cares for it" (Eph. 5:29).

This command is not a mandate to alleviate all the poverty and suffering in the world, or even in our own country. We could not accomplish that task if we tried. It is a mandate, however, to provide loving help to those who become our "neighbor" by crossing our path of life in the providence of God. Doing so is more than philanthropy; it is manifesting "the love of God . . . shed abroad in our hearts by the Holy Spirit" (Rom. 5:5, KJV).

This command to "love your neighbor as yourself" is simply a shorter version of the Golden Rule, "Do to others what you would have them do to you" (Matt. 7:12; cf. Luke 6:31).

Ask yourself: Who is my "neighbor"? What is his or her need? And how can I help meet that need today?

JUDGE NOT

A conductor got on a train and began checking tickets as the train left the station. Soon he announced to the passengers, "Everybody please get off at the next stop. You are on the wrong train." The passengers looked at each other in amazement. They began to check and found that it was the conductor who had boarded the wrong train.

So it is with judging others. While you are pointing one finger at another person, four are pointing at yourself.

The Apostle Paul warned against judging one another about "disputable matters" (Rom. 14:1) such as eating meat and observing special days (vv. 2-8). These issues may not be pertinent to us today; but in many other matters Christians judge each other, because "man looks at the outward appearance" (1 Sam. 16:7; cf. 2 Cor. 10:7a).

This warning against judging each other does not include open and obvious sin. Sin on the part of Christians cannot be ignored or excused. Even in such cases, however, it must be dealt with biblically (Gal. 6:1). Discipline, when necessary, should be administered by the local congregation and be remedial, designed to restore to fellowship and service.

The reason we should not judge other believers "on disputable matters" is that the others are servants not of us but of the Lord (Rom. 14:4) and "the Lord is able to make him stand."

Every Christian will be judged by God in due time. Paul wrote, "We will all stand before God's judgment seat" (v. 10). This will not be to determine whether or not we are saved; that was settled when we received Jesus Christ by faith. It is when our lives as Christians will be judged to determined which rewards we will receive from the Lord (v. 12; 1 Cor. 3:10-15; 4:1-5; 2 Cor. 5:10). In ancient Corinth, the "judgment seat" was the place where awards were presented to those who had run the race.

What about you? Are you being faithful to the Lord? Will you receive rewards at the judgment seat of Christ? Live today not to judge others, but in light of the fact that you will be judged.

WHAT LEADS TO PEACE

The pastor of a small rural church had died. The denominational leader sent to conduct the funeral was amazed to see the sanctuary crowded to the doors. The whole countryside had turned out to show respect. The leader asked a farmer the secret of the pastor's popularity.

"He wasn't much of a preacher," the farmer explained, "but he was such a wonderful man to make peace between neighbors."

This country preacher fulfilled Paul's exhortation to "make every effort to do what leads to peace" (Rom. 14:19). The exhortation, however, is to every Christian. God desires that His children "live in harmony with one another" (12:16). As a result Paul wrote, "If it be possible, as far as it depends on you, live at peace with everyone" (v. 18).

One way to achieve this objective is to "stop passing judgment on one another" (14:13) with regard to "disputable matters" (v. 1). Unfortunately, most of us tend to think that our way of doing things is the right way, even the only way. As a result, we are quick to discredit, even to criticize any other way. We need to be open to other ways.

Also important in doing "what leads to peace" is being sensitive to the convictions of other believers. You should "make up your mind not to put any stumbling block or obstacle in your brother's way" (v. 13). This is a part of spiritual maturity. One of the qualifications for the "overseer" is not being "quarrelsome" (1 Tim. 3:1-3; cf. 2 Tim. 2:24). Positively stated that means being peaceable.

One of the virtues that make up "the fruit of the Spirit" is "peace" (Gal. 5:22). Certainly in addition to the "peace of God" (Phil. 4:7), this means peace with our brothers and sisters in Christ and with those outside of Christ. Paul urged us within the body of Christ to "make every effort to keep the unity of the Spirit in the bond of peace" (Eph. 4:3). The Lord Jesus said, "Blessed are the peacemakers, for they will be called sons of God" (Matt. 5:9).

Ask yourself: Is there someone with whom I need to make peace? What specific steps can I take this week to accomplish that goal?

SPERONDEO

A husband, wife, and their grown son immigrated from Sicily to southern Illinois, where the two men worked in a coal mine. An explosion killed the father and maimed the son. While he was recovering in the hospital, he and his mother trusted Jesus Christ as their Saviour. They changed their surname to Sperondeo — "My hope is in God." This was his inspiration to complete college and graduate study and become a college professor. His name was the motto of his life.

This should be the motto of every child of God. In every disheartening circumstance of life, the Christian, like the psalmist, should repeat the refrain, "Put your hope in God" (Ps. 42:5, 11; 43:5). God "in His great mercy . . . has given us new birth into a living hope" (1 Peter 1:3; cf. vv. 13, 21). For this reason Paul stated that for believers the Lord is "the God of hope" (Rom. 15:13). Hope, a feeling that what one desires will happen, is native to human experience. Without hope all desire to live departs.

Hope in the spiritual sense, however, is different. It is found only through faith in the Lord Jesus Christ. Hope of acceptance by God apart from faith in Christ is just wishful thinking. Paul described the Gentiles as "separate from Christ" and "without hope" (Eph. 2:12).

"Through our Lord Jesus Christ," on the other hand, we who trust in Him "have peace with God . . . access by faith into this grace" and we "rejoice in the hope of the glory of God" (Rom. 5:1-2). This is "the hope held out in the Gospel" (Col. 1:23).

Our faith makes this hope sure and certain (Heb. 11:1). In this life, however, we have not experienced this hope. As Paul explained, "Hope that is seen is no hope at all. Who hopes for what he already has? But if we hope for what we do not yet have, we wait for it patiently" (Rom. 8:24-25). As a believer your hope of spending eternity in heaven conformed to the image of Jesus Christ is "an anchor for the soul, firm and secure" (Heb. 6:19). Through the indwelling Holy Spirit this hope can enable you to survive the storms of life and to "overflow with hope."

For you: Keep looking to the Lord in trust so that you may enjoy this hope.

CONTAINER OR CONDUIT?

A teacher asked her students if a beaker filled with small stones was full. When they said yes, she took a glass of water and poured it into the beaker until it overflowed.

Again she asked if the beaker was full. When the students hesitantly agreed that it was, the teacher took a saltshaker and dissolved quite a quantity of salt in the water.

So it is with the blessings of Christ, which Paul called "the unsearchable riches of Christ" (Eph. 3:8). God's blessings are endless. Each new day brings new discoveries. We never plumb the depths or scale the heights of God's blessings.

Lewis Sperry Chafer in his *Systematic Theology* lists thirty-three things the believer receives by the grace of God as a result of his faith in the Lord Jesus Christ. He calls these "the riches of divine grace."

Our inability to exhaust the grace of God and the blessings of Christ is because of God's infinity. Trying to exhaust His grace is like attempting to pour the infinite into the finite. It is like trying to empty the ocean with a teacup; it is impossible.

When the Apostle Paul, however, wrote about his desire to visit Rome and to minister to the Christians there, he wanted to "come in the full measure of the blessing of Christ" (Rom. 15:29). He was confident that he would so come. As you minister to others this is no doubt your desire as well.

How can we be as confident as Paul that our ministry will provide "the full measure of the blessing of Christ"? We need to be a conduit, not just a container. A container can hold only so much, but a conduit can continue to receive because it passes on what it receives.

It's a fact: The Christian who shares with others the blessings of Christ will desire and will receive more for himself. Are you a container or a conduit?

GREET ONE ANOTHER WITH A HOLY KISS

When Lord Louis Montbatten made a trip to Toronto, he asked for a list of all the drivers, waiters, and others who would serve him during his stay, with a few details about each one. He had an aide read the list of names and information to him slowly. During his entire stay Admiral Montbatten called by name each person who served him and chatted with him knowledgeably.

The Apostle Paul must have had a memory like that. In addition, he must have been a person who valued people and friendships. Rome was a city that Paul had never visited, and yet he sent greetings to twenty-eight individuals, plus several households and groups of saints (Rom. 16:3-16). For most of those mentioned Paul had a specific word of commendation. Paul kept up with these individuals and knew that they were in Rome.

Paul not only extended his personal greetings to these many friends but also sent greetings from eight of his associates (vv. 21-24) in Corinth where the letter was written (cf. 16:1; Cenchrea was the port of Corinth), Paul could never be accused of not being "a people person."

Some churches have a reputation of being cold and unfriendly. Perhaps you think the church you are attending is unfriendly. Perhaps it is thoughtlessness, as members who know one another tend to chat together and forget to welcome those they do not know.

The answer, however, might be in this thought-provoking verse:

> I went out to find a friend
> But could not find one there;
> I went out to be a friend
> And friends were everywhere!

Paul's advice to the Roman Christians was "greet one another with a holy kiss" (16:16), the form of greeting among believers in that day.

The message for us today is: "Be friendly." What better place to begin than in church with visitors.

DON'T THANK ME

Scottish singer and songwriter Harry Lauder gave a concert in Chicago. Every seat in the vast auditorium was filled. At the close of the stirring concert the audience stood en masse and applauded enthusiastically. Then the audience cried in unison, "Thank you, thank you, thank you."

Lauder stilled the crowd and then said humbly, "Don't thank me. Thank the good God who put the songs in my heart."

Lauder obviously recognized that all natural talents and abilities, no matter how carefully trained and developed, are in reality gifts from God. The same is true of all spiritual gifts bestowed on believers in the Lord Jesus Christ (1 Cor. 12:7-11).

That response of Harry Lauder echoes the answer in the *Westminster Shorter Catechism* to the question concerning the chief end of man. That answer reads, "The chief end of man is to glorify God and to enjoy Him forever."

The Apostle Paul had the same perspective. He closed the Epistle to the Romans—his great theological treatise on the Gospel as "the power of God for the salvation of everyone who believes" (Rom. 1:16)—with the words, "to the only wise God be glory forever through Jesus Christ! Amen" (16:27).

The infinite wisdom of God is displayed in His plan of salvation (11:33-36) that enabled God to preserve His righteousness and yet justify (declare righteous) "those who have faith in Jesus" (3:26). The doxology that ends the doctrinal portion of the epistle also closes with "to him [God] be the glory forever! Amen" (11:36).

Think about it: How can finite beings—even redeemed sinners—glorify the infinitely glorious God? First, by our praise and thanksgiving to Him for His salvation and His blessings. Second, by our lives of devoted service to Him as His children. Third, by our witness, proclaiming the Gospel of God's grace in Jesus Christ to the ends of the earth.

September

Devotional readings in the Prison Epistles
by John A. Witmer

ADOPTED AS HIS SONS

The English government refused to recognize Nana Sahib as peshwa (ruler) of the Maharatta kingdom around Cawnpore because he was the adopted son of Baja Rao, the previous peshwa. According to Hindu law, however, adoption secures all the rights and privileges of sonship, political as well as property. Their support of Nana Sahib led to the Sepoy rebellion of 1857.

The Apostle Paul is the only one of the New Testament writers who used the figure of adoption to describe the Christian's relationship to God the Father through faith in the Lord Jesus Christ. In Ephesians 1:5 Paul wrote that believers have been "adopted as [God's] sons through Jesus Christ."

In ancient Greek practice adoption frequently involved a purchase or redemption of the one adopted, illustrative of the redemptive death of the Lord Jesus. According to the Greeks, the one adopted had both the privileges and the responsibilities of an adult son. This was a higher position than that of a natural son who was a minor (cf. Gal. 4:1-2). The Christian is both a child (literally "born one") of God by regeneration (John 1:12-13) and a son by adoption.

Through Jesus Christ, God has redeemed us who believe so "that we might receive the full rights of sons" (Gal. 4:5). As a result, "God sent the Spirit of His Son into our hearts, the Spirit who calls out, '*Abba,* Father' " (v. 6). So, "since you are a son, God has made you also an heir" (v. 7), "heirs of God, and co-heirs with Christ" (Rom. 8:17).

Even though God "has blessed us in the heavenly realms with every spiritual blessing in Christ" (Eph. 1:3), we do not experience our full inheritance as sons of God now. In this life we "groan inwardly as we wait eagerly for our adoption as sons, the redemption of our bodies" (Rom. 8:23). Not only so, but the whole creation "waits in eager expectation for the sons of God to be revealed" (8:19-21).

A fact to remember and act on: Adoption as sons involves the responsibilities of adulthood in the family as well as the privileges. In the family of God this means spiritual maturity. This means submission to the indwelling Spirit of God so that we live in His power (Gal. 5:16) and are led by the Holy Spirit in doing the will of God.

GETTING TO KNOW YOU

Sir Isaac Newton, discoverer of the law of gravity, described himself and his great knowledge of science "like a boy playing upon the seashore, and diverting myself by now and then finding a pebble, or a prettier shell than ordinary, while the great ocean of truth lies all undiscovered before me."

So it is with our knowledge of God even as believers and His children through faith in the Lord Jesus Christ. As recipients of eternal life through faith, we have begun to know God. Jesus said, "Now this is eternal life: that they may know You, the only true God" (John 17:3).

Knowing God, as well as knowing any person, is more than having information about Him. It involves having a personal relationship, with fellowship and communion. In Scripture the verb *know* describes the most intimate relationship between husband and wife (Gen. 4:1; Matt. 1:25, KJV).

Unbelievers and "the heathen" are described as ones "who do not know God" (1 Thes. 4:5; 2 Thes. 1:8). They have information about God, some of it accurate, but they have no relationship with Him. The demons know and even believe "that there is one God" (James 2:19), but, having no relationship with Him, they "shudder."

Coming to know God through faith in Jesus Christ and entering into a relationship with Him is only the first step. The widely known song "Getting to Know You" expresses the idea. That is why Paul prayed that God "may give you the Spirit of wisdom and revelation, so that you may know Him better" (Eph. 1:17).

Keep in mind: The ministry of the indwelling Holy Spirit is essential in increasingly making God the Father known to us as believers. So is the Word of God as we read and meditate on it and apply it in our lives. It is God's message to us (2 Tim. 3:16-17). As God strengthens and guides and provides in the circumstances of life, we get to know Him better, too. You will never get to know God fully, however. Even in His presence in heaven for eternity you will continue to get to know Him better.

GOD'S WORKMANSHIP

If you have ever struggled to express your thoughts in poetic form, you know how difficult it can be. When you finally get the words to rhyme, the meter doesn't scan. When the meter is correct, then you can't find the proper rhyme word. Even a brief poem requires hours, perhaps even days, of deep thought and arduous work.

What does writing a poem have to do with Christians? you ask. Paul said believers "are God's workmanship" (Eph. 2:10). The Greek word translated "workmanship" is transliterated as the English word *poem.* It means "a thing made," which is what a poem is.

It seems strange to think of God laboring to produce a Christian. It did involve, however, an eternal plan of salvation (Eph. 1:4; 1 Peter 1:20; Rev. 13:8). It involved the incarnation of God's Son (Gal. 4:4), His life of ministry as God's Messiah, His sacrificial death and resurrection, and the ministry of the Holy Spirit in conviction and regeneration. The Triune Godhead—Father, Son, and Holy Spirit—all participate in the making of a Christian.

God also had a purpose in mind when He undertook the project of making Christians. We were "created in Christ Jesus to do good works." These are not things we necessarily consider good works, but things that God so designates. In fact they are things "God has prepared in advance for us to do." As we are controlled by the Holy Spirit day by day, we will do the "good works . . . God prepared" (Eph. 2:10).

Questions: As a believer are you properly thankful that God has made you one of His "poems"? Do you praise Him for His grace in including you in His eternal plan of salvation? Are you concerned that you fulfill in your life the "good works" that He "prepared for you to do"? Are you achieving God's designed purpose?

GOD'S HOUSEHOLD

Some years ago a Chinese student had just finished his medical training in the United States. He would soon return to his homeland to start his practice. He was having a farewell dinner with a Christian family that had entertained him frequently, making him feel one of them.

"Dr. Tong," his host asked, "what is the thing that has impressed you most about America?" With a sweeping gesture to include the family around the table, Tong replied without hesitation, "This is the most wonderful thing I have seen in America."

The Christian family and home is indeed wonderful. It is so because it emulates "God's household," the best family of all, when its members are all "members of God's household" (Eph. 2:19).

Later in Ephesians Paul prayed to God "the Father, from whom every family in heaven and earth is named" (3:15, ASV). God is the prototype Father because He stands as Father in so many relationships.

God is Father of His eternal Son by personal relationship. He is Father of the angels and of mankind by creation. He is Father of Israel by covenantal promise. And He is Father of believers by grace through faith in His Son, the Lord Jesus Christ.

In fact, believers are more than "members of God's household." As the writer to the Hebrews stated, "Christ is faithful as a Son over God's house. And we are His house" (3:6; cf. 10:21). Peter also pictured believers corporately as "being built into a spiritual house" (1 Peter 2:5).

Though all Christians are "members of God's household," each one has different functions and responsibilities to perform. Paul wrote, "In a large house there are articles . . . for noble purposes and some for ignoble. If a man cleanse himself from the latter, he will be an instrument for noble purposes" (2 Tim. 2:20-21).

What about you? Are you a member of God's family? If so, are you a clean "article" and "instrument" in His hands?

IT'S A MYSTERY

Joanna Southcott claimed to be the bride of Christ and that she would become the mother of the second Messiah. At the height of her popularity she had 100,000 followers. She died of a brain disease about ten weeks after she failed to give birth to the second Messiah promised on October 19, 1814.

Before her death she left a box with instructions that it not be opened till its contents were needed to solve a great world crisis. When the box was finally opened in 1928, it contained a dicebox, novel, puzzle, lottery ticket, lady's nightcap, and a horse pistol.

Kept hidden for more than a century, Joanna's mystery box was as false as her spiritual claims.

"The mystery of Christ" stands in sharp contrast. As Paul explained, "This mystery is that through the Gospel the Gentiles are heirs together with Israel, members together of one body, and sharers together in the promise in Christ Jesus" (Eph. 3:6; cf. 2:14-22).

In the Bible a mystery is not a truth that is hard to understand. It is a truth that has been unrevealed previously but now is openly revealed and proclaimed (Col. 1:26).

That God would send His anointed (Messiah, Christ) was no secret in Old Testament times; it was a prominent theme of prophecy (Isa. 61:1-3). That the Gentiles would be blessed through Israel and her Messiah was no secret in the Old Testament; it too was a theme of prophecy (Gen. 12:3; Isa. 49:5-6).

That Gentile believers would share as heirs with Israel, be members of one body, and co-sharers in the promise, however, was never revealed in the Old Testament. It is "the mystery of Christ" (Eph. 3:4; cf. Rom. 16:25; Col. 2:2).

Take note: Other thrilling facets of that mystery are the truth of the indwelling Christ, "the hope of glory" (Col. 1:27) and the mystery of the translation of the church (1 Cor. 15:51-57). Enter into "the mystery of Christ" now openly revealed.

BEING A GUEST OR BEING AT HOME

Many Christian homes have a room called a "prophet's chamber" (cf. 2 Kings 4:9-10) to give hospitality to visiting ministers and missionaries. The visitor stays a night or two or at most a couple weeks. No matter how warm and generous the hospitality is, the visitor is still a guest, not a member of the family, not "at home."

So it is with the Lord Jesus Christ in the life of the Christian. At the moment of faith, the Lord Jesus begins to live within the believer (Col. 1:27). Paul wrote, "Christ lives in me" (Gal. 2:20). In fact Christ is the new life principle of the believer (Col. 3:4).

For many Christians, unfortunately, the indwelling Christ is treated as a guest instead of the head of the home. He is restricted to His "prophet's chamber" and perhaps never invited into certain other areas of the person's life.

That is not what God intended or what the Lord Jesus desires, but He is too gracious to go where He is not invited and welcomed. He waits patiently till He is invited to take control. Meanwhile, that believer misses the blessing of his Saviour's control of his whole life.

The Apostle Paul's prayer for the Ephesians and for you and me is that through the Holy Spirit "Christ may dwell in your hearts through faith" (3:17). The verb translated "dwell" is an intensive form that implies "to settle down and be at home." This means no longer to be a guest but to be head of the home.

Please note: For this prayer to be fulfilled, the individual Christian must turn over control of his life to the Lord Jesus Christ. In biblical terms this means "to offer your bodies as living sacrifices, holy and pleasing to God—this is your spiritual act of worship" (Rom. 12:1). Then indeed Christ will be at home in your hearts through faith.

WORKS OF SERVICE

The new pastor preached his first sermon, a challenging call for Christians to "gird up their loins" for spiritual service and living.

After he preached the same sermon the second and the third Sunday, a committee from the congregation waited on him. "Don't you have any other sermons?" the spokesman asked.

"Of course," he replied, "but you haven't done anything about the first one yet."

Unfortunately, many Christians think that Christian ministry is the job of the pastor. "Isn't that what we pay him for?" they ask. Of course, the pastor will visit the sick, evangelize the unsaved, and counsel those in need.

The primary work of pastors and teachers, however, along with apostles, prophets, and evangelists, is "to prepare God's people for works of service" (Eph. 4:12).

When Paul spent more than two years in Ephesus, "all the Jews and Greeks who lived in the province of Asia heard the word of the Lord" (Acts 19:10). Obviously, Paul did not evangelize this large province by himself or even with his team. Visitors to Ephesus, the metroplex of the province, who became Christians returned home and evangelized their towns and villages.

Those "works of service" God intends His people to do are varied. Their purpose is "so that the body of Christ may be built up" (Eph. 4:12). Witnessing to unsaved family, friends, and neighbors so that they trust Jesus Christ certainly fulfills that objective. So does praying faithfully for missionaries and supporting Christian ministries financially.

Deeds of Christian love like visiting lonely older believers and providing meals for families in need of food because of a birth, a death, or sickness also help build up Christ's body.

A challenge: Look for opportunities to do "works of service" for Christ and His body.

DON'T LIVE LIKE GENTILES

When American forces captured Okinawa in World War II, the typical island village was a filthy place. The inhabitants were ignorant and poverty-stricken. The village of Shimmabuke was different. Its streets and homes were spotlessly clean. Its citizens were friendly and polite.

Thirty years before, an American missionary had stopped at Shimmabuke on his way to Japan. He won two men to Christ, Shosei Kina and his brother Mojon, and gave them a Bible. Through them the entire village became Christians and the village life was transformed.

This shows the transformation in personal and societal lifestyle that the Bible and salvation through Jesus Christ can make. It explains why the Apostle Paul urged the Ephesians to "no longer live as the Gentiles do" (4:17). The Ephesian believers were new creations in Jesus Christ and needed to live like it.

Paul continued to describe the lifestyle of the unregenerate Gentiles (vv. 18-19; cf. Titus 1:12). Before their conversion this had been the lifestyle of the Ephesian Christians (Eph. 2:2-3; cf. Col. 3:7). Paul had taught them of their need as God's children to change.

Once again in our secular age it has become necessary to instruct new converts about an appropriate Christian lifestyle, one honoring to God. Christian influence on society at large has been lost to such an extent that new believers must be told to "no longer live as the Gentiles do."

In addition it is important that Christians maintain a lifestyle consistent with their profession. We are in the world, but we are not to be of the world (John 17:14-16; Rom. 12:2). Christians are to "shine like stars in the universe" as they "hold out the word of life" (Phil. 2:15-16). This demands a distinctive lifestyle.

Ask yourself: If I were accused in court of being a Christian, would there be enough evidence to convict me?

IMITATORS

The British Museum contains an intriguing artifact from the classical Greek period, a piece of parchment used as a child's copy book. At the top the master had written the Greek alphabet in perfectly formed letters.

The first line of the student's writing was a good reproduction of the teacher's example. The succeeding lines, however, simply reproduced the one above it, not the master's example at the top. As a result each line got progressively worse until the letters were barely legible.

This is the problem we face as Christians when we pattern our lives after other believers, even great Christian leaders, rather than after the Lord Jesus Christ. Paul told the Ephesians and us, "Be imitators of God ... as dearly loved children" (5:1).

You might point out, however, that Paul urged his readers on several occasions to follow his example (1 Cor. 4:16; 11:1; Phil 3:17) and commended the Thessalonian Christians for becoming "imitators of us and of the Lord" (1 Thes. 1:6). Implicit in such commands is the idea "as I follow the example of Christ" (1 Cor. 11:1).

The generation to which Paul and the other apostles ministered had only the Old Testament and the verbal ministry of the apostles concerning the Lord Jesus Christ until the New Testament was completed. As a result, the apostles' personal examples of Christian character and life were strategic.

Now in Scripture God has given us the finished portrait of Himself and of our Lord Jesus Christ. We need to "fix our eyes on Jesus, the author and perfecter of our faith" (Heb. 12:2).

A reminder: Obviously, others can be examples of Christlikeness. Each of us should strive in the power of the Holy Spirit to reflect the Lord Jesus. But the Lord Himself always remains the pattern to imitate.

SUBMIT!

Two mountain goats met on a precipitous path, one descending and the other ascending the trail. At first they backed off as if they would lunge at each other to fight for the path. This would have meant death for both goats.

Then the goat below lay down in the path and allowed the one above to walk over his back. Then he got up again and both goats went safely on their way.

This illustrates the Apostle Paul's command to the Ephesian Christians and to us, "Submit to one another," adding, "out of reverence for Christ" (5:21). The Lord Jesus is the supreme example of submission (Phil. 2:5-8; Heb. 10:5-7; 12:2; 1 Peter 2:21-23).

Significant is the fact that submission to one another is one of the manifestations of the believer's being filled with the Holy Spirit (Eph. 5:18). When the Holy Spirit is in control, He will reproduce the Lord Jesus' spirit of willing submission in us.

Prerequisite to our willingness to submit to one another as Christians is our submission to God in consecration to Him and His will (Rom. 12:1-2). We take the step of submission by offering our "bodies as living sacrifices," which is our "spiritual act of worship" (v. 1).

Only after we have said to God, "Your will, nothing more, nothing less, nothing else," do we have the mindset that will lead us to submit to one another. Then our order of priority will be "God first, others second, myself third."

What about it? Paul spelled out the principle of submission in marital relations, filial relations, and employment relations (Eph. 5:22–6:9), but it applies to all interpersonal and social relationships. Is it evident in your life?

YOUR WAY OR HIS WAY?

In a large youth rally the evangelist had finished an impassioned plea for the young people to receive Jesus Christ as their Saviour. Among those who responded to the invitation was a girl who asked this startling question, "I want to know how I can be a Christian and have my own way."

Unfortunately, many professed believers are like that girl. They want to do the will of God, or so they say, but only if it coincides with what they want to do.

That attitude is contrary to Paul's dictum to be "doing the will of God from your heart" (Eph. 6:6). This is part of the apostle's instruction to Christian slaves to obey their masters (v. 5) and "serve wholeheartedly" (v. 7).

Doing God's will from your heart requires knowing the will of God. Part of knowing is easy because God plainly states His will for all His children—"be sanctified" (1 Thes. 4:3), "give thanks" (1 Thes. 5:18), do "good" (1 Peter 2:15).

Determining God's will for your life individually and in specific situations, however, is more difficult. The first step is submission of your life to God (Rom. 12:1-2), committing yourself to Him to do His will no what matter what it may be. God reveals His will only to those committed to doing it, not to those who want to consider it. This commitment to do God's will should be renewed each morning, by asking God to lead you that day.

Keep in mind: Finding the will of God in a specific situation requiring decision and action involves the agreement of three factors—the Word of God, the inward conviction produced by the Holy Spirit, and the trend of circumstances. Then, having decided, do "the will of God from the heart"—zealously to the best of your ability.

AT WAR

When World War I broke out, the War Ministry in London sent a coded message to a remote British outpost in the heart of Africa: "War declared. Arrest all enemy aliens in your district."

This prompt reply was received: "Have arrested ten Germans, six Belgians, four Frenchmen, two Italians, three Austrians, and one American. Please advise immediately who we are at war with."

The Apostle Paul left no doubt as to the Christian's enemy. He wrote, "Our struggle is . . . against the rulers, against the authorities, against the powers of this dark world and against the spiritual forces of evil in the heavenly realms" (Eph. 6:12).

Because the Christian's warfare is against the devil and his evil hosts, the apostle twice commanded us, "Put on the full armor of God" (vv. 11, 13). Our armor is not our own; it has been designed and provided by God. Only God's armor will enable the Christian to take his "stand against the devil's schemes" (v. 11) and "to stand firm" (v. 14).

The English word *panoply* is a transliteration of the Greek word translated "full armor." It involves both the equipment for the protection and defense of the soldier and his weapons for attack (cf. 2 Cor. 6:7).

The provisions of God for the Christian in his spiritual warfare are primarily defensive since the devil is the aggressor (1 Peter 5:8). The believer is to "resist the devil" (James 4:7; cf. 1 Peter 5:9), not attack him.

This protective armor includes "the belt of truth" and "the breastplate of righteousness" (Eph. 6:14), the sandals of "the gospel of peace" and "shield of faith" (vv. 15-16), and "the helmet of salvation" (v. 17). The Christian's sole offensive weapon is "the sword of the Spirit, which is the Word of God" (v. 17).

Note: Make sure you are fully equipped with the "full armor of God" and at ease with it so you can "stand firm."

PARTNERS

A couple in Ohio was supporting a girl in a mission school in India. One Saturday they received a letter from the missionary indicating the girl would have to be dismissed unless her attitude changed. Her rebellious spirit was infecting the other girls.

That night the couple prayed for their girl. At the same time it was Sunday morning in India. During the Sunday School lesson the girl broke down and trusted Jesus Christ as her Saviour. As a result, the whole class trusted Christ that morning.

Support in prayer is part of what Paul had in mind when he commended the Philippian Christians for their "partnership in the Gospel" (Phil. 1:5; cf. v. 19). Another part of their partnership was sending Epaphroditus from Philippi to minister to Paul under house arrest in Rome (2:25-30).

The Philippian Christians also sent a financial gift for Paul with Epaphroditus (4:18; cf. vv. 10, 14). Apparently, it was the only church that helped Paul financially (vv. 15-16). Paul boasted to the Corinthian believers of his ministering without charge even though he had the right to be supported by those to whom he ministered (1 Cor. 9:3-18).

This privilege of "partnership in the Gospel" is available to every believer. The first place to exercise it is in your local church with your pastor, other ministerial staff if you have them, and lay leaders. In addition to financial support of your local church, become partners with your ministerial and lay leaders in prayer and in helpful service.

You can also have "partnership in the Gospel" with Christian schools at all academic levels and with all types of missionary agencies from local rescue missions to children's and youth ministries to overseas mission boards.

Amazing! By support in prayer, service, and finances, your "partnership in the Gospel" can reach around the world.

TO LIVE IS CHRIST

An aged Christian woman had once known much of the Bible by memory. As advancing years stole her memory, she could recall only one verse: "I know whom I have believed, and am persuaded that He is able to keep that which I committed unto Him against that day" (2 Tim. 1:12, KJV).

Even that verse slowly slipped from memory until she repeated only, "That which I have committed unto Him." Finally on her deathbed she quietly whispered over and over, "Him, Him, Him," until she passed into Christ's presence.

She had the same perspective on life the Apostle Paul expressed when he wrote to the Philippians, "For to me, to live is Christ" (Phil. 1:21). Those words should be the life motto of every Christian, for several reasons.

First, the Lord Jesus Christ is the source of the spiritual life of the believer. Jesus told the Samaritan woman, "The water I give him will become in him a spring of water welling up to eternal life" (John 4:14). As the "living Bread that came down from heaven" (John 6:51), Jesus gives eternal life (vv. 53-54, 57-58).

Second, the Lord Jesus Christ is the life principle residing within the person who believes in Him. Paul declared, "Christ lives in me" (Gal. 2:20; cf. Rom. 8:10) and he spoke of "Christ, who is your life" (Col. 3:4).

What both Paul and the aged woman were saying, however, is that serving and exalting the Lord Jesus Christ were the single consuming goal and purpose of their lives, of all that they did and said. Paul wrote, "We take captive every thought to make it obedient to Christ" (2 Cor. 10:5).

True: If we aim at nothing in life, we will hit it every time. On the other hand if we focus on a single objective, our success will astound us, especially if our perspective is "to me, to live is Christ."

THE MIND OF CHRIST

An interesting study is how the changing public attitude toward alcohol consumption has affected the related terminology. What were saloons before Prohibition became bars and taverns after its repeal. In more recent years such places have become lounges.

Similarly, some years ago the early evening hours were known as the cocktail hour. Then that period became the happy hour. Now it is called the attitude adjustment hour. It still has the same effect of loosening both the tongue and the inhibitions.

There is a proper biblical call for attitude adjustment. Paul wrote to the Philippians, "Your attitude should be the same as that of Christ Jesus" (2:5).

What was the attitude of Christ? First, He did not insist on His rights and prerogatives (vv. 6-8). This runs counter to the prevailing attitude today, unfortunately sometimes even among Christians. If mankind received what it deserves from God, everyone would be doomed.

Second, the Lord Jesus was submissive to the will of God the Father (Heb. 10:5-7). Not only was He initially submissive to His Father's will, but Jesus was also continually obedient to God the Father. Jesus said, "I always do what pleases Him" (John 8:29; cf. v. 28; 12:49).

Third, Jesus' attitude was one of service and ministry to others (Phil. 2:7). He told His disciples, "The Son of Man did not come to be served, but to serve" (Matt. 20:28). He demonstrated this attitude by washing the disciples' feet (John 13:1-17).

Remember: Achieving the attitude of Christ is impossible in one's own strength. It requires the power of God operative through the Holy Spirit (2 Cor. 3:18). As you permit the Holy Spirit to control your life, walking day by day in His strength, you can have "the mind of the Lord" (1 Cor. 2:16).

WORKING OUT YOUR SALVATION

Norman Harrison was talking with a nurse who was confused about salvation and works. "Suppose I offered to give you a diamond worth $10,000," he told her. "Then when you demurred, saying you only had $50, I explained again that the diamond was a gift and extended it to you in my hand. Finally you took it. That is salvation by grace through faith."

Continuing his explanation, Dr. Harrison said, "If, sometime after I gave you the diamond, I asked you to care for my sick child, out of gratitude you would be happy to help. You cannot be saved by works, but once you are saved you will joyfully work for God."

Paul advised the Philippian Christians to "continue to work out your salvation with fear and trembling" (2:12). The salvation we have received as a gift from God by faith we need to express in our daily lives.

Whether Paul was encouraging the Philippians individually as believers or corporately as a local church is unsure and makes little difference. The exhortation applies both ways. These Christians faced serious problems both from outside (1:29-30) and inside their fellowship (3:18-19; 4:2-3). They would solve their problems both individually and corporately by continuing to work out their salvation.

Solving these problems could not be accomplished, however, in their own wisdom and strength. That would produce only "wood, hay, or straw" (1 Cor. 3:12) that would be "burned up" (v. 15) at the judgment seat of Christ (v. 13). Paul reminded them that they do not work alone, "for it is God who works in you to will and to do according to His good purpose" (Phil. 2:13; cf. Eph. 2:10).

A reminder: God will give you many opportunities to "work out your salvation" in solving the problems of life. Continue to seize such opportunities to glorify Him.

THAT I MAY GAIN CHRIST

All three Synoptic Gospels record how a man (Luke calls him a "ruler," 18:18) asked Jesus what he must do "to inherit eternal life" (v. 18; cf. Matt. 19:16; Mark 10:17). When Jesus recited the social commandments of the Mosaic Law, the man replied, "All these I have kept since I was a boy" (Luke 18:21).

Jesus then instructed him to "sell everything you have and give to the poor.... Then come, follow Me" (v. 22). At this the young man "went away sad, because he had great wealth" (Matt. 19:22). His wealth meant more to him than Jesus Christ.

Before his conversion, the Apostle Paul was much like that young man. He wrote that "as for legalistic righteousness," he was "faultless" (Phil. 3:6). Saul of Tarsus was not wealthy, but he was a proud Benjamite and a zealously religious Jew (vv. 5-6).

There the comparison ends, however. When Saul weighed all this against salvation in Christ, what had been profit became "loss for the sake of Christ" (v. 7). In fact he wrote, "I consider them rubbish, that I may gain Christ" (v. 8). Christ alone constitutes true spiritual and eternal wealth.

To "gain Christ" does not mean to merit Him or to get Him as a prize in a race. Instead to "gain Christ" means "to be found in Him" with "the righteousness that comes from God and is by faith" (v. 9).

One of the marks of the child of God is that he has "no confidence in the flesh" (v. 3). Paul demonstrated how this is necessary to become a Christian. It is also necessary, however, for the Christian as well. As a believer something else may be replacing Christ as first.

A truth: Each of us needs to examine our heart and make sure the Lord Jesus Christ is supreme, realizing that in comparison to Him everything else is as rubbish.

CITIZENS OF TWO COUNTRIES

When Dr. Thomas Lambie, a medical missionary in Ethiopia, wanted to buy property for a mission station, he discovered that Ethiopian law prohibited the sale of land to foreigners. Motivated by his love for Christ and for the Ethiopian people, Dr. Lambie relinquished his United States citizenship and became an Ethiopian citizen so he could buy the land for his mission station. Later the United States government restored his citizenship to honor him for his great work in Ethiopia.

Dr. Lambie recognized that, important as earthly citizenship is, for the Christian "our citizenship is in heaven" (Phil. 3:20). Believers are "aliens and strangers in the world" (1 Peter 2:11; cf. Heb. 11:13). God "has rescued us from the dominion of darkness and brought us into the kingdom of the Son He loves" (Col. 1:13).

That does not mean that Christians renounce their earthly citizenship with its privileges as well as its responsibilities. The Apostle Paul was justly proud of his Roman citizenship (Acts 22:25-29) and demanded his rights as such (16:37-40; 25:10-12).

A Christian is distinctive because he is a person with two countries. He owes allegiance to an earthly government (Rom. 13:1-7) and also to the Lord Jesus Christ, "the King of kings and Lord of lords" (1 Tim. 6:15; Rev. 19:16).

Normally the two citizenships of the Christian do not conflict. In fact believers, being citizens of heaven, are frequently the best and most responsible earthly citizens as well. Only when earthly authorities make demands contrary to Christian belief and the Word of God must the believer say, "We must obey God rather than men" (Acts 5:29).

Don't forget: Do your best to be a good citizen of both realms.

REJOICE!

Franz Joseph Haydn, the Austrian composer, was asked why his church music was always so cheerful. He replied, "I cannot make it otherwise; I write according to the thoughts I feel."

He continued, "When I think upon God, my heart is so full of joy that the notes dance and leap as it were from my pen. Since God has given me a cheerful heart, it will be pardoned me that I serve Him with a cheerful spirit."

Haydn had caught the joyful spirit of Paul's Epistle to the Philippians. At least a dozen times in the letter Paul used the words *joy* and *rejoice,* reaching a climax in his command, "Rejoice in the Lord always. I will say it again: Rejoice" (4:4; cf. 3:1).

To underscore the need for continuous rejoicing by the Christian, in addition to the word *always,* Paul used the present imperative, which in Greek implies continuing action—"keep on rejoicing." Whatever their circumstances, Christians can rejoice because their rejoicing is "in the Lord," not in their circumstances.

Paul illustrated this truth in his own life. He wrote to the Philippians from Rome, where he had been for most of two years (Acts 28:30) under house arrest "with a soldier to guard him" (Acts 28:16; cf. Phil. 1:14). Despite this "struggle" (1:30), Paul wrote that he rejoiced because Christ was preached (1:18) and he said, "I will continue to rejoice."

The Philippian Christians also were suffering for their faith in Christ (1:29-30), but Paul commanded them to keep on rejoicing in the Lord despite their trials. Happiness comes from circumstances, from what "happens," but joy comes only from the Lord.

For you: Demonstrate your faith in the Lord Jesus Christ by rejoicing "in the Lord always."

ALL YOUR NEEDS

During the Great Depression the bank in which my father was an officer was forced to close. False rumors about its stability sparked a run of withdrawals that exhausted its cash reserves before it could liquidate other assets.

I was convinced my father would be out of work. I knew I had to get a job as a boy of twelve to help support the family. A nearby corner grocer hired me after school and Saturdays for a dollar a week to sweep the floors and deliver groceries.

When I told my father, he replied, "I appreciate your concern and desire to help, Son, but I am trusting the Lord to meet our needs. We belong to Him, and He will take care of His own."

God honored my father's faith. He never went a day without employment throughout the entire Depression.

With similar confidence Paul wrote to the Philippian Christians, "My God will meet all your needs" (4:19). This was the encouragement those believers needed because they were far from affluent (2 Cor. 8:1-5). Out of their meager resources they had sent an offering to Paul in Rome (Phil. 4:14-18). Paul assured them that God would reimburse them.

Two important details about this promise must be observed. First, God will meet "all your needs," not your desires. Jesus said, "Your Father knows what you need" (Matt. 6:8), and His understanding of our needs may be different from ours.

Second, God will meet our needs "according to His glorious riches in Christ Jesus." God's supply is not "out of" but "according to His glorious riches." God is "able to do immeasurably more than all we ask or imagine" (Eph. 3:20).

Do it: Whatever your needs are right now, trust God to meet them and look for His supply.

THE POWER OF PRAYER

At Saint Catherine's Monastery near Mount Sinai two young monks about twelve centuries ago took vows between them of lifelong unceasing prayer. In adjoining cells one prayed while the other slept. A metal chain fastened to the wrist connected them through the wall between their cells. A tug on the chain signaled the beginning and end of each one's praying.

Visitors are told the story and shown the skeletons of the two monks in caskets, still connected by the metal chain. They carried the Apostle Paul's command to "pray continually" (1 Thes. 5:17) beyond what he intended or practiced himself.

Paul carried on a great ministry of intercessory prayer. He wrote to the Colossian Christians that he and Timothy "have not stopped praying for you" (Col. 1:9). This did not mean that he prayed for the Colossians continuously, but that regularly he interceded for the Colossians as well as for others.

Paul is an example to all Christians of a faithful and consistent prayer life. Most of his letters mentioned his praying for his readers and some of them include at least one specific prayer. Despite his travels and ministry and work as a tentmaker, he took time to pray for his converts.

Furthermore, Paul did not pray in generalities — "God bless the Colossians" — but with specific requests appropriate to the group and its needs. Since the Colossians were disturbed by the Gnostics, who claimed to have unusual spiritual insight, Paul prayed for God to fill the Colossians "with the knowledge of His will through all spiritual wisdom and understanding" (1:9).

Because he knew the power of prayer, Paul also asked his converts to pray for him (Eph. 6:19-20; Col. 4:3-4; 1 Thes. 5:25; 2 Thes. 3:1).

For you: Follow Paul's example and develop a consistent ministry of prayer and intercession.

WHO IS SUPREME?

A Christian painter was producing his interpretation of the Last Supper. It was to be his masterpiece to the glory of Jesus Christ. Every detail was perfect even to the jeweled cup on the table before the Lord.

When the artist heard spectators admiring the beautiful cup, he painted it out and replaced it with a common clay cup. To protesters he explained, "I want attention focused on the Lord, not the cup."

That is also the intent of God the Father, whose purpose was that "in everything He [Jesus] might have the supremacy" (Col. 1:18).

In teaching the supremacy of Jesus Christ, the Apostle Paul was refuting the false Gnostic view that Christ was only one of a line of spirit beings between God and mankind. Instead, Paul taught that "God was pleased to have all His fullness dwell in Him" (1:19), that is, Jesus Christ.

Christ's supremacy is demonstrated first by the fact that "He is the image of the invisible God" (v. 15). In addition, He is the active agent of God in all His creation (v. 16). He is also the cohesive energy that holds all creation together (v. 17).

Jesus Christ is supreme in God's redemptive program as well as in His creation. In this program He is "the head of the body, the church" (v. 18). As such He exercises authority over the body, the church (Eph. 1:22), as well as being organically united with all the members of the body, giving direction and motivation to them all.

By His resurrection from the dead Jesus Christ is also "the Beginning" of a new race of human beings (v. 18; cf. 1 Cor. 15:20, 22-23). He has been exalted "far above all rule and authority" (Eph. 1:20-21; cf. Phil. 2:9-11) and will be manifested as "King of kings and Lord of lords" (1 Tim. 6:15; Rev. 19:16).

A question only you can answer: "Does Jesus Christ have supremacy in my heart and life?"

FULLNESS IN CHRIST

The incipient Gnosticism the Christians at Colosse faced had a powerful psychological appeal, especially to new or superficial believers. The Gnostics claimed that faith in Jesus Christ was fine but not all that God offered. They offered the additional knowledge that supposedly made spiritual experience complete. Many cults and sects today have a similar appeal.

The Apostle Paul refuted this false teaching by emphasizing first that Jesus Christ was enough, in fact all that God provided. He pointed out that "in Christ all the fullness of the Deity lives in bodily form" (Col. 2:9; cf. 1:19). The word translated "fullness" represents the complete crew needed to sail a ship. As a result, everything it takes to make God "lives in bodily form" in Jesus Christ.

In response to Philip's request, "Lord, show us the Father, and that will be enough for us" (John 14:8), Jesus replied, "Anyone who has seen Me has seen the Father" (v. 9). The writer to the Hebrews wrote, "The Son is the radiance of God's glory, and the exact representation of His being" (Heb. 1:3).

Paul continued his refutation, however, by telling the Colossian Christians, "You have been given fullness in Christ" (Col. 1:10). As Peter explained, "His divine power has given us everything we need for life and godliness through our knowledge of Him" (2 Peter 1:3).

The obvious conclusion from Paul's argument for the Colossian believers and for us is that we need nothing and no one beyond the Lord Jesus Christ. Paul wrote of "Christ, in whom are hidden all the treasures of wisdom and knowledge" (Col. 2:3).

A challenge: Let each of us as believers resolve to translate the treasure we have in Christ into living reality in daily experience.

ALIVE WITH CHRIST

In 1974 peasants digging a well accidentally discovered part of the terra cotta army of 6,000 soldiers and horse-drawn war chariots of China's first emperor, Ch'in Shih Huang Ti.

Life-size and so realistic they seem alive, these pottery warriors are inanimate works of art. They may illustrate unregenerate human beings who, though alive physically, are spiritually "dead in . . . transgressions and sins" (Eph. 2:1; cf. v. 5; Col. 2:13). This was the condition of each of us as Christians before we trusted the Lord Jesus Christ.

The analogy is especially interesting because God created man "from the dust of the ground" (Gen. 2:7) just as these clay soldiers were formed. God proceeded, however, to breathe "into his nostrils the breath of life, and the man became a living being."

Man's sin of disobedience brought the judgment of both physical and spiritual death (Gen. 2:16). Adam and Eve were expelled from Eden and were told that in physical death they would "return to the ground . . . for dust you are and to dust you shall return" (Gen. 3:19).

God's remedy for both physical and spiritual death for mankind is found in the redemptive death and resurrection to newness of life of the Lord Jesus Christ. Every time a spiritually dead human being appropriates God's remedy in Christ by faith, as Paul wrote the Colossians, "God made you alive with Christ" (Col. 2:13; cf. Eph. 2:4).

The believer is still subject to physical death, but by faith in Jesus Christ he is now spiritually alive forever. In addition, he will share in the physical resurrection or transformation when the Lord Jesus Christ returns.

For you: Rejoice, praise God, and share with others the life you have received in Jesus Christ.

THE PEACE OF CHRIST

Two artists were commissioned to paint their concepts of peace. One painted a tranquil scene of a placid lake surrounded by trees, its surface without ripples from the wind. On the far side cattle contentedly grazed in a meadow.

The other artist painted a raging waterfall cascading over the rocks. Black storm clouds filled the sky. In a cleft in the rocks, however, sat a bird on her nest brooding her eggs, protected from both the torrent and the impending storm.

This latter scene portrays the peace Christians enjoy in the Lord Jesus Christ. The world about us is in turmoil. We are engaged in a spiritual warfare with the devil and his hosts (Eph. 6:11-12). We are encouraged, however, as Paul wrote the Colossians to "let the peace of Christ rule in [our] hearts" (Col. 3:15).

Our spiritual life begins with peace. Paul told the Roman believers, "Since we have been justified through faith, we have peace with God" (Rom. 5:1). Once rebels against God and His enemies (v. 10), we now can enjoy peace and harmony.

Paul also wrote to the Colossians that "you were called to peace" (Col. 3:15). This refers to harmony in our interpersonal relationships with other believers (cf. Phil. 2:2-4) first of all. It also applies to our relationships with others. Paul wrote to the Romans, "If it is possible, as far as it depends on you, live at peace with everyone" (Rom. 12:18). The Lord Jesus pronounced a special blessing on "the peacemakers" (Matt. 5:9).

In his exhortation to "let the peace of Christ rule in your hearts," however, Paul was speaking of inner personal tranquility of heart and mind and life (cf. Phil. 4:7, 9). This is part of the fruit of the Holy Spirit (Gal. 5:22).

Today and every day: In the turmoil of life let the Spirit control you and let the peace of Christ make the decisions ("rule") in your life.

YOUR SPIRITUAL SERVICE

As a boy H.A. Ironside worked for a Christian cobbler after school and Saturdays to help his widowed mother. His job was to pound the water out of the leather soles with a wooden mallet before they were sewn on the shoes, a tedious task.

Another cobbler who did not pound his soles told him the soft soles wore out and had to be replaced sooner, giving him more income. When Harry suggested this technique to his employer, the godly Scot replied, "Son, I do not repair shoes for the money I make; I do it as a spiritual service to glorify God."

The Apostle Paul had that same idea in mind when he reminded the Christian slaves at Colosse, "It is the Lord Christ you are serving" (Col. 3:24; cf. vv. 22-23; Eph. 6:5-7). The reminder applies to Christian employees today.

Any legitimate occupation for Christians can be a spiritual ministry, a means of serving Christ. The word translated "worship" in the clause "we who worship by the Spirit of God" (Phil 3:3) literally means "do spiritual service." It was applied to the Levites who erected and took down the tabernacle and those who drove the wagons on which the tabernacle was carried from place to place in the wilderness.

A worker may respond, however, "I've got to please my boss or I'll lose my job." The best way to please one's boss is to follow Paul's directions, "Whatever you do, work at it with all your heart, as working for the Lord, not for men" (Col. 3:23). If that doesn't please your boss, you need to change jobs.

Do any task as to the Lord: You will transform it into a spiritual ministry that will glorify God and satisfy you.

THE GOSPEL ACCORDING TO YOU

Gordon Maxwell, a missionary to India, asked a Hindu scholar to teach him the language. The man replied, "No, Sahib, I will not teach you my language. You would make me a Christian."

Maxwell explained that he simply wanted to be taught the language. The man still refused. He explained, "No man can live with you and not become a Christian." Such was the impact of Maxwell's life and testimony.

That is the kind of life the Apostle Paul had in mind when he wrote to the Colossian Christians, "Be wise in the way you act toward outsiders" (Col. 4:5). The way we act toward unbelievers can either enhance our profession of faith in Christ or damage it; it can either attract others to the faith or repulse them.

The Apostle Peter gave his readers similar advice. He wrote, "Live such good lives among the pagans that, though they accuse you of doing wrong, they may see your good deeds and glorify God" (1 Peter 2:12). He commanded them to "show proper respect to everyone" (v. 17), reminding them that "it is God's will that by doing good you should silence the ignorant talk of foolish men" (v. 15).

To the Ephesian Christians Paul wrote, "Be very careful, then, how you live—not as unwise but as wise, making the most of every opportunity, because the days are evil" (Eph. 5:15-16). Wise living before the unsaved involves our conversation as well as our actions (Col. 4:6).

Give this thought: A poet, reminding us that "you are the only Bible a careless world will read," asks the pointed question, "What is the Gospel according to you?"

SERVANTS FOR LIFE

In ancient Israel a man or woman could sell himself to a fellow Israelite as a slave. He would serve for six years and be released from servitude the seventh year (Ex. 21:2; Deut. 15:12-14). He was then "to be treated as a hired worker" (Lev. 25:40).

If, because of affection for his master and his family, the man did not want his freedom (Ex. 21:4-5; Deut. 15:16), then his ear was pierced with an awl at the doorpost and he served his master for life. He was bound to his master by his vow of love.

The Apostle Paul used this terminology when he identified Epaphras, a Colossian, as "a servant of Jesus Christ" (Col. 4:12). The word translated "servant" is literally "slave." He used the same word with a prepositional prefix to speak of Tychicus (v. 7).

Paul spoke of himself as "a servant of Jesus Christ" (Rom. 1:1) and "a servant of God" (Titus 1:1). So did James (James 1:1), Peter (2 Peter 1:1), and Jude (Jude 1). Because of their love for the Lord Jesus, they had vowed to serve Him as slaves for life.

In a sense the servitude of these apostles to the Lord is in loving response to His servitude during His earthly ministry. In describing Christ's condescension, Paul said He took "the very nature of a servant [slave]" (Phil. 2:7). Jesus told His disciples, "The Son of Man did not come to be served, but to serve" (Mark 10:45; Matt. 20:28).

Every Christian should consider himself "a servant of Jesus Christ" (cf. 1 Cor. 7:22-23), bound to the Lord for life by cords of love because of the eternal salvation He has provided (cf. Rom. 12:1).

RSVP: Jesus invites us to take His yoke on us. He promised, "My yoke is easy and My burden is light" (Matt. 11:29). What is your response?

SHARE IT

A businessman had a couple of hours between flights at a busy airport. He thought, *How can I be used by the Lord here?*

He had a supply of Gospel tracts. Inside each one he put his business card. Then he distributed them, explaining to each recipient that the booklet told how to become a Christian and inviting them to come talk with him or write him.

When he had to catch his plane, people were standing in line to talk with him and for weeks he got letters of inquiry at his office.

This Christian was active in sharing his faith, what the Apostle Paul encouraged Philemon to do (Phile. v. 6).

Philemon had apparently been active in sharing his faith in the past because a church met in his house (v. 2). At that time Paul had not visited the city of Colosse where Philemon lived (Col. 2:1). Much of the evangelism there had been carried on by believers like Philemon.

At least two reasons exist for Paul's prayer that Philemon be active in sharing his faith. One obviously is that more persons would hear the Gospel and receive Jesus Christ as their Saviour. Paul did not mention this reason.

The second reason, the one Paul did give, is the benefit that comes to believers when they share their faith. Paul told Philemon to share his faith "so that you will have full understanding of every good thing we have in Christ" (v. 6). When we witness, our understanding and appreciation of the riches of God's grace in Christ increase!

For you: The Apostle Paul would say to each of us as he did to Philemon, be "active in sharing your faith."

REFRESH MY HEART

After seven years in a small, struggling pastorate in Wainsgate, John Fawcett was called to London to succeed the famous Dr. Gill. His parishoners came to say "good-bye" as the Fawcetts loaded their meager possessions in the wagon.

Touched by the outpouring of Christian love, Mrs. Fawcett said, "Oh, John, I just can't bear this. They need us so badly here."

"God has spoken to my heart, too," John replied as he directed the unloading of the wagon. "We cannot break these wonderful ties of fellowship." This experience inspired his writing the hymn, "Blest Be the Tie That Binds."

Paul had the joy of Christian fellowship in mind when he asked Philemon to "refresh my heart in Christ" (Phil. v. 20). That communion would be demonstrated if Philemon responded favorably to Paul's request concerning Onesimus.

Onesimus had been a slave of Philemon. He had run away after apparently stealing from his master. In Rome he had met Paul, who was under house arrest awaiting his appeal to Caesar. Onesimus trusted Jesus Christ as his Saviour.

Now Paul had sent him back to Philemon, asking him to forget the past and receive Onesimus as a brother in Christ (vv. 10-16). Doing this, Paul wrote, would "refresh my heart in Christ." Paul expected a positive response from Philemon because he had already commended him for having "refreshed the hearts of the saints" (v. 7).

What you can do: Each day be on the lookout for Christians whose hearts you can refresh. Amazingly, your heart will be refreshed in Christ too.

October

Devotional readings in Paul's Letter to Titus
by Gene A. Getz

Some of the material in these readings is adapted from the author's Saying No When You'd Rather Say Yes *(Ventura, CA: Regal Books, 1983) and is used by permission.*

A SERVANT—BUT FREE

Recently, when a friend of mine sat down in a restaurant, the waiter said to him, "I am your servant." That's unusual. Few people want to think of themselves as servants. They prefer more significant positions and titles.

The Apostle Paul did not hesitate to call himself God's servant (Titus 1:1). The same is true of Peter, James, and Jude, who identified themselves as "servants of God" or "servants of Christ" (James 1:1; 2 Peter 1:1; Jude 1).

The Greek word *doulos* translated "servant" means a bondservant or a slave, one who gives himself up totally to do someone else's will. This, of course, describes Paul's attitude toward his Heavenly Father. Following his conversion, he had no other goal for his life but to do the will of God. This relationship set him "free"—free to become what God wanted him to be.

How can a person be a servant and yet be free? This is a divine mystery. Only one relationship on earth makes it possible—a relationship with God through Jesus Christ and a relationship with other members of the body of Christ who have experienced the same relationship with God. Only as a person becomes rightly related to the Lord can he begin to experience true freedom in his relationships with other people. And the way of freedom comes through servanthood—total commitment to the God of the universe whose Son first became our Servant (Phil. 2:7).

For your consideration: Paul was a special kind of "servant of God" because of his apostleship. But God's will for all believers is that they too become His servants. Do you desire to do His will? Is your life conformed, not to the world's system but to Jesus Christ? Are you "eager to serve" (1 Peter 5:2)? Are you *God's* servant?

COMMISSIONED AND SENT

An apostle in New Testament days was a special person, called by God and especially gifted to help launch the church of Jesus Christ. Along with the New Testament prophets, the apostles had a foundational ministry (Eph. 2:20). They were eyewitnesses of Jesus Christ and received their calling and commands directly from Him.

When stating his credentials, Paul called himself "an apostle of Jesus Christ" (Titus 1:1). This means he was a delegate or messenger of Christ. Why did Paul identify himself in this way in most of his epistles? He wanted others to know that his authority as Jesus' messenger came directly from God and that He was specifically set apart to communicate the "truth that leads to godliness" (v. 1). He was committed to encouraging others to have "faith and knowledge" (v.2), a trust in and knowledge of the Lord that results in "eternal life." The "preaching" of this truth was "entrusted to me," Paul wrote, "by the command of God our Saviour" (v. 3).

To what extent are you involved in an "apostolic ministry"? Don't misunderstand. I am not suggesting that you are to strive to be another Apostle Paul, Apostle Peter, or Apostle John. Today there are no apostles, at least not in the New Testament sense. Though we do not receive direct revelations from God as they did, we have at our disposal the revelation they received, which is recorded for us in the Bible. And the command given to all believers is to *communicate* God's message to all mankind. This is what the Great Commission is all about (Matt. 28:19-20).

How do you answer? To what extent are you taking seriously the Great Commission? To what extent are you involved in sharing Christ with those who do not know Him personally? To what extent are you involved in helping other Christians grow in the grace and knowledge of Jesus Christ? God called the apostles to launch the church, to lay the foundations. What are you doing to further the building process?

BE LIKE TITUS

When the late Richard Seume, chaplain at Dallas Theological Seminary from 1971 to 1985, conversed with a male student, he would often address him as "son." This expressed his fatherly concern for the students who, of course, were younger than he. Similarly, Paul addressed Titus as his "true son" (Titus 1:4), probably to point out the fact that Paul had led Titus to the Lord. And yet the apostle did not put himself above Titus. He wrote that they shared a "common faith," that they were equals in Christ.

Though Titus was evidently a young man, he was mature emotionally and spiritually. This seems obvious because of the heavy responsibilities Paul gave him. For example, Paul allowed Titus to go to Corinth to minister to Christians there who were well known for their carnality. Titus demonstrated his maturity when he helped them shed many aspects of worldliness (2 Cor. 7:5-15).

Titus was positive and enthusiastic. When Paul needed a man to confront those worldly Christians in Corinth, Titus voluntarily accepted the challenge. Paul wrote, "Titus . . . is coming to you with much enthusiasm and on his own initiative" (2 Cor. 8:17).

Titus was also a self-starter. He thrived on difficult assignments. And he did not run away from opportunities, difficult though they may have been, to serve the Lord Jesus Christ. This is evident from his willingness to accept the challenge to visit the Corinthian church. Anyone with lesser stature would have gladly given the "opportunity" to someone else.

For today: Like Titus, we too should have a positive attitude toward serving the Lord. Look for opportunities that will strengthen you, challenge you, and help you develop. This may be difficult; we all tend to shirk experiences that stretch us. But serving the Lord and others willingly, positively, and with enthusiasm can benefit both ourselves and those we serve.

GETTING STRAIGHTENED OUT

Paul left Titus on the island of Crete to "straighten out what was left unfinished" (Titus 1:5). Many expositors say this was a directive to organize churches, especially since Paul followed this initial injunction with a reference to appointing elders. Obviously, elders were to be appointed. But Paul was concerned that these Christians' lifestyles get straightened out. As relatively new believers, the Christians in Crete had received little instruction on how to live for the Lord. Like the Corinthians, they were so ingrained in ungodly and pagan living that it took time to move them toward maturity. Also false teachers were already leading them in the wrong direction. These false teachers were anything but godly. So the best way for the believers to counteract these negative influences was to get their own lives straightened out.

To give these new, immature Christians models of Christlike behavior, Paul instructed Titus to "appoint elders in every town." Evidently, Paul had already directed Titus to care for this matter before he left Crete, but he wanted to be sure Titus (and all the other Christians in Crete) knew exactly how to select the men best qualified.

Check yourself: Today the church of Jesus Christ desperately needs men and women to emerge as mature Christians. Where are you in the process of developing the kind of reputation Titus had? To do this, sit down with a mature Christian friend you trust and ask that person to give you feedback regarding areas of strength and weakness in your life. Then set up goals in areas where you need to improve.

BEING BLAMELESS

Paul began his list of qualifications for elders with an overarching characteristic—to be "blameless" (Titus 1:6). Obviously, he was not referring to "perfection," for no one, apart from Jesus Christ, has lived a perfect life. Rather, Paul was speaking of a "good reputation," of being "above reproach."

Timothy stands out as a vivid illustration of this quality. When Paul went to Lystra before his second missionary journey, a number of the Christians there were talking about a dynamic young man named Timothy. Luke recorded that believers from Lystra and Iconium "spoke well of him" (Acts 16:2). In other words Timothy had a good reputation as a Christian. He was "blameless" in the eyes of those in the Christian community. There were no specific flaws in his life that would bring reproach to the cause of Christ. So Paul invited Timothy to be his missionary companion, and this resulted in a deep, lasting relationship and ministry together.

Titus was also this kind of man. Mature in many ways, he maintained pure motives, evidencing compassion and concern for people (2 Cor. 8:16) and demonstrating a positive attitude toward the ministry (v. 17). There is no better way in which to develop a good reputation among Christians and non-Christians alike.

Be blameless. This quality and the other qualifications for elders are standards all of us should strive for, whether we are in positions of church leadership or not.

A daily challenge: Stand firm for what is right. Be above reproach. Don't compromise your convictions in order to be accepted by others. Be teachable and open to correction, but never in any way that violates God's will.

MORALLY PURE

Christians differ on what Paul meant by the qualification "the husband of but one wife" (Titus 1:6). The Greek simply says "a one-woman man," which leaves us with a certain ambiguity that must be interpreted contextually.

I believe Paul was saying that a husband who serves as an elder in a church must be sexually related to only one woman, loyal to his wife and morally pure. Since it was relatively common for men in the first century to have more than one woman in their lives besides their legal wives, Paul had to deal with this issue specifically. This kind of lifestyle is prevalent in our day too, but it was an even more open and accepted practice then.

Loyalty to one's wife should characterize all Christian husbands. Nearly every New Testament epistle warns against premarital and marital sexual sins. In sexual ethics Christians are to live above the standards of the world. To be mature spiritually, allow no compromise in this area of your life.

Today's moral standards are rapidly declining. Though we may not have reached the depths to which the Greek and Roman cultures fell, we are moving in that direction. The influence of literature, movies, music, and television are all contributing to and reflecting the moral decadence all about us.

What about your own life? Are you—as a husband, wife, or single person—maintaining a life of purity? Whether married or single, what we sow we will reap. Marital unfaithfulness and sexual promiscuity, whether in mind or body, run counter to God's will. They are sin. Be faithful in this area of your life—in your thoughts as well as your actions.

A WELL-ORDERED FAMILY

Many children and teens tend to be wild, to disobey their parents, to resist adult influence and directives. But they *need* not be that way! They can be trained to be disciplined, self-controlled, and obedient. In fact, if a person is to be an elder in a church, his children must be believers and must not be "wild and disobedient" (Titus 1:6).

Paul viewed a well-ordered home as a true test of a man's maturity and ability to lead other Christians, especially a home that has passed the test of time. When the entire family is committed to Jesus Christ and the wife is dedicated to her husband and grown children respect and love their father, this is strong evidence that this man is mature. Only then is he qualified to manage the church of God (1 Tim. 3:5).

The fact that some grown Christian children go astray from God's will does not always mean a man has not been a good father. The home is not an island. The world's influences are sometimes felt, no matter how effective the Christian environment in the home. And once children leave home, Satan can sometimes gain access to their lives, without meaning the parents were ineffective child trainers.

A well-ordered household usually reflects maturity in the parents. But a "black sheep" in a family does not always mean a Christian father will not make a good spiritual leader in the church. However, if a wayward son or daughter hurts the reputation of the father in a particular community, it would be wise for that father not to maintain a prominent position in the church.

No family is perfect. And in every family periods of stress may result in periodic straying from "the straight and narrow." The important thing is that in the eyes of others there is steady, overall progress toward spiritual maturity.

What about it? If you are a Christian father, are you moving in that direction? Is your well-ordered family a reflection of your spiritual maturity?

AN OVERBEARING PERSONALITY

"Since an overseer is entrusted with God's work, he must . . . not [be] overbearing" (Titus 1:7). "Overbearing" people are "those who follow the corrupt desire of the sinful nature and despise authority" (2 Peter 2:10). They are "bold and arrogant"—or "self-willed" (NASB).

An "overbearing" Christian is a person who is "a law to himself." He insists on having his own way. Others are always wrong; he is always right. He is his own authority.

It is easy to see why this kind of person should not be appointed to spiritual leadership in the church. Just as this kind of man as husband and/or father causes conflict in his family and discourages his own wife and children, so he can easily do much harm to the family of God. All it takes is one person with this characteristic to generate disunity in the body of Jesus Christ. "Shepherds of God's flock" are not to be "lording it over those entrusted to" them (1 Peter 5:3).

Every believer should evaluate his life in light of this biblical standard. Ask yourself, am I overbearing? That is, do I allow my old nature to take control in my relationships with others? For example, do I insist on having the last word in every discussion? Do I find it difficult to agree with others? Do I force my opinions on other people? Affirmative answers to these questions are evidences of an overbearing attitude.

A challenge: If this is evident in your life, begin to put into practice this instruction—"Do nothing out of selfish ambition or vain conceit, but in humility consider others better than yourselves. Each of you should look not only to your own interests, but also to the interests of others" (Phil. 2:3-4).

FLYING OFF THE HANDLE

Elders must not be "quick-tempered" (Titus 1:7). A "quick-tempered" person is one who readily "flies off the handle" or "loses his cool." He does not deal with the ordinary functions and frustrations of life with emotional stability. Losing control, he "strikes out" at others, if not physically, at least verbally.

A quick-tempered Christian can be devastating to the cause of Christ. He is a bad example and model, and he hurts others and stunts their spiritual growth.

Paul wrote, " 'In your anger do not sin': Do not let the sun go down while you are still angry" (Eph. 4:26). In other words Christians should deal with their anger. It should be kept under control. But a quick-tempered person is "out of control." In fact, getting angry, losing your temper is downright foolish. "A quick-tempered man does foolish things" (Prov. 14:17). "A quick-tempered man displays folly" (v. 29).

To determine if you are needing help in this area, ask yourself these questions: Am I quick-tempered? That is, do I easily lose control of my temper? Do I speak before I think? Do I find it difficult to be objective about a situation when I am the object of criticism? Do I hurt people easily? Do people hesitate to ask me about sensitive issues?

If you answer yes to any of these: Ask God to help you overcome this problem. Also commit these verses to memory: "But the wisdom that comes from heaven is first of all pure; then peace-loving, considerate, submissive, full of mercy and good fruit, impartial, and sincere. Peacemakers who sow in peace raise a harvest of righteousness" (James 3:17-18).

ARE YOU ADDICTED?

Paul also wrote that elders must "not [be] given to drunkenness," and must not be "violent" (Titus 1:7). New Testament Christians were often tempted to revert to their former way of life in the matter of drinking. Because wine was a common beverage with meals, they were easily tempted to overindulge.

A mature Christian should not allow himself to be dominated or controlled by anything that will harm his body, cloud his thinking, or hinder his testimony for Jesus Christ. As Paul wrote, "So whether you eat or drink or whatever you do, do it all for the glory of God" (1 Cor. 10:31).

To be "violent" means to be a "striker," that is, one who physically strikes out at another person. Note the progression in Paul's list of negative characteristics—a person who is overbearing may become quick-tempered. A quick-tempered person may lose control when he is under the influence of alcohol, and as a result he may become violent.

Yet a "verbally" pugnacious person is certainly as destructive as a person who becomes physically violent. To inflict psychological pain can be even more devastating than inflicting physical pain. Verbal abuse can leave scars in others' lives that are not easily erased.

Questions for you: Are you addicted to anything that affects your psychological and physical well-being? What about food? What about drink? What about other habits?

Are you a pugnacious type of person? Do you strike out at others physically or verbally? Do you ever resort to subtle ways of hurting people, even though it may appear to be a "gentle" approach? For example, do you gossip about people under the guise of personal concern? Ask the Lord to help you avoid these problems of addictions and violence—to have "gentleness and self-control" (Gal. 5:23).

MONEY-MAD

The world seems to be "money-mad." Everyone wants more money. Even millionaires say they never have enough. Some people seem to be able to make money more easily than others. But the important thing is not *how much* you make, but *how* you make it. If you gain money by dishonest means, you disqualify yourself from being an elder.

False teachers or leaders in Crete had impure motives regarding material things. Besides "teaching things they ought not to teach," they were doing it "for the sake of dishonest gain" (Titus 1:11). To counter this problem, Paul directed Titus to appoint spiritual leaders who would *not* be "pursuing dishonest gain" (v. 7).

Money in itself is not evil. Neither is it wrong for spiritual leaders to accept money for their work. In fact, Jesus Christ Himself made it clear that "the worker deserves his wages" (Luke 10:7). And Paul specifically taught that "the elders who direct the affairs of the church well are worthy of double honor" (1 Tim. 5:17). That is, elders or pastors who spend much of their time in the ministry, especially in teaching and preaching are to be remunerated for their work. "Those who preach the Gospel should receive their living from the Gospel" (1 Cor. 9:14).

What then causes a spiritual leader to have a bad reputation? If we are overbearing, quick-tempered, given to much wine, and violent, and if we pursue money dishonestly in clever, underhanded ways, we bring reproach on the name of Christ. When we are entrusted with God's work, we should be free from these problems. But even if we are not spiritual leaders, all Christians need to be sure these characteristics are not part of their lives.

Think about—and act on—these verses: "If you owe taxes, pay taxes; if revenue, then revenue; if respect, then respect; if honor, then honor. Let no debt remain outstanding, except the continuing debt to love one another, for he who loves his fellow man has fulfilled the law" (Rom. 13:7-8). Don't be a "lover of money" (1 Tim. 3:3).

LOVING WHAT IS GOOD

Evil. Wicked. Bad. Sinful. These words easily describe our culture. Many people seem bent on being as bad as they can. They "love" to sin. Men love darkness, Jesus said, because what they do is "evil" (John 3:19). By contrast, Christians—and especially church elders—are to love "what is good" (Titus 1:8). This means pursuing good rather than evil. In fact, Paul wrote that a mature Christian is to "overcome evil with good" (Rom. 12:21). And again Paul said, "we are God's workmanship, created in Christ Jesus to do good works" (Eph. 2:10). This is to be the "normal" Christian life, and our efforts in doing good are to be directed "to all people," not just to fellow Christians (Gal. 6:10). One way to show our love for what is good is to "be hospitable" (Titus 1:7), another qualification for elders.

An elder's primary ministry is to shepherd, teach, and manage the flock of God. But, as with all believers, he is to have a ministry to all people, attempting to lead "them to a knowledge of the truth . . . that they will come to their senses and escape from the trap of the devil" (2 Tim. 2:25-26). One of the best ways to achieve this goal is to love "what is good." This is one reason Paul emphasized the fact that an elder "must also have a good reputation with outsiders" (1 Tim. 3:7).

Do you? All Christians need to have a "good reputation" with unbelievers. We need to ask ourselves, what is my reputation with those who don't know Christ? Do they respect me? Or do they question the things I do? Do they question my attitudes and the things I talk about? Do I love what is good? Could I write "good" over what I read, what I see, what I listen to, what I say, what I do?

"Finally, brothers, whatever is true, whatever is noble, whatever is right, whatever is pure, whatever is lovely, whatever is admirable—if anything is excellent or praiseworthy—think about such things" (Phil. 4:8). Love what is good!

UNDER CONTROL

Elders must be "self-controlled ... and disciplined" (Titus 1:8). "Self-control" is an important mark of maturity in a Christian's life and one Paul was uniquely concerned about, especially in his letter to Titus. In fact, he used this word five times to emphasize the significance of this quality in the lives of *all* Christians (1:8; 2:2, 5-6, 12).

What is self-control? It means being in control of yourself physically, psychologically, and spiritually. English translations convey the meaning of the Greek word by the words "sensible," "sober," and "of a sound mind." Putting it another way, a self-controlled Christian is not in bondage to sinful desires, impulses, or passions.

Being "disciplined" is closely related to "self-control." Paul illustrated this quality in his first letter to the Corinthians. "Do you not know that in a race all the runners run," he asked, "but only one gets the prize?" (1 Cor. 9:24) Then he applied this athletic illustration to the Christian life: "Everyone who competes in the games goes into strict training" (v. 25). "Strict training" involves self-discipline. Anyone who wants to participate successfully in athletics must get ready both mentally and physically. He must carefully and consistently discipline himself—controlling his appetite, withdrawing from harmful activities, using his time wisely, exercising rigorously.

The Christian life is to be a disciplined life. Thus Paul wrote of himself: "Therefore I do not run like a man running aimlessly; I do not fight like a man beating the air. No, I beat my body and make it my slave" (1 Cor. 9:26-27).

True of you? Are you self-controlled and disciplined? Are you sensible, sober, and of a sound mind? Today keep yourself under control and discipline yourself—with the Lord's help and strength.

UPRIGHT AND HOLY

To be "upright" and "holy" (Titus 1:8) means to be experiencing practical holiness. Paul, Silas, and Timothy demonstrated these qualities in their lives when they served in Thessalonica. Later, when Paul wrote to that church, he said, "You are witnesses, and so is God, of how *holy, righteous,* and *blameless* we were among you who believed" (1 Thes. 2:10).

These three New Testament leaders were living models of Christianity. They wanted the new believers in Thessalonica to see the righteousness of Jesus Christ flowing through their lives. And no doubt they achieved this goal; otherwise, they could not have written about it and called on God as their witness. This is also why Paul could write to the Corinthians, "Follow my example, as I follow the example of Christ" (1 Cor. 11:1).

More than any others, these two qualities—being upright and holy—summarize the life of Christ. This is the kind of person He was, even in His humanity. This is what made Him a great and acceptable High Priest (Heb. 7:26). He demonstrated for us what it means to "live in this world" without being "a part of this world." Besides being our Saviour from sin, He also is our example for living a life not dominated by sin. Though He was perfect and we are imperfect, yet by His grace and strength we are to emulate His life (Phil. 2:5).

Remember, "put off your old self, which is being corrupted by its deceitful desires . . . be made new in the attitude of your minds; and . . . put on the new self, created to be like God in true *righteousness* and *holiness*" (Eph. 4:22-24).

Talk to God: Ask the Lord to help you be righteous or upright, to be fair and just in all your dealings with other people, not taking advantage of them. And ask Him to help you be holy, set apart from the eroding influence of sin and dedicated solely to Him.

THE TRUSTWORTHY MESSAGE

In Titus 1:9 Paul used an important word to describe the content of Christianity. He called it "trustworthy"—a word meaning "reliable, dependable, faithful." In other words we can trust what God has said; and even more significant, we can be sure God has said it.

The most important reason the message of Christianity is clear and trustworthy relates to the One who is the Essence of Christianity—Jesus Christ Himself. The trustworthy Christian message involved His birth, life, death, resurrection, and ascension. So many were the witnesses to these events that only the totally ignorant can rationally deny them.

To those who were exposed to the miraculous process that accompanied the revelation of this message, there was no question that the message was indeed trustworthy. God did not leave it to chance. He wanted the whole world to know He had indeed spoken.

Those who were teaching false doctrine in Crete were discouraging others and leading them astray. In every situation there will be people who distort God's truth. As Paul wrote in Titus 1:9, Christians are responsible to "refute those who oppose" sound doctrine. Only those who know sound doctrine and who "hold firmly" to it can carry out this responsibility.

Time for action: Therefore, it is not only what we believe about the Bible, but what we do with it. Are you holding firmly to it? Are you using it to "encourage others"? Do you know it well enough to refute those who oppose it?

Perhaps this last question is key: How well do you know the Bible? We cannot use it if we do not know it. And we cannot know it if we do not read it and study it.

BEWARE! FALSE TEACHERS

Another Gospel. That's the title of a book written by Ruth A. Tucker (Grand Rapids: Zondervan Publishing House, 1989). The book surveys the developments and analyzes the unbiblical teaching of more than two dozen cults and false religious groups. False teachers abound! And in Crete false teachers abounded. There were "many" such "rebellious people" (Titus 1:10). They had permeated the church, and something had to be done to counteract their negative influence, which had reached destructive proportions.

Paul classified them as "rebellious" or "unruly." If they were ever subtle and secret, they were so no more. They were directly opposed to true Christian principles. Paul also called them "mere talkers"; that is, individuals who talked a lot, but whose words had very little substance. Though they were communicating constantly, they were saying nothing significant compared with the "trustworthy message" (v. 9) revealed by Christ and the Holy Spirit.

Paul also said these people were "deceivers." Their motives were false and deceitful. Closely related to these traits were their works. They were "ruining whole households by teaching things they ought not to teach" (v. 11). And their motive was money; they were teaching false doctrine "for the sake of dishonest gain." Like many other Cretans, they were liars, evil, and gluttonous (v. 12). They were corrupt in their thinking (v. 15), and though they claimed to be followers of the Lord, "their actions" showed otherwise (v. 16). Two thoughts stem from these verses.

Two thoughts to keep in mind: First, it is important that mature Christian leaders have the same qualifications outlined for elders in 1 Timothy 3 and Titus 1. If they don't, immature leaders will arise and create problems, and will do the church more harm than good. Second, if you are a new believer, it is important that you become grounded in sound doctrine as soon as possible. If you aren't, false teachers may lead you astray.

REFLECTING SOUND DOCTRINE

"Teach . . . what is in accord with sound doctrine" (Titus 2:1). Paul's approach in this letter brings into focus a serious error prevalent in some Christian circles today. Some believe and teach that emphasizing "sound doctrine" will *automatically* result in godly living. But if this were true, Paul would not have spent most of this letter spelling out what should *accompany* sound doctrine — what that lifestyle should be for Christian leaders and all members of Christ's body.

Knowing the Bible without "living the Bible" simply produces more people who know the Bible but don't live it. And when this happens, the basic message of Christianity, though accurate doctrinally, soon becomes purely academic and is eventually nullified.

People need to listen to people who not only *know* what they believe but are also *living* what they believe. Paul instructed Titus to be sure to exemplify in his own life what he was teaching and to be sure to exemplify the message even by the way he taught it. This again points out why Paul throughout this letter emphasized "lifestyle" more than pure doctrine as a means of helping people mature spiritually. What people need today more than anything else is to see and experience the Word of God "fleshed out" as each member of the body of Christ functions and as the church builds itself up in love (Eph. 4:16).

What about your life? How much of the Word of God is being "fleshed out" in the way you live? How much are you contributing to building up the body of Christ in love? How much are you "living the Bible"?

A PROFILE FOR OLDER MEN

"Teach the older men to be temperate, worthy of respect, self-controlled, and sound in faith, in love and in endurance" (Titus 2:2).

Being "temperate" means having a proper perspective on life, a perspective that in turn affects our mental and emotional stability and reactions. "Self-control" zeros in more specifically on our fleshly appetites. A Christian—in this case, an older man—is not to be in bondage to fleshly desires, impulses, and passions.

"Worthy of respect" involves living in such a way that others respect us. We can be worthy of respect only because we have earned it through imitating Christ's way of life.

To be "sound in faith" focuses on our attitude of trust in God the Father and His Son, Jesus Christ. To the extent that we have confidence in our Lord, we are "sound" (literally spiritually healthy) in the area of faith. If we are in a constant state of doubt and unbelief, we are certainly not "sound in faith."

Being "sound in love" is the hallmark of Christian maturity. When referring to faith, hope, and love, Paul clearly stated that the greatest of these is love (1 Cor. 13:13). To be sound in love, then, means to live like Christ, for love characterized His life. Being "sound in endurance," means persevering in the face of difficulties.

Take note: Unfortunately, getting older is no guarantee we will stabilize in our Christian lives. Our emotional state sometimes overshadows our spiritual condition. Competition often threatens an older man more than it does a younger man. And in some instances, boredom also sets in because of too much leisure time. If you are an older Christian man, evaluate your life in the light of these six marks of spiritual maturity. Ask the Lord to help you become godly as you become older.

A PROFILE FOR OLDER WOMEN

"Likewise, teach the older women to be reverent in the way they live, not to be slanderers or addicted to much wine, but to teach what is good" (Titus 2:3). Women who claim to follow Christ should exemplify His lifestyle. This kind of consistent living is of course to characterize all Christians, whether men or women. This is why Paul began this verse directed to women with the transitional word "likewise," which refers back to what he has just said to older men. It is as if he was going to say to "older women" the same thing that he had just said to "older men." In essence this is what he did, while adding some pointers especially for women.

Paul focused in on two overarching positive qualities. First, older Christian women are to be "reverent in the way they live," and second, they are to "teach what is good." Godly living forms the basis for effective verbal teaching. A life lived in accord with sound doctrine enables Christian women to communicate effectively with younger women on how to walk in the will of God, to teach younger women "what is good."

How to use the tongue appropriately is a recurring problem for all humans. Though it is certainly an area of weakness for both men and women, Paul specifically said women were "not to be slanderers." Before sharing information about anyone, ask yourself, Will this build the person up? Is it a kind thing to say? Have I ever felt envy toward this person? If so, are my motives pure?

Questions to reflect on: To what extent are you leading a consistent Christian life? Are you "worthy of respect"? What do younger women see when they observe how you live? What do they see when they observe your attitude toward your husband, your children, your neighbors, and your enemies?

A PROFILE FOR YOUNGER WOMEN

One of the first things Christian young married women were to learn was to "love their husbands" (Titus 2:4). Why was it necessary for Paul to write this? Wouldn't young wives naturally do this? First, many of these women may have been married to men they really were not attracted to. Perhaps in Crete, as in some cultures today, marriages were arranged by parents, regardless of romantic feelings.

Second, many women in the first century were used as marital conveniences to produce offspring. In these circumstances women usually had no sense of commitment, security, or fondness.

Young mothers are also "to love their children" (v. 4). Bearing children as a result of "dutiful performance" doesn't set a good stage for a love relationship between mother and children. Every mother—particularly every young mother—at times experiences feelings of resentment toward her children. These feelings are normal. However, constant and persistent resentment indicates a serious problem that needs to be resolved.

Two lessons emerge from the study of biblical love. First, actions are to take precedence over feelings. Positive feelings often emerge in the process of doing what we know we must do. Second, feelings of affection can be learned. Paul implied this in Titus 2:4. And in most instances, affection is learned through example such as seeing it demonstrated in older women who model this kind of relationship with their husbands.

Questions: As a married woman and/or mother, to what extent are you loving your husband and/or your children at the "action" level? To what extent are you attempting to learn to love more deeply at the "feeling" level? Some people do not learn to love at the feeling level because thy have not dealt with feelings of anger and bitterness. Is this true of you? Loving your husband and your children will give you greater happiness. It will also help keep people from maligning the Word of God (v. 5) as they see your consistent walk with the Lord.

A PROFILE FOR YOUNGER MEN

Paul also instructed Titus to give specific directions to young men regarding their lifestyle (Titus 2:6-8). But he prefaced those instructions by exhorting Titus to "set them an example." Why did Paul add this? Probably because he knew the young men in Crete would be more critical of Titus since he was one of their peers. Titus would need to take unusual precautions to be sure that what he taught was exemplified in his own conduct.

In Titus' teaching he was to "show integrity, seriousness, and soundness of speech" (Titus 2:8). The Greek word rendered "integrity" means to be "uncorrupt." Though it is difficult to know how this differs from "seriousness and soundness of speech," I personally believe Paul was encouraging Titus to be sure he "practiced what he preached." Titus was not to teach young men one thing and live something else. If he did, he certainly would not win a hearing.

If you are a young man, take a lesson from Titus: Work hard at becoming mature. This kind of lifestyle is not automatic. It takes effort. It means eliminating bad habits and establishing good ones. It means being open to correction. It involves having a teachable spirit. Become a serious student of the Scriptures, learning God's Word and what His will is for your life. Also become a functioning part of the body of Christ, learning to relate to others in unselfish ways, "doing," as Paul wrote Titus, "what is good" (v. 8).

Remember what Paul wrote to another young man, Timothy: "Don't let anyone look down on you because you are young, but set an example for the believers in speech, in life, in love, in faith, and in purity" (1 Tim. 4:12).

A PROFILE FOR SLAVES

Human slavery is a horrible thing. Slavery in America in the pre-Civil War days is a blight on American history. Paul never revolted against slavery, though the Bible implies that it is wrong. But Paul did tell Christian slaves how to live. Apparently, in Crete they were less submissive than they should have been. Perhaps they saw their new freedom in Christ as a rationale for disobeying their non-Christian masters.

Of course, when Paul encouraged "slaves to be subject to their masters in everything" (Titus 2:9), he was assuming that when obedience to man conflicts with obedience to God, we owe our allegiance to God, no matter what the cost (Acts 5:29).

Why should Christian slaves submit to non-Christian masters? "So that in every way they [the slaves] will make the teaching about God our Saviour attractive" (v. 10).

To "make . . . attractive" renders the Greek word *kosmeō*, translated "adorn" in some Bible versions. We derive the English word *cosmetics* from *kosmeō*, which was also used in New Testament days to describe arranging jewels in the best way so as to show their full beauty. Slaves, then, were to live in such a way as to make the Gospel attractive. Their conduct was to be like "cosmetics" to the Gospel. From these verses, we can identify principles for employer-employee relationships today.

Ask yourself: At work do I do what is expected of me or am I shirking my responsibilities? Am I consistently on time for work? Do I overextend my coffee breaks? Do I complete assignments as told? Am I loyal to the company? Do I listen carefully when I'm told what to do? Most important, how much does my life make the Word of God attractive to others?

GOD'S GRACE

In Titus 2:11 Paul wrote of "the grace of God that brings salvation." What is grace? It is God's unmerited favor toward mankind, especially toward those who respond to His infinite love through Jesus Christ.

Paul added that this grace "has appeared to all men." But how has it been revealed? The answer: Jesus Christ "gave Himself for us" (v. 14). God's grace was certainly obvious in the Old Testament—when He chose Abraham, when He chose the nation Israel to be His own special people, and when He continued to love them and bless them in spite of their disobedience. This indeed was God's grace. But it reached its fullest manifestation when Christ came into the world and died on the cross.

Christ is the perfect embodiment of God's grace. The sinless Son of God became the perfect sacrifice for sin. His life, His death, His resurrection, and His ascension all reveal God's grace.

That grace continues to be evident to us today through the Bible. Just as Christ taught men who He was and why He came, so the Bible, God's Word, continues to reveal God's favor to all people.

Isn't it true? Understanding God's grace should make an indelible impression on every believer. Can we do less than to respond obediently to God's grace when we understand that grace? His grace should give us a desire to please God, to conform our lives to His will, to "say 'No' to ungodliness and worldly passions, and to live self-controlled, upright, and godly lives" (v. 12). We ought to be all the more eager to reject ungodly living in view of the approaching return ("the glorious appearing," v. 13) of Jesus "who gave Himself for us" (v. 16) to purchase us from a life of "wickedness" and to make us His very own (v. 14). Are you living in the light of these glorious truths?

AUTHORITATIVE OR AUTHORITARIAN?

Before discussing another aspect of Christian living, Paul summarized his exhortations to Titus. By his words, "Do not let anyone despise you" (Titus 2:15), Paul ended this section as he began in verse 1. However, he added that Titus should communicate these spiritual concepts with confidence: "Encourage and rebuke with all authority."

Paul had spelled out for Titus what the apostle had learned by direct revelation from God about Christian living. And he wanted Titus to teach these truths to others with the same degree of authority—as if he too had received them directly from God. Adhering to God's trustworthy message (1:9), Titus need not be intimidated nor have his confidence undermined. He had no reason to be "ashamed of the Gospel" (Rom. 1:16).

We too have an authoritative message—the Bible—to communicate to others. We need not apologize nor be ashamed of it. Though not everyone will receive it, we must not be intimidated. When we are speaking God's truth and some reject it, they are rejecting God, not us.

Consider: We are to be authoritative without being authoritarian. We are to know what we believe, communicating it without reflecting a "know-it-all" attitude.

We must be sure when we "encourage and rebuke with all authority" that we are speaking the truth. And as we grow in knowing the Scriptures, God can use us to be "speaking the truth in love" (Eph. 4:15) so that no one will "despise" us (Titus 2:15) nor the Lord.

RELATIONSHIPS TO GOVERNMENT

How are Christians to relate to the government? What should be their attitude, especially if the leaders are opposed to Christianity? The New Testament addresses this problem (Rom. 13:1-7; Titus 3:1-2; 1 Peter 2:13-17).

Before the Cretan Christians were saved, they probably rebelled against the governmental "rulers and authorities" (Titus 3:1). As "liars, evil brutes," and "lazy gluttons" (1:12), they would have had poor attitudes toward authority figures. And how a person lived before salvation sometimes carries over into his conduct as a believer.

Paul said Christians are "to be subject" to government officials, "to be obedient," and "to be ready to do whatever is good" (cf. loving "what is good," 1:8; teaching "what is good," 2:3; being "eager to do what is good," 2:14; and "doing what is good," 3:8, 14). Submission involves accepting advice and counsel and, if necessary, yielding to another person's admonitions and commands. It is difficult to differentiate between submission and obedience. Certainly the two words together reinforce the importance of doing what is expected of a good citizen.

However, Paul added balance to these instructions when he told Titus to remind the believers "to be ready to do whatever is good." He implied that at times all Christians, like the apostles in Jerusalem, "must obey God rather than men" (Acts 5:29). We are to do "good," not "evil." However, if Christians readily do what is good, their conduct will quickly reduce or perhaps eliminate the times government leaders will ask them to do what is "not good" (see 1 Peter 3:13; Rom. 13:1-5).

For you: Every Christian, then, must examine his or her attitude toward governing authorities, whether those officials are Christians or not.

A GOOD REPUTATION

In Titus 3:2, Paul turned his attention to the behavior Cretan Christians should exhibit toward all non-Christians. He outlined four qualities of life.

First, they were to "slander no one." That is, they were not to use abusive language and speak reproachfully of non-Christians, no matter what the occasion. Second, they were to "be peaceable." The Cretan believers were not to stir up trouble in the non-Christian community. Rather, they were to do everything they could to create peace without violating their Christian convictions.

Third, they were to "be considerate." This refers to demonstrating a spirit of "gentleness" toward believers. Fourth, they were to "show true humility." They were not to treat non-Christians with an attitude of superiority, pride, or arrogance.

These four qualities help make it possible for Christians to "have a good reputation with outsiders" (1 Tim. 3:7). Even those who despise us and accuse us of doing wrong may see our good deeds and eventually "glorify God" (1 Peter 2:12; cf. Matt. 5:16).

Your answers? Do you ever slander non-Christians? How do you treat non-Christians in the office where you work? What do you say behind their backs? It is at times necessary to "speak out" on issues of right or wrong, but it is possible to do so without slandering another person. True, maintaining Christian standards may cause difficulty and misunderstanding, but we can help prevent that by avoiding anger, resentment, and insensitive actions and attitudes.

THE PAST

How would you describe unsaved people? Paul wrote that before salvation, he, Titus, and Christians in Crete were "foolish, disobedient, deceived and enslaved by all kinds of passions and pleasures" and living "in malice and envy, being hated and hating one another" (Titus 3:3).

A bleak picture. But true. Non-Christians have no spiritual understanding, no enlightenment of heart and mind by the Holy Spirit. Therefore because believers were once in this condition, reasoned Paul, they, of all people, should understand non-Christians and be sensitive to them.

Unbelievers, Paul said, are disobedient; that is, they violate God's will. Everyone except for the Lord Jesus Christ is guilty of disobeying God.

Many of us may not be guilty of the pagan lifestyle described by Paul—being foolish, deceived, giving in to passions, and being guilty of malice, envy, and hatred (vv. 3-4). But it is only God's kindness, love, and mercy (v. 5) that keeps us from "stepping over the edge" and experiencing the depths of sin into which many have fallen.

A reminder: We are all sinners, no matter what our past. We have all fallen short of God's standard (Rom. 3:23) in some area of our lives. And it took Christ's death on the cross and His shed blood to save *us* too. Only by His grace are we "justified" and made "heirs ... of eternal life" (Titus 3:7). This in itself should cause us to respond with compassion toward those who do not know Christ as their personal Saviour. Are you gracious and sensitive toward unbelievers at work, in your neighborhood, perhaps even in your family? They too need God's grace.

STRESS WHAT IS PROFITABLE

"You can trust his word! If he says it, he'll do it!" That's what we like to hear about people. We want others to be reliable, trustworthy.

That is also true of God's Word. When Paul wrote, "This is a trustworthy saying" (Titus 3:8), he was referring to God's revealed Word—a message that could be trusted and relied on because of its divine source.

Earlier, Paul had instructed Titus to be sure those who were chosen as elders in Crete were men who held "firmly to the trustworthy message" (1:9). Then Paul, writing to Titus about this "trustworthy saying," said, "I want you to stress these things" (3:8). Here Paul probably had in mind everything he had written in this letter—the truth regarding his own calling as an apostle, qualifications for spiritual leaders, how to handle false teachers, godly characteristics for all Christians, and the theological basis for their Christian walk. By stressing these things, Titus would help believers "devote themselves to doing what is good." Such things, Paul said, are "profitable for everyone."

A challenge: To what extent do you stress those things that are profitable, both in your own life and for others? A more basic question is this: To what extent do you accept the Bible as authoritative in your life? To what extent have you both received it and committed your life to it?

Some Christians believe the Bible is God's Word, but they have not brought their lives under its complete authority. They acknowledge its trustworthiness, but they have not responded with "full acceptance." What about you?

PROFITABLE OR UNPROFITABLE?

To make sure that Titus clearly understood his task, Paul also spelled out those things he was to avoid and *not* to stress. Many false teachers were emphasizing these very things. Many of the false teachers were evidently Gentiles who had mixed certain aspects of Judaism with elements from their pagan religions and had produced a syncretistic message that was appealing but dangerous. And in some subtle way it caused people to pay money in order to get involved (1:11).

We do not know specifically what the false teachers then were teaching. There may have been variations in their doctrines. This can also be said about false teachers and their messages today.

Titus was to avoid these "foolish controversies and genealogies" because false doctrine always leads to "arguments and quarrels" (3:9). On the other hand, God's truth spoken in love leads to doctrinal stability, unity in the faith, and Christian love (Eph. 4:11-16). Put another way, God's Word is "excellent and profitable" (Titus 3:8); but false doctrine is always "unprofitable and useless" (v. 9).

What's your thought? To what extent do you avoid what is "unprofitable"? Some Christians dwell on peripheral issues and secondary matters in the Christian faith. They get emotional satisfaction from creating controversy. Rather than making "every effort to keep the unity of the Spirit through the bond of peace" (Eph. 4:3), they do what they can to create divisions and disunity. Paul classified this kind of behavior among Christians as "worldly" (1 Cor. 3:1-3). Are you involved in what is profitable or what is unprofitable?

DEALING WITH DIVISIVE PEOPLE

The false teachers in Crete were corrupt in "both their minds and consciences" (Titus 1:15). And they were "divisive" (3:10). Such persons must therefore be stopped, Paul said. If they were not, many more immature Christians would be led astray.

How do you deal with such a person? Paul said he must be warned, not only once but at least twice. And then if he does not respond, we must break fellowship with him. We are to "have nothing to do with him." We are not to allow ourselves to get involved in his unprofitable activities.

Some divisive people, however, will not respond to gentle warnings; they will continue in their ways. And if such a person does that, we "may be sure that such a man is warped and sinful; he is self-condemned" (v. 11). He has brought judgment on himself and must be silenced. In such cases Paul himself did not hesitate to deal with the problem firmly.

Elders and pastors are not the only ones to deal with these problems. All Christians are responsible to teach and counsel others (Col. 1:28; 3:16). However, a Christian must not try to take "a speck of sawdust" out of his brother's eye when he has a "plank" in his own eye. Jesus said one who tries to do that is a hypocrite (Matt. 7:3-5). However, spiritual problems in our own lives do not give us an "escape route" for avoiding our responsibility for others.

A reminder: As members of the body of Christ we are to care for others, helping them walk in the will of God, so that they do not "live unproductive lives" (Titus 3:14).

PAUL'S FINAL GREETING

Paul ended his letter to Titus with three succinct, personal statements (3:15). First, "Everyone with me sends you greetings." We can only speculate about who was with Paul. Titus no doubt knew and could relate this information to the Cretan Christians. Otherwise, Paul would have probably mentioned specifically who these people were.

Second, "Greet those who love us in the faith." Some translate this, "Greet those who love us as Christians." Rather than referring to the Christian faith, Paul may have been referring to those who loved him and his co-workers "faithfully." In other words, Paul wanted to be remembered in a special way to those who were spiritually and emotionally involved with him in the ministry.

Third, "Grace be with you all." Here Paul included all the Christians at Crete. This final greeting was a common one for Paul. It was also a common greeting in the Gentile world, even among non-Christians. But every Cretan Christian knew Paul's final words represented more than social protocol. Grace to Paul was a constant reminder of every Christian's position in Christ (cf. 2:11; 3:7) and of the fact that they were brothers and sisters in the family of God. God's grace—not anything they had done—gave them this position with God and with each other.

And so it is with us today! We can be grateful for the grace of God, His grace "that brings salvation" (2:11) and that teaches us "to live self-controlled, upright, and godly lives" (2:11), "while we wait for . . . the glorious appearing of our great God and Saviour, Jesus Christ, who gave Himself for us" (2:13-14).

November

Devotional readings in the Epistle of James
by J. Ronald Blue

READ THE INSTRUCTIONS

It seemed simple enough. In fact, splashed across the cardboard container was the reassuring statement, "Some assembly required. Wrench provided." I was sure that I could have this gleaming new swing set in place in our backyard and ready for use in a matter of minutes.

Four hours later I sat defeated in the middle of twisted metal bars, mismatched parts, and a bent useless wrench. The problem? I had failed to read the little paper titled, "Assembly Instructions." When all else fails, read the instructions!

A layman's "logic" is not always sufficient for the complex task of swing-set assembly. In like manner, human ingenuity falls short in putting the pieces of life together. We live in a world of broken relationships and twisted morals. There are a thousand man-made suggestions of how to put it all together. Detailed instructions are needed from the manufacturer. "How shall we then live?" is a question to be answered not by some novice handymen but by the Divine Designer. We need His enlightenment.

The little Epistle of James provides the help we need to put faith into action in everyday life. Writing to first-century Christians who had been dispersed into a corrupt and confused world, James offers clear, practical instructions on every aspect of life.

James deals with what we are, what we feel, what we say, what we do, and what we have. Here is a handbook that offers heavenly solutions for successful living in a messed-up world.

You will be blessed from God's instructions that can revolutionize your character, convictions, communication, conduct, and contribution to society around you. In five short chapters the Epistle of James will teach you to be what God wants you to be, to feel what He wants you to feel, to speak as He desires you to speak, to act in a way He would have you act, and to give as He would have you give. In short, this brief letter tells Christians how to live.

Remember: When all else fails, read the instructions.

"HE'S MY BROTHER"

The little boy in tattered clothing was trudging through the snow. He bore the weight of a companion on his back. The caption under the drawing was touching: "He's not heavy; he's my brother."

Family ties provide a mystical glue that binds people together. I have one brother. Even though he is four years older than I and lives about a thousand miles away, we are still close companions. After all, he is my brother.

You would think that James would open his letter by identifying his unique family relationship to the Lord Jesus Christ. James was the half-brother of Christ. He was one of the children born to Joseph and Mary after Jesus' virgin birth (Matt. 13:55).

James mentioned his half-brother, but he did not boast of his family relationship. Instead, he identified himself as a "bond-servant" of Christ (James 1:1). James subjected himself to the authority of the One he knew to be God in the flesh. Literally, James said he was a "slave" of Christ. Jesus is not simply a brother. Christ was James' Owner, his Master.

In like manner, Christ is our Owner. He is our Master. He bought us; He redeemed us. He merits our worship; He deserves our obedience.

For you: As you engage in your activities today, think of the One who bought you, who died for you so that you could enjoy the fullness of life in Him. Recognize His leadership. Yield to Him as your Lord and Master. As you serve Him, He will bless you. He will lift you up when you fall. He will carry you through every trial. Can you hear Him say, "You are not heavy; you are My child"?

ARE YOU READY FOR THE TEST?

There is something fearful about an exam, especially when it is unannounced. Students seem to panic when the professor announces, "Close your books and take out a sheet of blank paper." At that moment students' faces turn white and minds turn blank. Who is ever ready for a test?

How can learning be measured without some kind of test? I give tests to my students at Dallas Seminary. I don't give tests to see if the students will pass out. I give tests to see if they can pass.

In like manner, God tests His children. He wants to measure our progress. He wants to see if we can pass. The Lord is especially adept at giving unannounced quizzes. When we least expect to be examined, He puts a test in our path.

What should be our reaction to God's tests? James wrote, "Consider it all joy, my brethren, when you encounter various trials" (1:2). James did not say "if" you encounter trials. Tests will come whether we are ready for them or not.

How can a person accept trials with joy? James tells how. Focus on the value of the test. It will produce endurance and ultimately will develop Christian maturity (vv. 3-4). Trials are tests and tests serve a vital purpose. Through tests God's child is able to measure spiritual progress. Instead of fearing the tests, and complaining about them, the believer should rejoice that by God's power and His grace, victory can be achieved.

Take note: You may be in the midst of taking one of God's exams right now. Rather than be demoralized by the trial, focus on the outcome that can be yours to enjoy. The Lord wants you to pass His test. In fact, He is ready to help you pass. He can lift you above the circumstances of your trial, give you the endurance you need, and then reward you with the glowing grade of "mature and complete" (v. 4). With the Lord you are ready for every test.

MAY I HELP YOU?

The most successful retail merchants have learned that a key to effective sales is a friendly clerk who is ready to serve every customer. A cheerful and sincere, "May I help you?" can mean the difference between a financial boom or bankruptcy.

In the frustrations and complexities of life, Christians are in great need of someone to come alongside and say, "May I help you?" We are especially vulnerable when faced with the strain of trials. It is not easy, and at times humanly impossible, to find the way through the maze that entraps us.

James has the answer for the believer caught in a seemingly impossible trial. The same One who has permitted the test stands ready to give assistance in finding an answer to the test. "But if any of you lacks wisdom, let him ask God" (1:5). When human wisdom is wanting, divine wisdom is available.

It is encouraging to note that the request for wisdom from God is always granted. God "gives generously to all." Verse 5 says, "it will be given to him." James warned, however, that the believer must ask with confidence. The doubter who is driven about like "the surf of the sea" cannot expect God to answer his request (vv. 6-7).

Why not now? Take advantage of God's offer of assistance. In the midst of life's confusing choices and especially in the time of trial, ask for God's wisdom. He promises to provide help. He who made you now asks, "May I help you?" You can be sure He will help you if you ask Him. Ask right now in faith, in no way doubting. He has made the promise. You can count on Him.

MARATHON ENDURANCE

I have always admired distance runners. Those who run the marathon and finish the race are all winners as far as I am concerned. Their endurance is incredible to me. Somehow they keep their legs moving when everything in their body says "Quit!" Even those who win no trophy receive my utmost admiration and praise.

The Christian life is a marathon. The sprinters may look good for awhile but they may not even finish the race. We need to develop the stamina and discipline of a distance runner. The present circumstances must be viewed in the light of eternal consequence.

James encouraged believers to recognize the transitory nature of social and economic position in the race of life. Those who are of "humble circumstances" need to rejoice in their high spiritual position (1:9). The rich man must glory in "his low position" before God (v. 10). At best, life is but a blade of grass that withers in the autumn years and dies. The temporary pursuits that seem so important will fade away (v. 11). It is not status or wealth that counts ultimately. It is the believer's eternal position in the Lord that is essential. Only in Him can anyone cross the finish line.

Getting back to the theme of trials and testing, James gives marathon advice. "Blessed is a man who perseveres under trial" (v. 12). Nothing helps more in the midst of trial than to keep thinking of the goal. Distance runners know how to drive their energy toward the finish line.

Right now: Thank the Lord for the security you have found in Him. No matter what your present situation may be, the goal is always in view. Persist. Keep on. You will be approved. You will receive the crown of life "promised to those who love Him" (v. 12). Show to the world and to yourself marathon endurance. Be a winner in Christ.

DON'T BE DECEIVED

I thought I had a good excuse. I had not taken any of the mulberries from the tree. My childhood friend Roger was the one who had picked them and offered them to me. I knew the tree was off limits, but once the mulberries had been picked it seemed only natural to eat them. So I blamed Roger.

From the Garden of Eden into the twenty-first century the human race continues to pass the blame for its sin. It seems reasonable. If God would like to have us live uprightly, why does He allow us to be tempted? Certainly we cannot be blamed.

James didn't mumble about this well-used game. "When tempted, no one should say, 'God is tempting me.' God cannot be tempted, nor does He tempt anyone" (1:13). Temptation is not from God nor does it originate out there in the world. The source is within. Each person is "tempted . . . by his own desire" (v. 14). Lust then gives birth to sin and sin brings forth death (v. 15). The unmentioned father of this sordid offspring is Satan. But we dare not blame him either. We are the ones who foster the inner desire that leads us to a sinful decision that is ultimately so destructive.

"Don't be deceived, my dear brothers," James warned (v. 16). We must not let external trials push us down nor dare we let internal temptations pull us down. The place to win over sin is in the heart and mind.

Begin today to conquer sin: Apply James' key lesson. Don't let lust lodge in your life. Pull the weeds of evil desire from your soul so that the good things of the Lord may fill your mind and heart. Don't be deceived. Temptation is not the culprit. Attack the problem of sin at the very root, inside you.

THE FATHER OF LIGHTS

It was absolutely breathtaking. As the Word of Life Collegians concluded the Passion Play in an open-air concert, the Northern Lights suddenly burst into action across the night sky. God's fireworks provided a heaven-sent finale that seemed like a prelude to the rapture.

Turning from the grotesque scene of Satan's offspring born in the mire of lust, sin, and death, James fixed his view upward to the glories of God's rich gifts. "Every good and . . . perfect gift is from above, coming down from the Father of the heavenly lights" (1:17). Evil lurks in dark corners. Righteousness shines forth in brilliance.

In God there is no changing "like shifting shadows" (v. 17). God does not change. He is eternally holy and pure. His light neither flickers nor is His glory ever eclipsed. In the midst of trials or temptation it is important to fix our gaze on Him.

James gave an important reminder of God's amazing grace: "In the exercise of His will He brought us forth by the word of truth, so that we might be, as it were, the firstfruits among His creatures" (v. 18, NASB). It is beyond human understanding that we should be counted as His children. By His will and through His Word, we are the living evidence of His work of grace.

Question: Do you sense the value of your life? You are one of the "firstfruits." It is important that you pass the tests of adversity and resist the temptations of iniquity. Bask in the light of God's glory. Reflect the light of His grace. Focus on the "good things" and the "perfect gifts" that come down to us from the Father of heavenly lights.

TWO EARS AND ONE MOUTH

It is a significant observation in human anatomy. Two ears and one mouth may be a clue to God's design for people to listen twice as much as they speak.

James had considerably more to say about the tongue later in his practical epistle, but he attacked the problem early with sound advice. "Everyone should be quick to hear, slow to speak, and slow to become angry" (1:19). There is a pressing need for listeners in the world. Most people are quick to speak and slow to listen. People seldom listen when emotions rise. Outbursts of anger engage the tongue and only serve to burn the ears of others.

In a plea to his "dear brothers" James issued a stern warning: "Man's anger does not bring about the righteous life that God desires" (v. 20). A mouth that is driven by anger is a violation of God's righteous design. It is controlled by pride and passion and is therefore at enmity with God.

By contrast, the believer should lay aside "moral filth" and "evil" of a flesh-driven passion. God's child is to "humbly accept the Word planted" in him (v. 21). By giving an ear to God's voice in Scripture, both normal conversation and outbursts of anger can be brought under control. God's Word "can save you" (v. 21). It saves unbelievers from the penalty of sin, and it also has the power to save a believer from the practice of sin.

For you: Take advantage of every opportunity to listen today. Ask God to use His Word in your life to control your tongue and to restrain your emotions. Give your ears a day of special honor. Let your tongue have a day of rest. Put uncontrolled anger to death. Watch God use you as you humbly and lovingly focus on the concerns of others.

MIRROR, MIRROR ON THE WALL

Mirrors can be disturbingly honest. Even the mirror of the Snow White story ultimately told the wicked queen the bitter truth. She was not, after all, the fairest of them all.

At least the wicked queen was moved to action by the truth communicated by her mirror. She immediately sought to eliminate Snow White. Sadly enough, most believers see their blemishes reflected in the mirror of God's Word and do nothing to correct them.

James made his point clear: "Do not merely listen to the Word, and so deceive yourselves. Do what it says" (1:22). We should be quick to hear the Word; but even more important, we should be ready to act. Those who do not apply the truth deceive only themselves. No one else is fooled!

One who is merely a hearer of the Word is like a man who looks in a mirror, sees a problem in his grooming or his clothing, but then goes on his way without correcting it. In fact, he simply forgets about it (vv. 23-24). Obviously, he simply does not care how he looks. He hardly needs a mirror; it does nothing for him.

The believer needs to look intently into God's "perfect law" and then become an "effectual doer" of what he sees. James concluded, "He will be blessed in what he does" (v. 25). These are the believers who bridle their tongues, who care for orphans and widows, and keep clean in a corrupt world (vv. 26-27).

Careful: Don't miss the blessing of applying God's truth to your life. Use the reflection from the Word to bring restoration in your life. Let God's mirror put you in motion today as a witness and a blessing to others.

OUR HONORED GUEST

He was definitely a VIP. Colonel Jim Irwin had been to the moon! People of Segovia, Spain flocked to see him in the public appearance we had arranged in conjunction with the regional conference of evangelicals. He was our honored guest.

Notoriety is natural. But it should not become a controlling force in the church. James pleaded with the brethren, "As believers in our glorious Lord Jesus Christ, don't show favoritism" (2:1). There is only one "Superstar," the Lord Jesus Christ. All believers are dusty planets designed to reflect His light. Class distinctions and social status are not a part of His design for the church.

To pay special attention to one who wears fine clothes while relegating a poor man in dirty clothes to a place of inferiority was condemned by James (vv. 2-3). James asked, "Have you not discriminated among yourselves and become judges with evil thoughts?" (v. 4) Prejudice is a serious matter. It is a judgment call made on the basis of favoritism rather than on God's righteous standards.

James' teaching here is very convicting. Most of us are guilty of judgments made on the basis of external appearance. We give honor to some and turn our backs on others. We lack spiritual discernment.

To apply: Ask God for His help to see people not simply for what they appear to be but for what they are or can be in the Lord. Help stamp out prejudice. Make Christ the honored guest of your life. He will help you cause others to feel accepted and to sense their eternal worth before the Lord.

FROM RAGS TO RICHES

I was moved by his story. He came to the United States as a young lad with nothing but a few dollars in his pocket. Through hard work and a great deal of ingenuity, this lowly Italian immigrant became the founder and chief executive officer of Tropicana. Most of all, Anthony Rossi was a man rich in faith. His "from-rags-to-riches" story has an eternal touch.

Mr. Rossi would be the first to tell you that his greatest riches are to be found in the Lord Jesus Christ. "Yet people seem to be more enamored with my financial success," he told me. The Epistle of James corrects this misplaced admiration. "Listen, my dear brothers: Has not God chosen those who are poor in the eyes of the world to be rich in faith and to inherit the kingdom He promised those who love Him?" (2:5)

To show preferential treatment to those who are rich in earthly goods and look down on the poor is a grave error. James revealed the unrighteous actions of many rich people to prove his point. "Is it not the rich who are exploiting you? Are they not the ones who are dragging you into court? Are they not the ones who are slandering the noble name of Him to whom you belong?" (vv. 6-7)

God's "royal Law" demands impartial love (v. 8). Respect and compassion towards others should not be influenced by their material wealth. "But if you show favoritism, you sin and are convicted by the Law as lawbreakers" (v. 9).

A challenge: Be sensitive today to those around you. Apply God's "royal Law." Love your neighbor without the taint of materialistic partiality. The one in rags might just be the richest of all.

THE LAW OF LIBERTY

I dislike stoplights. I could get to my destination so much faster if stoplights did not exist. I like the freedom to keep going, but the law says when the light is red I must stop. This is an infringement on my liberty! Down with the law of the stoplight! Give me liberty or give me death!

The law of the stoplight is a law of liberty. If it were not for this law, I could well be dead. Red lights are designed for my protection. Furthermore, if I run a red light and a policeman serves me with a ticket for my offense, it does little good to argue that I have stopped at hundreds of stoplights in my lifetime. I am a transgressor of the law, a law of liberty to protect me from death.

God's Law is a law of liberty. It is written for our good. To stumble in one point of His Law is to be declared guilty (2:10). James used an extreme example to support his point, "If you do not commit adultery, but do commit murder, you have become a lawbreaker" (v. 11). Obviously, you do not have to be both an adulterer and murderer to be guilty. One offense will do.

Rather than try to excuse ourselves from the Law, we should follow James' call for positive action. "Speak and act as those who are going to be judged by the Law that gives freedom" (v. 12). We need to see the wonderful liberation given us in abiding by God's precepts. The apparent restrictions are to give us fullness of life. Rather than use God's Law in judgment over others, we should rejoice in His mercy to us (v. 13).

Beginning today: Enjoy the blessings of living under God's Law of liberty. Speak and act in accord with His commands and discover the freedom that only He can offer. Be governed by His perfect Law of liberty.

DEAD FAITH

In my brief career working at the Ohio State University eye clinic, I was invited one day by a colleague to visit the morgue in the basement of the university hospital. Curiosity won and I accompanied him. It was quite apparent that the body on the morgue table was dead. There was no movement, no pulse, no breath. There was simply no evidence of life. The man was dead!

Life is always accompanied by some vital signs. So true faith is always accompanied by some evidence of works. James asked a key question, "What good is it, my brothers, if a man claims to have faith, but has no deeds? Can such faith save him?" (2:14) Dead faith is useless faith.

James gave an illustration of how dead faith might respond. "Suppose a brother or sister is without clothes and daily food. If one of you says . . . , 'Go, I wish you well; keep warm and well fed,' but does nothing about his physical needs, what good is it?" (vv. 15-16)

Contrary to those who see in this passage the necessity of works for salvation, James was simply stressing the vitality of true faith. The Apostle Paul emphasized the essence of faith; James focused on the evidence of faith. James wrote, "Faith by itself, if it is not accompanied by action, is dead" (v. 17). If there are absolutely no vital signs, faith is pronounced dead. Paul agreed. We are "created in Christ Jesus to do good works" (Eph. 2:10).

To put into practice: If you know Christ as your Saviour, let your faith shine forth. Let people see the vibrancy of your faith, a living faith that makes a difference in the way you live.

FAITH THAT WORKS

Every time I walk through the jet way and into the massive chasm of a jumbo jet I am amazed. It is hard to believe that the gigantic hunk of metal, all the luggage, and all the people will rise into the air. Yet I sit down, fasten my seat belt, and by faith anticipate arrival at my destination.

Faith is no mystery. Everyone lives my faith. But not all faith works. Boarding a jet is not blind faith. It is faith in a pretty reliable means of travel. Faith in my ability to reach my destination by flapping my arms would rightfully be declared stupid. Misplaced faith simply does not work.

Biblical faith always works. James wrote, "But someone will say, 'You have faith; I have deeds.' Show me your faith without deeds, and I will show you my faith by what I do" (2:18). Saving faith works.

True faith is not mere intellectual assent. James pointed out that demons believe in God. To believe in airplanes will not get a person to his destination. Faith without a boarding pass is useless.

True faith was seen in Abraham, who showed his trust in God by offering up Isaac, and in Rahab, who demonstrated her trust by protecting the spies (vv. 21-25). James reiterated his point, "As the body without the spirit is dead, so also faith without deeds is dead" (v. 26).

Do it: Rejoice that you have your faith in One who takes you to your destination with far greater security than any airline. Live in His assurance. Let Him work through you today. Let everyone see that you have a faith that works!

WATCH YOUR STEP

One little split-second slip can have disastrous consequences. My mother-in-law always moves with due caution. Nonetheless it happened. She slipped and fell. The result? A broken hip. A fall takes only a second. Healing takes months, even years.

James followed his counsel on how to be what God wants us to be (chap. 1) and how to feel what God wants us to feel (chap. 2) with some very sound advice on how to speak as God wants us to speak (chap. 3). He began with a warning: "Not many of you should presume to be teachers, my brothers, because you . . . will be judged more strictly" (3:1). A teacher can hardly claim ignorance to the rules he is teaching. He is responsible not only for his teaching but also for obedience to the rules he communicates. If he falls, he will certainly be judged more strictly.

Who does not fall? James added, "We all stumble in many ways" (v. 2a). The real test, however, is to keep from falling in what a person says. "If anyone is never at fault in what he says, he is a perfect man, able to keep his whole body in check" (v. 2b).

God has carefully designed the tongue to be held in a cage of teeth with two trap doors called lips, yet it still manages to escape and cause us to stumble.

Do your best today: Control your tongue. Let your speech be a blessing and encouragement to those around you. Don't let your tongue get loose and cause you to fall. The wounds could take years to heal. Take heed to James' warning. Watch your step.

THE O'LEARY THEORY

It is said that Mrs. Patrick O'Leary's cow caused the famed Chicago fire of 1871. Her cow kicked over a lantern that started a fire that raged for over 24 hours, destroyed 17,450 buildings in 3⅓ square miles, claimed 300 lives, and left over 90,000 people homeless. One careless kick, one small flame, and an entire city was almost totally consumed.

A small force can yield catastrophic results. James gives three illustrations to support this principle: little bits turn gigantic horses, a small rudder puts huge ships on a new course, and a small flame can consume an entire forest. "The tongue is a small part of the body, but it makes great boasts" (3:3-5).

In fact "the tongue also is a fire, a world of evil among parts of the body." This little piece of muscle is capable of defiling the entire body. It "sets the whole course of [a person's] life on fire, and is itself set on fire by hell" (v. 6). James' lesson on the anatomy of the tongue is alarming. Hell's fire can turn a tongue into a torch that consumes and destroys all in its path.

We need to be alert to the danger of an uncontrolled tongue. No spark from hell dare ignite our tongues and turn us into some kind of demonic dragon spewing forth consuming fire. Harmful gossip and conceited boasting must not issue from our lips. Instead we should speak words of encouragement and enlightenment, of grace and blessing.

Seek God's help: Control your tongue. Make sure no fire escapes from your mouth today. May your words bless, not burn, those to whom you speak.

KILLER WHALE "SHAMU"

It was certainly impressive. At the trainer's command the giant killer whale swam to the side of the tank and then opened her mouth wide while a spectator stuck his head into the massive cavern. Shamu defied her killer instinct. Her big jaws did not smash closed until the volunteer's head was no longer in jeopardy.

The most unusual species of animals can be trained. James acknowledged this amazing fact. "All kinds of animals, birds, reptiles, and creatures of the sea, are being tamed and have been tamed by man" (3:7). There is one animal organ, however, that remains untameable: the human tongue. "But no man can tame the tongue" (v. 8a).

James called the tongue "a restless evil, full of deadly poison" (v. 8b). Not that the tongue itself is evil or full of poison. The tongue is a mere muscle designed to move at the command of its trainer. The problem is in the evil the tongue can issue and the poison it can spew forth.

Killer whales can be trained to respond to commands with total consistency. The human tongue is restless and unreliable. It is full of vicious venom that can strike out when least expected. No one can tame the tongue.

We need to recognize how vulnerable we are before our own tongue. It will take more than our own human effort to keep our tongue in check. We must seek God's help.

Talk to the Lord: Ask Him to keep your tongue under control today. Pray that your tongue will be kept from chilling, killing comments. Let Him fill your mouth with words of kindness.

DON'T DRINK THE WATER

They are the most common words of advice to a world traveler heading toward an undeveloped area: "Don't drink the water." In primitive regions the water is usually contaminated. It all depends on the source. Some springs provide pure, clean water. This is the water that is bottled under sanitary conditions and sold to tourists willing to pay the high price. Water from rivers or standing pools, however, is bound to be dirty.

Water sources are usually reliable. The tongue is not. James stated, "Out of the same mouth come praise and cursing." The same tongue blesses God and curses men. James concluded, "My brothers, this should not be" (3:10).

Three easily answered questions follow. "Can both fresh water and salt water flow from the same spring? Can a fig tree bear olives, or a grape vine bear figs? Neither can a salt spring produce fresh water" (vv. 11-12). There is more order in the natural world than in man. The tongue is disturbingly inconsistent. Like the tongue of some dreaded reptile, man's tongue is forked and issues both refreshing words and bitter words, both blessing and cursing.

Decide now: Let your tongue flow with the sparkling water of life in your conversation. Ask God to give you supernatural consistency in the words you speak today. Don't let foul talk and distasteful language contaminate your communication (Eph. 4:29).

IS IT IN GEAR?

The first-time driver raced the engine wildly, but the car did not budge. The noise was deafening. The exhaust poured out clouds of black smoke. All to no avail. There was one simple problem. The car was not in gear!

Ultimately, the problem with a loose tongue is that it is disconnected from the mind. Winsome talk demands some wise thought. That is why James asked in his letter, "Who is wise and understanding among you?" Gracious speech will come from one who is filled with "the humility that comes from wisdom" (3:13). Humble character brings forth wholesome conversation.

The jealous, selfish, arrogant person will lie. These earthly, natural, demonic forces are destructive in every way (vv. 14-16).

By contrast, "the wisdom that comes from heaven is first of all pure; then peace loving, considerate, submissive, full of mercy and good fruit, impartial, and sincere" (v. 17). A mind consumed by these rich qualities will move a tongue to speak words of grace and peace. "Peacemakers who sow in peace raise a harvest of righteousness" (v. 18).

The way to control our talk is to cultivate our thought. The roar of cursing and the black billows of evil speech are simply a result of not putting the mind into gear before the tongue starts wagging.

Right now: Ask for wisdom that comes down from heaven. Let God make both your life and your lips a rich blessing to everyone you meet today.

WORLD WAR III

World wars have marred the history of planet earth. Nothing is more devastating than warfare that engulfs the whole world. Surely two global confrontations are enough. Actually the third world war is in progress. It is a war that engages all mankind in spiritual battle.

What exactly causes war? James asked and answered this key question: "What causes fights and quarrels among you? Don't they come from your desires that battle within you?" (4:1) War, just like temptation, is born within man. Pleasure, desire for self-gratification at all costs, drives an individual to battle anyone who may stand in the way.

The drive for prideful satisfaction can result in horrendous consequences. "You want something but don't get it. You kill and covet" (v. 2a). James already presented this disastrous formula; desire yields sin and sin brings forth death (1:15). The result may be fights rather than murder. "You quarrel and fight. You do not have" (4:2b).

Quarrels, conflicts, fights, murder, and war all come from the same source: a lustful, envious, self-gratifying heart. When a person cannot get what he wants, he turns to violence to get his way. James suggested a better way. "You do not have, because you do not ask God" (v. 2c). If God wants His child to have something, He can grant it. Fights are never warranted in God's program.

Live by God's rules: Steer clear of being part of World War III. Keep personal desires subdued. Don't fight; pray. Enjoy God's peace today.

UNANSWERED PRAYER

One of the most disturbing experiences in the Christian life is to pray for a specific request and seemingly never receive an answer. Why do prayers go unanswered? Surely God is big enough to supply anything we might request.

James gave two reasons why we do not receive what we desire. First, "You do not have, because you do not ask God" (4:2). This may be our greatest problem. We ask God for nothing and get it every time. But what about those things for which we do ask and do not receive. Second, "When you ask, you do not receive, because you ask with wrong motives, that you may spend what you get on your pleasures" (v. 3). God denies requests that are not good for us.

Requests driven by worldly desires must be denied. "You adulterous people, don't you know that friendship with the world is hatred toward God?" A "friend of the world" is "an enemy of God" (v. 4).

The solution is to be controlled by the Spirit in our prayer requests so that we ask for what is in God's good pleasure to give to us (v. 5). Prayer is simply a declaration of dependence on the Father. We seek His power, His protection, and His provision in accord with His purpose.

In your time of prayer right now: Focus first on the One to whom you are talking. Fall in love with the Lord and declare your devotion and dedication to Him. Then ask for what you know to be within His will. For any other requests, be sure to acknowledge your desire for His will in the matter. Desire His good pleasure, not yours. Then face the day with confidence that He will answer.

YIELD

Frankly, I just did not see the sign. Nor did I see the taxi bearing down on the intersection. Fortunately, the taxi swerved. It would have been a terrible collision. The taxi driver was furious. At the next intersection, while I waited for the light to turn, I felt my car door open, and there was the irate driver with a screwdriver in his hand ready to kill me. I apologized profusely. I did what the sign had said to do. I yielded. Finally, the taxi driver's passenger subdued him. I now see yield signs.

Our Christian conduct is governed in large part by one big yield sign. God opposes the proud but "gives grace to the humble" (4:6). "Submit yourselves, then, to God," James wrote. "Come near to God." As we yield to God we turn from sin. In fact, we can resist the devil and he will flee (v. 7).

The best way to avoid a collision with the world is to yield to God. If we humble ourselves before Him and confess our sins to Him, He will cleanse our hands and purify our hearts (v. 8). To be crushed by sin is, of course, no laughing matter (v. 9). We must steer clear of the road of destruction.

The answer is simply, "Humble yourselves before the Lord, and He will lift you up" (v. 10). Yield your life to Him in sincere humility. He will protect you from the devastating consequences of sin. In fact, He will lift you up. He will exalt you.

Yield to the Lord right now: Confess your sins to Him. Rejoice in His cleansing. Stand tall in His exaltation and move forward in His protection.

JUDGE NOT

It is so easy to be judgmental. Flaws in other people seem to stand out. Surely we need to demonstrate "tough love" and confront our Christian friends. We need to straighten them out before they get bent out of shape. Generally, however, the "tough love" is "tight law" and confrontation becomes condemnation. Instead of lifting up the fallen, we tear down the frail. We judge.

James attacked the judgmental spirit. "Do not speak against one another, brethren. He who speaks against a brother, or judges his brother, speaks against the law, and judges the law; but if you judge the law, you are not a doer of the law, but a judge of it" (4:11, NASB). God's Law, that is, His Word, was not given as a club for us to use on others. It was given for us to obey. We must follow God's precepts; not judge them.

There is only One who can rightfully serve as Judge. It is the One who gave the Law. He is the "One who is able to save and to destroy" (v. 12a). God serves as the executive, legislative, and judicial branch of His kingdom. We have no place on the bench. We are assigned to no court. James rightfully asked, "Who are you to judge your neighbor?" (v. 12b) God is the Judge. We are His subjects. Our greatest desire should be to serve Him and obey Him.

While we can rightfully remind each other of God's judgment, we dare not assume His role as judge over one another. We must not usurp His authority.

Consider this: To acknowledge your limitations is actually very liberating. You need not judge others. You are free from this awesome responsibility. You can relate to others with love and acceptance. There is joy in a nonjudgmental approach to life. Live in the freedom God has given you.

"D.V." IS STILL IN VOGUE

It is not commonly seen in correspondence anymore. The simple letters "D.V." used to appear with frequency. They served as a symbol of the Latin phrase *Deo volente* meaning "God willing." A century ago, "D.V." following a description of one's plans was a sign of culture and, even more important, a sign of dependence on God.

Our modern society needs to get back to "D.V." James would agree. "Come now, you who say, 'Today or tomorrow, we shall go to such and such a city, and spend a year there and engage in business and make a profit' " (4:13, NASB). This statement seems innocent enough. The problem lies in the attitude behind the statement. There is no acknowledgment of the Lord. He is completely left out of the plans.

We must realize that all our plans are tentative. We do not know what the future holds. Life is a "mist that appears for a little while and then vanishes" (v. 14).

"Instead," James continued, "you ought to say, 'If it is the Lord's will, we will live and do this or that' " (v. 15). We are totally dependent on God for life itself, to say nothing of our plans. To leave Him out is to be arrogant, self-sufficient, and boastful. God calls this evil (v. 16). Every plan we devise must include a "D.V." God willing, we will live and engage in activities. But only if God is willing.

Think it over: You may feel that the "D.V." is self-evident. It is automatic. Why belabor the point? James answered that question. "Anyone, then, who knows the good he ought to do and doesn't do it, sins" (v. 17). Sin is not merely the wrong things we do; it includes the good we may fail to do. To fail to recognize the Lord in our plans is sin. Count Him in. "D.V." is still in vogue.

RUST PREVENTION

For those who live in Yankee land, undercoating has been one of the great inventions of mankind. Salt that is strewn across the icy city streets is a marvelous aid to bringing a car to a stop, but the same salt serves to eat the car alive. Rust moves in and before long the body needs considerable repair. Rust prevention is the answer. It is well worth whatever it costs.

How do we get rust prevention for the rest of our possessions? James spoke to the issue. "Come now, you rich, weep and howl for our miseries which are coming upon you. Your riches have rotted and your garments have become moth-eaten. Your gold and your silver have rusted; and their rust will be a witness against you" (5:1-3a, NASB).

James had given counsel on who we are (chap. 1), what we feel (chap. 2), how we talk (chap. 3), and what we do (chap. 4). Now he turns to what we have (chap. 5).

James was not tolerant of the rich. He attacked not the possession of wealth but the obsession with wealth. Actually, there is no rust prevention for the goods we accumulate on earth. Everything falls apart sooner or later.

To try to find security in garments and gold is futile. These will rot and rust, and the rust "will consume your flesh like fire. It is in the Last Days that you have stored up your treasure!" (5:3b, NASB) To hoard goods and put confidence in stuff is hopeless. There is no undercoating for the junk of this world.

Heed James' words: Be free from the bondage of materialism. Hold on to your possessions very lightly. Use the resources God has given you wisely, but don't let them control you. It is not what you have but what has you that counts. Invest in eternity. There is no rust there.

MONEY TALKS

I simply refused to take the advice of this experienced traveler to Mexico. He informed me that a few well-placed dollars tucked into a passport would eliminate any delay at the border. Noting my hesitancy, he said, "It's like a tip given in advance. Money talks." The tip looked too much like a bribe to me. I would not do it.

Money talks, all right. Ill-gained wealth and improperly used money will speak out against us in heaven. James wrote, "Look! The wages you failed to pay the workmen who mowed your fields are crying out against you" (5:4a). We must be exceedingly cautious in our use of money.

Those who have been cheated join in the heavenly accusation before "the ears of the Lord Almighty" (v. 4b). The unjust employer is found guilty. "You have lived on earth in luxury and self-indulgences" (v. 5). Too often there is abuse rather than wise use of money. Christians are to be noted for honesty and generosity in their finances. Ostentatious living and opulent luxury are but evidence of open lust, of self-indulgence. Indeed money talks. It condemns.

Those who achieve excessive wealth will often use their money to remove all obstacles. "You have condemned and murdered innocent men, who were not opposing you" (v. 6). Once more in the Epistle of James the chain reaction occurs—lust leads to sin and sin leads to death (1:15). Money does more than talk. It taints. It corrupts.

Don't become enamored with money: Be wise in its use. Make money your servant, not your master. To hoard it or adore it is to let it destroy you. Wrongly used money will speak out against you. Money talks.

PATIENCE IS A VIRTUE

Twice as true as it is repeated is the little phrase, "Patience is a virtue." In a society that is constantly on the run, patience is a rare commodity. If you don't believe it, put a person on hold for about twenty minutes and see if he is still on the line when you reconnect. Most will slam down their phone in less than ten minutes.

Christians need a good dose of patience in this frenzied world. James wrote, "Be patient, therefore, brethren, until the coming of the Lord. Behold, the farmer waits for the precious produce of the soil, being patient about it, until it gets the early and late rains. You too be patient; strengthen your hearts, for the coming of the Lord is at hand" (5:7-8, NASB). Instead of demanding an immediate return on our labors, we need eternal perspective. The real harvest comes in heaven, not on earth.

Impatience often turns vocal. "Do not complain," said James. Instead of griping at one another, we need to encourage one another. "The Judge is standing right at the door" (v. 9, NASB). The Lord's return is imminent. We should live in hope and expectancy.

The wait for eternity is not without trials. James referred to the prophets and to the patriach Job as great examples of those who endured suffering with patience and hope. The outcome is significant. From it we can see that "the Lord is full of compassion and merciful" (vv. 10-11). God always rewards those who patiently endure.

Could it be true? You may feel cheated when you look at rich people around you. Your patience is running out. You feel like you have a legitimate gripe. Don't complain. Enlarge your vision. Lengthen your view. Your pay may be meager, but the rewards of serving the Lord are out of this world. Have patience. God will bless you richly.

LIFT UP THE FALLEN

Frankly, I could not get up. I was playing "capture the flag" with the youth when it happened. We were about to free one of our players from "prison" when a guy who looked like he ought to be playing for the Green Bay Packers crashed down on my leg. I could not get up without help. I hobbled around until after I had spoken at the campfire. Then they took me to the hospital. I had a broken leg.

Christians are often able to get up on their own with help from the Lord. "Is any one of you in trouble? He should pray. Is anyone happy? Let him sing songs of praise" (5:13). Prayer and praise are direct channels to God's help and blessing.

But what happens when a believer is wounded to the extent he cannot get up without help from other Christians? James instructed, "He should call the elders of the church, to pray over him and anoint him with oil in the name of the Lord. And the prayer offered in faith will make the sick person well; the Lord will raise him up" (vv. 14-15a).

These verses are usually taken to refer to physical healing. More likely, they refer to spiritual healing. The Greek word translated "sick" in verse 15 is used only one other place in the New Testament and there it is translated "weary" (Heb. 12:3). When a believer is downcast, dejected, spiritually broken, he needs others to come and help lift him up.

To James' Jewish audience, the anointing oil was associated with cleansing. "If he has sinned, he will be forgiven" (v. 15b). Restoration is assured. Cleansing is guaranteed. The Lord will raise him up.

If you are down today: Call for help. Your friends or church leaders are ready to help lift you up. If you have a friend who is down, offer assistance. Lift up the fallen.

THE RED TELEPHONE

I received orders to report to Clarksville, Tennessee. I wondered what the Unites States Navy was doing in Tennessee. I soon discovered that it was a top-secret base. Once I had received my clearance, I stood guard duty in what we affectionately called "the pit." There was a red telephone there with a direct line to the Pentagon. I never did use that phone, for there was never an emergency.

We as Christians have a red telephone. It is a direct line to the Creator of the universe. Why don't we use it more? The power for cleansing and healing is to be found through prayer. "Therefore, confess your sins to each other, and pray for each other, so that you may be healed. The prayer of a righteous man is powerful and effective" (5:16).

Perhaps one of the greatest problems in the church today is the lack of effectual prayer. We have fantastic programs, gifted personnel, and visionary plans; but it all seems to rattle around with little or no power. Prayer is the missing ingredient. The red telephone gathers dust. "After all, it is only for dire emergencies." We say, "Why bother God? Everything is under control."

To show the tremendous power of prayer, James cited the example of Elijah, who "was a man just like us." The prophet prayed "that it would not rain, and it did not rain on the land for three and a half years. Again he prayed, and the heavens gave rain" (vv. 17-18).

Don't miss the power of prayer, individually and corporately: If your church has a prayer meeting, plan to attend this week. Right now, take advantage of the red telephone. Spend some time in prayer. Watch God work.

ON THE WRONG ROAD

It was after midnight when the student called to tell me he and several others were stranded. Their VW camper had broken down. He asked if I could come rescue them. "We are just beyond Lake Ray Hubbard on Interstate 20 at a Fina station." I told him I'd be right there. I jumped into our car and zoomed off to the rescue.

I knew right where they were—so I thought! I started down Interstate 20 but then reasoned, "Lake Ray Hubbard? That is not on I-20. That's on I-30." So I traveled for miles and miles on I-30 and never did find the Fina station. I was on the wrong road. I did not realize that Lake Ray Hubbard exists from both I-20 and I-30. Hours later I found them right where they said, on I-20!

It is a frustrating thing to be on the wrong road. All too often believers make a wrong turn and head away from God and His blessing. James advised, "My brethren, if any among you strays from the truth, and one turns him back, let him know that he who turns a sinner from the error of his way will save his soul from death, and will cover a multitude of sins" (5:19-20, NASB).

We need each other. When one falls, others need to lift him up. When one sins, others can pray for his cleansing. When one strays, others should be ready to give directions back to the truth. This could be the greatest gift of all.

Follow James' practical advice: Be a Christian of upright character (chap. 1), firm convictions (chap. 2), clear communication (chap. 3), holy conduct (chap. 4), and generous contribution (chap. 5). Give of your means and of yourself. Keep on the right road and direct others back to that road. You will be blessed beyond measure.

December

Devotional readings in the Epistles of John
by Kenneth O. Gangel

LETTER OF LIFE

Everyone likes to receive love letters; they seem so tangible and can be enjoyed over and over again. When friends express the feelings of their hearts, it makes us love them more and want to express that love in return. In our studies for this month, the Epistles of John give us a glimpse of his love for the Saviour and for other believers. These letters also tell how we are to share that love with one another.

The First Epistle of John is always referred to as a letter despite the fact that it has no address, no subscription, no reference to person or place, no direct trace of author, and no special destination. Yet the very fragrance of its pages suggests a warm, almost pastoral tone. The author appealed to his readers as though he knew well their background and personal traits.

Like the letters you and I might write, the vocabulary of 1, 2, and 3 John is simple (much like the Gospel of John), the approach very personal, and there are no quotations or other scholarly distinctives. Experts almost unanimously attribute all three epistles to John, primarily because of the close similarity with the fourth Gospel.

All three books display themes important to us in the late twentieth century—life, light, and love. John's Gospel presents the way of salvation, exhorting readers to believe. His epistles emphasize the results of salvation in those who have already believed. In John's day some distorted the message of Christ, claiming to have a superior knowledge about Him and His relationship with the Father. Some taught that Christ never really became a man but only seemed to have human form.

The presence of many cults and sects in our day, some of which teach the same heresies John faced, makes this first epistle as relevant to us as it was to those in the first century.

Assignment: As we study the truths of 1 John, may God give us the same encouragement, assurance, and joy that John prayed for the original readers so many years ago.

FOUR EVIDENCES OF THE INCARNATION

When we look at a newborn baby, we are looking at a miracle. Created by God, sent as a gift from Him, a beginning of a new life is marvelous to observe. Of course spiritual birth is a miracle too, and the Lord wants us to "see, hear, and touch" the Father in the form of His Son, Jesus Christ (1 John 1:1).

Interestingly, three out of four first words in John's Gospel and this first epistle are alike. In both books he emphasized up front that the truths about Jesus have been verified "from the beginning."

But just as quickly, John changed the direction of thought. In his Gospel he went on to prove Jesus' deity while assuming His humanity; here he assumed Christ's deity while writing to prove His humanity.

As a disciple and one of the inner band, John gave a firsthand, eyewitness account of the Lord's life. First, he *heard* the Lord speak of Himself and the Father. You may remember how frequently John recorded Jesus' emphasis on His own words. But John also stated that he *saw* the Lord with his own eyes. No one could convince him that Jesus of Nazareth was anything other than a complete human being.

The words *looked at* refer to more than casual investigation. In wonder and amazement, John had contemplated God's Messiah. John also *touched* the Word of life. Like a scientist he had the privilege of examining all Jesus' claims in the laboratory of life. The very life of God had been manifest, and John affirmed that everything Jesus said about Himself was true.

John saw and believed. But this same writer had already recorded the words of the Lord, "Blessed are those who have not seen and yet have believed" (John 20:29).

Take action: Surrender today any doubts you may have about the power and humanity of the Saviour. Accept John's four evidences of what God did for the world when He sent His Son to become a person like us so that His life might become ours—eternally.

FELLOWSHIP WITH THE FATHER

When asked by his Sunday School teacher for a definition of "fellowship," a little boy said, "I'm not sure, but I think it means several fellows in the same ship." He may have been more correct than that teacher probably gave him credit for at the moment. Christians are "all in the same boat," as we say in a popular idiom. That "boat" or "ship" is the church, the body of Christ. First John 1:3 reminds us that such blessed fellowship contains at least three dimensions.

First, all Christians participate in a joint relationship with each other, based on their collective faith in the message about our Lord and His work in their lives. The word *fellowship* appears four times in this first chapter, establishing a major theme within John's purpose (vv. 3 [twice], 6-7). This fellowship with each other is made possible by our joint fellowship with the Father and with the Son.

What characterizes this important relationship? It is personal, doctrinal, vital, mutual, and eternal. The Holy Spirit bonds believers together in spiritual love and interdependence. Some resist or distort that relationship, but such behavior makes it no less important that the world see God's people living together in loving harmony and peace.

What about it? Is anything distorting or preventing your full participation in this grand fellowship? If so, surrender it to the Lord for forgiveness and come join in the eternal, heaven-bond "ship."

O God, touch my heart today
And cleanse me from all sin,
Put Your love and joy inside
And keep it safe within
Until someone comes along
And needs my help
To lift their loads today,
Then may I reach inside my heart
And give love and joy away.

–Mildred H. Bell

From "The Power of Love," Salesian Missions, New Rochelle, NY 01801.

JOY—MARK OF THE CHRISTIAN

"I just want to be happy." This is a common plea heard by parents, pastors, and counselors around the world. This confused and confusing society seems to throw up obstacle after obstacle that obstructs human happiness. Some Bible teachers see a difference between human happiness and biblical joy, but real joy can be found only in the Lord, who indwells believers, not in material things.

Leon Bloy once wrote, "Joy is the most infallible sign of the presence of God." That is precisely what John wrote about in 1 John 1:4—how the Person and work of Jesus can complete our joy, that of his readers as well as himself. More properly, in the light of yesterday's study, that joy comes when Christians live in right fellowship with the Father, the Son, and other Christians.

This promised joy will be the result of the knowledge of the truth about Christ practiced within the fellowship of Christ's people. That joy extends from the inside, where the Holy Spirit creates it, to the service God allows us to render to others.

A.W. Tozer once spoke of such joy in the ministry of several of God's great saints: "George Mueller would not preach until his heart was happy in the grace of God; Jan Ruybroeck would not write while his feelings were low but would retire to a quiet place and wait on God till he felt the spirit of inspiration. It is well known that the elevated spirits of a group of Moravians convinced John Wesley of the reality of their religion, and helped bring him a short time later to a state of true conversion. The Christian owes it to the world to be supernaturally joyful."

Is this a joyful day for you? If not, ask the Father to awaken in your heart the complete joy of which John wrote so many years ago.

WALKING IN THE LIGHT

As I get older, one of the less welcome signs of age is the increasing light necessary for everything I want to see. Whether trying to read a newspaper or struggling across a dark street at night, I seem to need more light than what is available much of the time. John promised that in spiritual things at least, there need never be an absence or rationing level of necessary light.

Light is the second of the apostle's key words in this epistle. Used throughout Scripture as a synonym for infinite holiness, purity, and righteousness, the word demonstrates here that correctness of lifestyle comes only when we walk in the light shed by God Himself. People have no excuse for natural darkness (Eph. 5:8), willful darkness (John 3:19), or eternal darkness (Jude 13).

John presented light as a test of salvation. The logic of 1 John 1:5-7 runs something like this:

> *Claim:* "I have fellowship with God."
> *Conduct:* The claimant is living continually in sin and darkness.
> *Condemnation:* He is a liar; he does not practice the truth.

All the verbs in 1 John 1:7 describe a lifestyle, not an occasional act of grace or worship. The concept of cleansing stands strategically at the very heart of the doctrine of sanctification. "What can wash away my sin? Nothing but the blood of Jesus. What can make me whole again? Nothing but the blood of Jesus."

Reflect and act: Has your heart been washed clean by the blood of Jesus so that His light can permeate through the darkness of sin? If you are a believer, do you sometimes get defeated, lonely, and discouraged? Take the hand of the Saviour and allow His light to crowd out fear and illuminate every dark corner of your life.

THREE FALSE IDEAS OF SIN

Verses 6, 8, and 10 in 1 John 1 give us three false ideas of sin, obviously common in John's day and also quite prevalent in ours. Verse 6 describes an attitude that belittles sin by disregarding its seriousness and ignoring its consequences. People who flaunt such disregard for God's standards demonstrate their lying behavior; both words and conduct show they have chosen to remain outside God's grace.

The second error is referred to in verse 8, in which John warned that only self-deceived people deny they have a sin nature. Some religious movements teach that the sin nature is removed at sanctification, and people who have progressed to that point in their spiritual walk never sin again. Mistakes maybe, and perhaps a shortcoming or two, but no real sin! Such a view directly denies the truth of verse 8.

Verse 10 deals with acts of sin rather than the nature of sin, but both effect and penalty are the same. The result of no sin nature would be no acts of sin. But John said that one who holds such an unbiblical notion makes God a liar and demonstrates that His truth has no place in his life.

Tomorrow we will study the solution to erroneous views of sin and once again be moved to praise God for His grace. But today let's humbly acknowledge that the God who made us knows us well.

A reminder: The sin nature of Adam, passed on through the human race, is alive and well today, active in our lives as well. Confession means to agree with God's analysis of what is true and real rather than making excuses for our behavior. Yes, Lord, we have sinned because we are sinners; please forgive and cleanse us.

CONFESSION AND CLEANSING

How commonly we hear 1 John 1:9 used to invite unbelievers to trust Christ for salvation. Yet in its context it refers to the sins of Christians and technically does not apply to evangelism. Of course, the forgiving grace of the Saviour is offered to anyone who meets His conditions for that forgiveness.

We may need to clarify our thinking regarding the difference between repentance and confession. Repentance (*metanoia* in Greek) means turning one's direction and heading the other way. Generally speaking, repentance represents the posture needed by unbelievers, and confession is the posture needed by believers. "Confess" is from the word *homologeō,* which means "to say the same thing" God says about our sin.

John added that our God *is* two things and *will do* two things for us when we sin. First, He is *faithful;* He will always keep His promises (2 Tim. 2:13; Heb. 10:23). And our Heavenly Father is *righteous;* He will keep s62laws. The bridge between these two qualities can be found in His magnificent grace.

God *forgives* us and *cleanses* us. Both verbs indicate a single act. Since known sin in the life of a Christian is not habitual, John wrote that God deals with it completely and finally at the time we confess it. This holy God can forgive us legally since the penalty for past and even future sins was cared for by the blood of Jesus on the cross.

For what do you need cleansing today? What thought or behavior should come under that cleansing blood? If you are a member of God's family through faith in Christ, you need only agree with God about your sin, and His powerful grace will forgive it immediately. Praise His name for the truth and hope of 1 John 1:9!

HOLINESS THROUGH ADVOCACY

"Correction fluid is the magical liquid that covers over your errors, your typos, and your unfortunate slipups. You brush on the liquid and start all over again, your former mistakes obliterated by the forgiving fluid" (John V. Chervokas, "How to Keep God Alive from Nine to Five," quoted in *Christianity Today,* April 4, 1986, p. 55).

Surrounded by a sin-soaked society, we must struggle to maintain the kind of holiness commanded of God's people in Scripture. Such a lifestyle is possible only because of Christ's advocacy on our behalf.

Already we have seen two purposes of this epistle: fellowship (1:3) and joy (1:4). Now John added a third: "I write this to you so that you will not sin" (2:1-2). We know from Romans 6:1-2 that God's abundant grace is no excuse for continued sinning; it should be the aim of the believer to sin "not at all."

But since sinning is possible for believers, God has provided an Advocate who stands beside us on earth and pleads our case in heaven. As the God-man, Jesus understands our weaknesses and sinful tendencies. And He stands before heaven's throne as the anointed Messiah, the righteous One who has no sin of His own.

He became the "atoning sacrifice" (propitiation) for our sins (1 John 2:2; 4:10; cf. Rom. 3:25). The word *propitiation* means "to cover," and the Book of Hebrews details many legal aspects of how propitiation works in God's plan (Heb. 2:17; 9:12, 26). Jesus' work on the cross served the whole world, but His role as Advocate is limited to those who have accepted His offer of salvation.

For you: Thank God this day for our Righteous One, the One who can help us deal with sin.

OBEDIENCE TO CHRIST'S COMMANDS

How much do you know? Some folks think they never know enough, while others consider themselves more informed than they really are. *Know* is one of the key words in this epistle, especially when it emphasizes the knowledge Christians have of Christ. How do we know if we know Him? By how well we keep His commands (1 John 2:3, 5). The Greek word translated "commands" is not the common *nomos* (used fifteen times by John to refer to the Mosaic Law), but a word that means "precepts" or "charges."

This obedience serves as a test of salvation since some will claim they know the Lord while violating His commands. Such "liars" are obviously unsaved and have no truth in them. Notice the contrast between the Old Testament and New Testament in this passage. Moses said, "Do these things and live"; Jesus said, "Live, and because you have life, do these things." The love of God matures in the one who keeps Christ's Word.

Verse 5 introduces a fourth key word in 1 John—*love*. And here is another test of salvation; the one who truly knows the Lord "must walk as Jesus did" (v. 6). Christlikeness has always been the mark of genuine disciples. God designed us to live in harmony with each other, and Jesus clearly taught that love is the hallmark of the church.

How can we do it? The indwelling Holy Spirit produces the love of Jesus in our hearts. What a joy to know that "the darkness is passing" (v. 8). Though the amount of progress in one day may be difficult to measure, we can be confident that our Lord draws us closer as we keep His commandments and walk in the light.

Jesus showed His love to people by serving them when they were in need, healing them when they were sick, talking with them when they were lonely, and crying or praying with them in their sorrow.

A question for you: Is there someone today who needs Christ's demonstration of love through you?

WALKING AS HE WALKED

"The road is too rough," I said.
"Dear Lord, there are stones that hurt me so."
And He said, "Dear child, I understand;
  I walked it long ago."
—Olga J. Weiss (*Poems for Sunshine and Shadow,* vol. 2)

What does God want from us? What distinctives should mark Christians as they walk before a watching world? Following their Saviour, His people pattern their lives after His—walking as He walked.

John wanted his readers to know that their obedience links not to some new idea, some strange obligation God had placed on them, but rather the one they had known from the beginning. As we noticed yesterday, the central focus of the church emphasizes love—first to God, then to other people.

Walking is a common biblical metaphor for living. The one who claims to belong to the Lord must also adopt a lifestyle close to that modeled by the Lord Himself.

What might that mean for us? How do the Saviour's followers "walk"? What will be different in your life this day because you know Him? What will be different because you took time to study His Word?

Gentleness, kindness, truth, grace—all these and many more qualities marked the Lord's life and therefore should be seen in our lives as well. Once again, we need to be reminded that only the Holy Spirit can produce such a lifestyle in struggling, imperfect people like you and me.

SAVED AND UNSAVED

Someone once wrote, "The world can be divided into two groups of people, those who divide the world into two groups of people and those who do not." This may be true, but it's not very helpful. The Bible repeatedly divides the entire human race into two groups—the saved and the unsaved.

In his Gospel, John had talked about "whoever believes in Him" and "whoever does not believe." The former group will escape condemnation, but the latter group "stands condemned already" (John 3:18). Bible writers never waffle on the strict line separating those who have trusted Christ and those who have not.

Now John described these groups more thoroughly (1 John 2:9-11). The unsaved person claims to be in the light but hates his brother, walks in darkness, loses his way, and causes others to stumble. Like the blind fish in Mammoth Cave's Green River, persistence in darkness has blinded him.

In that same underground cave, electric lights have been installed so visitors can see the beauty of the stalactites and stalagmites. But when the lights are turned off, people experience total darkness, a darkness that can almost be felt and that leaves them feeling totally helpless. Spiritual darkness brings that kind of helplessness too.

The saved person, on the other hand, makes the same claim to walking in the light. But he reflects that light by loving his brother, he exercises spiritual vision, and provides no occasion of stumbling to himself or others (v. 10).

Where do you stand? If you truly walk in the light, the Lord needs you to reflect that light in love to your brothers and sisters in the body of Christ. Think of some practical ways you can do that today.

A WARM APPEAL TO CHRISTIANS

Now John switched his focus to three classes of people, people measured not by their relationship to the Lord but by the level of spiritual maturity they have attained (1 John 2:12-14). Almost every church, regardless of size, includes these three kinds of people. God's Spirit wrote through His apostle to speak to congregations in every century, including ours.

First, John addressed the "little ones," using titles that speak both of kinship (*teknia*) and subordination (*paidia*). These people are young in the faith; their sins have been forgiven "on account of His name." The metaphor of children emphasizes the biblical doctrine of adoption.

Next John turned to the "fathers," those who have become mature believers. These are identified as having "known Him who is from the beginning" (v. 13). Lest anyone think John limited this passage to men, the word translated "fathers" here could be rendered "parents" and appears just that way in Hebrews 11:23. Like Paul's injunction to older Christians in Titus 2:1-3, John expected mature believers to reflect their years of walking with the Lord.

Third, the passage speaks to energetic young men (1 John 2:13) on the way up. They are growing Christians who have overcome the wicked one and have become strong spiritually. New converts become growing Christians who turn into mature saints. No wonder the Bible says the church is like a family.

Think about it: Growing can be a painful process. Our children had some hard lessons to learn before they were ready to move out and be mature and responsible adults. Sometimes the pain was inflicted by the parents, but many times children need to face the results of their own sinful behavior. The joy comes when we get victory over sin and relationships can be restored in joy.

HOLINESS AND WORLDLINESS

Howard Hendricks tells the story of a flight from Boston to Dallas in the summer of 1987 which departed six hours late. Tired Friday-afternoon businessmen were steamed about the problem. The man across the aisle growled at the flight attendant every time she walked by. Since approaching him seemed a hopeless idea, Hendricks walked back to the galley to commend the flight attendant on self-control and the way she handled the situation. He asked her name, suggesting he wanted to write American Airlines and express appreciation. She responded, "I don't work for American Airlines; I work for Jesus Christ."

First John 2:15-17 may represent the most important teaching in the Bible on the subject of worldliness. In our day we have often described worldliness according to a list of "don'ts" which Christians should avoid. To be sure, serious Christians do avoid certain behaviors condemned in Scripture, but here John made it clear that worldliness is primarily attitude.

Loving the world is not some accidental mistake God's people might fall into on occasion, but rather a definite love relationship. John used one of his favorite words here, *agapē*, the strongest Greek term for love and the same word used of God's love in John 3:16. Sinful cravings (illegitimate desires), the lust of the eyes (sensory desires), and boastful speech (self-pride) all stem from our sinful natures and are at cross-purposes with our loving God.

Loving the world is futile, said John, because it is "being caused to pass away" while those who do the Father's will live forever.

Motivation stands at issue here: Loving the world displays a character inconsistent with the nature of God. Christians must show the world that they belong to a different kingdom and, by God's grace, can walk above the lure and attraction of worldliness.

APOSTASY AND CONFUSION

Absolute truth seems hard to find in these days of glass diamonds, simulated pearls, and instant foods. Even Christians develop fake relationships because we want others to think well of us. But only the Holy Spirit can produce true knowledge and help us live out God's absolute truth.

Virtually every New Testament writer viewed the days in which he lived as the "end times" or the "last hour." Teaching about the Antichrist was common, so John warned that many who represent his spirit and ideals already walked about in the world (1 John 2:18-27). Certainly their number has increased dramatically since John wrote these words.

Verse 19 helps us understand why some people who profess Christ leave the faith and go "out from us." They are apostate because they never had a life-changing experience with the Saviour to begin with. Now, as they reject the Gospel, they merely show their true colors. Their very departure marks them as never having been a true part of Christ's body.

True believers listen to the Holy Spirit and therefore know the truth. Only "liars" deny that Jesus is the Messiah come in the flesh. They reject Christ's incarnation and deity. Just as apostasy marks phony Christians, we identify true believers by their abiding and their anointing. Surely this "anointing" links back to verse 20 and refers to the Holy Spirit who lives in the born-again person.

A reminder: No human teacher is the *ultimate* source of a believer's instruction; the inner witness of God's Spirit leads us in His truth.

> Earthly props are useless
> On Thy grace I fall;
> Earthly strength is weakness
> Father, on Thee I call—
> For comfort, strength, and guidance
> Oh, give me all.

—John Oxenham

From "Faith," Salesian Missions, New Rochelle, NY 01801.

JESUS IS COMING!

How can Christians make right choices between worldliness and holiness? The coming of the Lord helps motivate us to select and live out righteous behavior. If we really believe that the Lord could come again at any time, we would behave in ways that would please Him (1 John 2:28–3:3). This includes living so that we will be "confident and unashamed before Him" (2:28), having done "what is right" (v. 29), and leading pure lives (3:3).

John expressed amazement at the kind of love it would take for us to become the children of God. Yet "that is what we are." Unsaved people cannot understand the reality of the new birth; they do not know Christ experientially. But those born of God, who live in His likeness, understand the spiritual nature. Through sanctification they become more like the Lord as they wait for His return.

And that return offers hope — the hope of seeing our blessed Saviour face to face. These wonderful verses emphasize the fact that a genuine expectancy of Christ's return will lead the true believer to self-examination, cleansing from sin, and a life of holiness (cf. 2 Cor. 5:10).

GOD'S SOLUTION FOR SIN

The headline in our local paper blared, "Two Killed, One Hurt in Church Shooting." Apparently when four deacons got into an argument, one pulled a gun and started shooting. Two were killed and one was seriously injured. Because sin had a place in the heart of a church leader, the entire church suffered the consequences.

According to John, habitual sinning stands contrary to the behavior of a genuine Christian. We see the emphasis on habit in the fact that almost every verb in 1 John 3:4-10 is in the present tense. Sin is lawlessness, John wrote, and Christ came to fulfill the Law and remove sinful lifestyles from those who turn to Him.

Once again, John measured hearts by what he could see in people's conduct. Someone who continually practices sinning demonstrates that he has never known the Lord experientially. He may know much about the Bible and the Gospel, but if the living Christ indwells him through the Holy Spirit, a pattern of perpetual sinning cannot occur.

In the opposite corner stands the habitual sinner, unable to shake such behavior because it demonstrates his connection to Satan (v. 10). Practicing righteousness reveals the new birth; practicing sin reveals a lost condition apart from God.

But how can we change? Within this immediate context the first answer has to do with trusting Christ for His life-changing power. If you are already a Christian, yet still bothered by sin, remember two things. First, God will allow you to experience no temptation that you can't handle with the resources He has provided (1 Cor. 10:13). Second, the process of confession and cleansing described at the end of 1 John 1 is available to all who call on His name.

THE LIFE OF LOVE

Among believers, love provides a test of life. John must have paid attention to the Lord's words in the Upper Room the night of the Crucifixion. There Jesus taught His disciples that the world would measure the reality of their relationship to Him by the way they related to each other (John 13:35). This central theme of 1 John 2 now reappears in 1 John 3:11-18.

Cain represents the opposite of love, the epitome of what happens when one cannot get along with other people for whatever reason. Cain hated Abel because they had different natures. In the same way the world will hate believers, sometimes even to the point of death. Anyone who habitually hates others contains within himself the characteristics of a murderer (Matt. 5:21-22).

How does God want His people to love? Not just in word (as important as that is) but in action and in truth. Who needs to know about your love today? Children? Parents? Husband? Wife? Brothers and sisters in your congregation? God will give you the courage and the wisdom to reach out in love to those who need to hear it and see it in you.

Icebergs may be beautiful to look at, but they are cold and foreboding. Yet some churches and Christians seem as calm and majestic in their orthodoxy as an iceberg. Remember, God gave us emotions, not to be wasted in flaunted extravagance, but to let those around us know how much we genuinely love them.

THE HOLY SPIRIT IN OUR LIVES

Clouds remind me of the Christian's conscience. A mass of small water droplets or tiny ice crystals floating in the air, they can reflect the beauty of a sunset, bring refreshing rain, or cover the earth with a blanket of white snow. A conscience filled and controlled by the Holy Spirit displays great beauty in the Christian's life.

Do Christians have consciences? Most people would argue that Christians should have the most highly developed, most sensitive consciences of anyone in the world. Yet 1 John 3:19-24 and other passages remind us that the role of the conscience in the believer is augmented by the Holy Spirit's ministry within us. Conscience no longer operates according to law, or social codes of morality, but rather as it is informed by the Spirit.

As the Holy Spirit assures us of proper decisions and behavior, He relieves us of guilt and uneasiness. As He convicts, however, we are turned to the Lord for forgiveness and cleansing. All this attaches closely to our prayer lives. If we keep clean at the Spirit's prompting, and keep His commandments, we can ask those things that are within His will and expect to have them.

To think about: Consider for just a moment the importance of the Holy Spirit's residence in your life. More than just a test of salvation, His presence becomes the key to godliness and contentment here on earth. Learn more about this great truth and practice this day the awareness of your resident Friend (Rom. 8:16; Gal. 3:14; Eph. 4:30).

TRY THE SPIRITS

A counselor was out with his group of young campers one dark night. With only a flashlight to guide them, the boys were frightened by the darkness and wanted to turn back. But the counselor assured them that even though the light would shine only a short distance in front of them, it was enough to lead them back to the camp one step at a time. Jesus, our Light, guides us through love and truth when we wander from Him. He loves us and draws us back again.

We come now to an important doctrinal section of 1 John. The apostle wanted to be sure his readers understood that love must be grounded in truth; so he encouraged them to be discerning about what they believed, especially regarding spiritual things (1 John 4:1-6). Acceptance of the Incarnation becomes the demarcation line for truth and error.

Though the spirit of the Antichrist already permeates the world, believers have overcome that force through the indwelling power of the Holy Spirit. False teachers, whether in John's day or ours, come out of society, and their teaching finds its basis in this world's systems. All false cults and heresies originate in the mind of man. Only the truth of Christianity comes from God through revelation.

So what can we expect? Opposition and strife. When we proclaim God's truth from His Word, we should anticipate that many will reject it and will scorn the messenger. Let's make sure we measure results by our relationship to the pure truth of the Gospel, not by some interpretation we happen to treasure. Remember, God holds us responsible for sharing the message; responses remain in His hands.

UNION WITH GOD

How do Christians best reflect the nature of God? Through church attendance? Through correct doctrine? Through their giving to missions? As important as all three may be for all of us, none represents the correct answer. John labored the point that we best show what God is like when we love other people (1 John 4:7-17). Yet we only know how to love because we have seen God's love in action; namely, that He loves us "and sent His Son as an atoning sacrifice for our sins" (v. 10).

This verse is the key to this section. The substitution Christ made for us—His death instead of ours, His life sacrificed in place of our sin—stands as the timeless and ultimate demonstration of what love must be. Love as a habitual order of life comes to us modeled by the Father and the Son. For emphasis John repeated much of what he had already told us in this letter.

The section closes by contrasting love with fear. Fear has to do with judgment, but love recognizes that Christ already took our punishment. Fear shows no confidence about eternity, but love reflects on our union with God through the Saviour.

Christians whose love has matured need have no fear of the world now or the judgment of the future. As patient foster parents slowly change an abused and frightened orphan into a trusting family member, so the Father's love to us can make us productive and confident members of the household of faith.

Let's remember: Our relationship with God is the foundation for our relationship with other people. We first experience His love for us; then we return that love as reflectors, demonstrating the love of the Father to others of His children.

LOVE OR FEAR?

A father burst into the bathroom one morning to find his three-year-old son playing with a straight razor. Thinking he might startle the boy and cause an accident if he cried out or moved quickly, the father simply reached into his pocket and pulled out a shiny quarter. "Son," he said softly, "if you'll give Dad that razor, I'll give you this brand new quarter." Immediately, the boy surrendered the dangerous tool and reached out for his promised reward.

The exchanging and rewarding role of love in the Christian life has been called "the expulsive power of a new affection." Rather than demanding that His children give up their worldly "toys" and desires, our Lord places within us an overwhelming love, making us willing to put Him first. Even fear, so common to many people in this world, must succumb to the power of His love (1 John 4:18-21).

Notice how verse 19 differs from what we customarily quote. We tend to say, "We love Him because He first loved us." But John wrote, "We love because He first loved us." Both statements are true, of course, but the context in this passage emphasizes love for other people, made possible by the expulsive and explosive power of a new affection.

> Love is an attitude, love is a prayer
> For a soul in sorrow, a heart in despair.
> Love is good wishes for the gain of another
> Love suffers long with the fault of a brother.
> Love gives water to a cup that's run dry.
> Love reaches low as it can reach high,
> Seeks not her own at expense of another.
> Love reaches God when it reaches our brother.

From "The Power of Love," Salesian Missions

KNOWLEDGE GROUNDED IN FAITH

"Seeing is believing," we say in our culture, and at least one state (Missouri) has cultivated a national reputation for a tough "show me" or "prove it" attitude. But John's writings turn that motto around (as we have noted before in this book) and make it say, "Believing is seeing." The particular item of faith here, as elsewhere in this epistle, is the Incarnation (1 John 5:1-5). What marks those people who truly belong to the Saviour? They believe that Jesus was the virgin-born Son of God come in human flesh, that is, He is the Messiah.

Furthermore, love for the children of God is attested by love for God. Whoever loves the Father will also love His children. This principle appears in reverse form in 4:20 where we learn that whoever loves God's children loves God. And how do we implement this love? By keeping His commandments.

"Faith is the victory" we sing, and the hymn comes directly from these verses. In the Greek text the word for "victory" and "overcome" is the same, appearing in noun form only here in the entire New Testament. We gain victory over the world, John wrote, because we participate in the overcoming power of Jesus Christ, the Son of God.

Sometimes, however, that victory does not seem very realistic. We get discouraged and even defeated by our own failures and the obstacles to faith all around us.

Please remember: When we are least sure of God's presence, we most need to accept it by faith and act on it. Let this be a day of overcoming for you.

THREE WITNESSES

Medical missionary Bill Barnett was sent by God to an island off Mozambique, where it is illegal to witness overtly. Authorities, however, allowed him to practice medicine and to answer questions. To keep the spirit as well as the letter of the law, he refused to discuss Christianity with anyone unless that person asked him three times, which happened with some frequency during the years of his ministry there. His life was a threefold witness!

Cerinthus, a popular heretic living during John's day, taught that the person of God came on Jesus the man at the time of His baptism and then left Him just before the cross. But John would have no such confusion of the Gospel; the Jesus who was baptized was the same Lord who died for our sins on the cross. According to 1 John 5:6-9, He came "by water" (baptism) and "by blood" (crucifixion).

How do we know this? How did these early Christians to whom John wrote this letter grasp and hold on to this and other truths? Because the Spirit testifies of such things and the Spirit is truth. Three facts witness to the truth: the presence of the Holy Spirit, the historical record of Jesus' baptism, and His death on the cross for us. The reality of these historical witnesses remains foundational to our faith. Our belief must be grounded in accurate historical record.

Think how many people know about the baptism and death of Jesus, even about His resurrection, and yet have chosen to reject the truth and meaning of those events because they resist the Holy Spirit's confirmation.

Keep in mind: No one becomes a believer, and no believer grows in faith without the necessary yieldedness to the Spirit's efforts to proclaim and explain truth. Trust Him to provide the wisdom and understanding you need today.

IN A NUTSHELL

As in 1 John 5:6-9, so in verses 9-13 "testimony" is a key word. John warned that rejecting the Spirit's testimony about the Gospel leads to lying and death. And what precisely is that testimony? "God has given us eternal life, and this life is in His Son. He who has the Son has life; he who does not have the Son of God does not have life" (vv. 11-12).

When I was a boy, my mother frequently taught children's Bible classes with a strongly evangelistic emphasis. One of the object lessons she used was a walnut shell, hollowed out and "stuffed" with the familiar ribbon in black, red, white, and gold colors. Calling it "The Gospel in a Nutshell," she would slowly pull out the ribbon while explaining sin (black), Christ's atoning power (red), righteousness (white), and heaven (gold).

Our verses for today also contain the Gospel "in a nutshell." Like the Gospel of John, this epistle centers in the Person and work of the Saviour. But John's Gospel was written to unbelievers to call them to faith in Christ; 1 John was written to call them to assurance (v. 13).

Remember: One valuable result of certain knowledge is prayer. If we know Him, and know that He hears us when we pray, then we can know that we already have what we asked for, if we have asked in His will.

A Christian praying in God's will is like a sailboat carried along by the force of the winds. Direction and mobility come when we adjust ourselves to the flow of His plans and timing.

THE SIN UNTO DEATH

Do you know of anyone who has sinned a "sin that leads to death"? First John 5:14-18 is a difficult passage, a passage on which scholars have different opinions. First, we need to notice that the sinner is a "brother," obviously a fellow Christian. Furthermore, God expects the praying friend to know whether the sin in question is "unto death" or not.

Some believe the sin leading to death is a denial of the Incarnation, since John emphasized that doctrine so strongly throughout this letter. Others prefer an interpretation that centers on physical death, perhaps from the punishment of God as in the case of Ananias and Sapphira. I tend to favor the latter view. John seems to be saying, "If you see another Christian sinning, pray that God will keep him alive if he has not sinned seriously enough to warrant death. But remember, not all sin results in death."

Interesting, isn't it, that John linked our prayer for fellow Christians with the confidence of answered prayer (vv. 14-15). So often we pray for ourselves, our needs, our wants, our hurts and struggles. That's fine, of course, but John reminded us to remember others as well.

A suggestion: Why not make your prayer time today one of special emphasis for brothers and sisters in Christ who may be involved in some sin known to you. Ask the Lord to keep them alive, to bring them to confession and cleansing, and to make them productive in His service once again.

KNOWING THE FATHER

Knowing God intimately will see us through the hard times. When we understand we are His children, that He has given us His truth, all else may crumble around us but we rely on the known God.

Certain knowledge stands as one of John's central goals in this epistle. Three of the last four verses in 1 John 5 begin with the words, "we know." What is this information of which the early Christians were so confident?

1. True Christians come only from God.
2. The whole world lies in Satan's control.
3. God's Son has come and explained the Father to us.
4. Jesus Christ is the true God and believers belong to Him.

The stern and final warning against idolatry (v. 21) suggests rather firmly that any concept of God apart from Jesus Christ is idolatry. In John's view, all agnostics, cultists, and others who deny the Incarnation and related truths of Christ's ministry should be labeled "idolaters."

How essential for us to recognize that idolatry can exist in the mind. We dare not limit it to images or carved religious objects. Even Christians, when they substitute some personal or cultural idea for the true biblical teaching about God, engage in a form of idolatry. Let us strive to follow only those worship patterns which we can establish from His Word.

He is with us in the twilight when the evening shadows fall.
He is with us in the morning when the daybreak comes to call.
He is with us in the noon day when the skies are bright and clear.
He is with us when the darkness of the storm clouds hovers near.
Give us faith to feel His presence as we walk from day to day.
Let us never fail to trust Him. He goes with us all the way.

—Dovie A. Owens
From "Another Day," Salesian Missions

TRUTH DEMONSTRATED

Lying seems to come easily to all of us. It begins when we are young children, quickly denying wrongdoing in order to keep from being punished. As adults we sometimes avoid telling the whole truth in order to advance our own cause or perhaps to save money. In 2 John 1-6, John took immediate aim at the importance of truth, reminding us that Jesus came to earth in truth and love.

Whether "the chosen lady" (v. 1) represents a local church or a real person, the central theme of this tiny epistle stands firm—truth. After a loving and doctrinal introduction, the apostle suggested three ways in which God's truth is demonstrated.

The first is the Father's own word establishing His truth through His commands. The Father's truth has also been shown firsthand through His Son who has revealed grace, mercy, and peace—qualities marking not only the life of our Lord but also the lives of those who follow Him.

Second, God's truth is also reflected by a group John called "some of your children." Was he referring to a remnant of the congregation or the young people of the church? Commentators vary in their views; but one thing is clear, the Bible commends all who live out their faith by walking in the truth.

Third, we see truth in the love of the saints. What is more important in a group of believers—truth or love? John argued that these two absolutely essential ingredients must be kept in balance. Just as Jesus came "full of grace and truth" (John 1:14), His people are expected to speak the truth in love, never compromising one for the sake of the other.

According to a legend, the Apostle John, more than 100 years old, preached, "Little children, love one another." Then he repeated himself twice more. Finally, he concluded, "It is enough. Little children, love one another."

Question: Are you walking in the truth? And are you walking in love? Ask the Lord to help you do both.

TRUTH VIOLATED

One day several young boys went hunting crabs, placing the ugly creatures in a wicker basket after they were caught. Several adults passing by on the beach noticed that the basket had no lid. One of them called to the boys, "Hey, you kids had better cover that basket or the crabs will get away."

"No they won't," replied the lad. "If one crab tries to climb up, the others pull him down."

This is the exact opposite of what John tells us should happen among believers whose task it is to help each other up. (From *Good Morning, Lord,* by Ron Hembree, Baker Book House, 1976.)

Yesterday we noted the importance of combining truth and love in our attitudes and behavior. Next, in 2 John 7-13, John emphasized that some people care for neither. These "deceivers" have abandoned the teaching about the Father and the Son; they go beyond the limits of pure doctrine and deliberately confuse and lead astray those who listen to them.

How should sincere Christians react to such false teachers? John issued two practical warnings: watch out so you don't lose your full reward, and don't welcome such people or assist them in any way. Apparently, John's immediate correspondents were already doing this, since he chose wording that suggested they should stop their behavior.

Like many of us, John felt that touchy matters of doctrine were best dealt with in person, so he deferred further discussion until he could see his friends. And at that visit he wanted to accomplish more than just theological correction; he wanted them all to experience real joy from their collective fellowship. What a grand picture of the body of Christ—demonstrating truth, avoiding violators of truth, and sharing loving joy with one another.

For you: Think of some realistic ways to do these things today, and then follow through in carrying them out.

GREETINGS TO GAIUS

Shirley has the gift of hospitality. Her home is always open to friends, travelers, and even strangers. The weekly Bible study meets in that home even when Shirley is out of town since several friends have keys to her house. Everyone knows her attitude: "Just make yourself at home." People who need a place to stay often bunk in at Shirley's for months at a time. She provides a good example of John's admonition in 3 John 1-8.

The only third epistle in the Bible urges believers to enjoy and exercise fellowship with those who walk in truth. Four times John referred to Gaius as "beloved," commending him for his hospitality to other Christians. And look again at verse 2; what condition would you be in if your physical health were as good or as poor as your spiritual health?

Gaius had made a ministry out of hospitality to itinerant preachers who were strangers to him. Their reports came back to John in Ephesus, creating a positive reputation for Gaius as one who put his love into practice. Because people like Gaius cared for the travel needs of these servants, the Gospel could be proclaimed without charge to the heathen. And those who offered them hospitality shared in the evangelism.

How are you doing? Some say hospitality is a dead art among believers today. Yet the New Testament consistently urges us to show such care for others, even strangers. Let's take passages like this seriously and "revive" hospitality among God's people in our day. If He has given you the resources, let it begin with you and your family.

DIOTREPHES AND DEMETRIUS

When a young man died of cancer in 1977, the memorial card for the funeral quoted these words by John Henry Newman:

> God has created me to render Him some definite service. He has committed some work to me which He has not committed to another. I have a mission. I may never know it in this life but I shall be told it in the next. Therefore, I will trust Him. Whatever I am, I can never be thrown away. If I am in sickness, my sickness may serve Him. If I am in sorrow, my sorrow may serve Him. He does nothing in vain. He knows what He is about.

The Apostle John ended his little letter with a contrast between two men (3 John 9-14). One represents precisely the opposite of what we learned yesterday from the example of Gaius. Diotrephes rejected John's earlier letter recommending hospitality, and also insisted that others behave as he did.

What kind of fellow must he have been? Obviously very arrogant and demanding. Perhaps he held some office and tried to control the congregation because of his own authority. John clearly condemned that kind of autocratic leadership.

The other is named Demetrius, and John urged Gaius to follow his example. Some believe Demetrius may have been John's courier, carrying this letter to Gaius, but such precise identification is impossible to know. The behavior of church members affirms or denies their claims. John encouraged Gaius (and us) to pattern our lives after the good examples.

Take a tip: When Dwight Eisenhower was a general, he used to demonstrate the art of leadership with a simple piece of string. Putting it on a table he'd say, "Pull it and it will follow wherever you wish; push it and it will go nowhere at all. It's just that way when it comes to leading people." The church needs leaders today—leaders who can "pull" by loving and caring, leaders like Demetrius and Gaius.

DYNAMIC CHRISTIAN LIVING

John did it again! Like the wonderful fourth Gospel, these three short epistles have shown us the dynamic of Christian life, the reality of what it means to "walk in the light." Surrounded on every hand by false teachers and enemies of the truth, the aging apostle taught his children how to follow the loving Son.

The central error he opposed in these letters distorted the Person and work of Christ and specifically the Incarnation and His relationship with God the Father. A sophisticated system of worldly wisdom tricked believers into considering error above truth. Proud and deceitful, these fake "prophets" taught that Jesus differed from other men only in that He was better and wiser.

How modern it all sounds! North American universities overflow with modern "Gnostics" who claim to know so much more than simple, Bible-believing Christians. Sects and cults proliferate in our society, many of them spreading heretical ideas about Christ which sound frighteningly similar to those John attacked almost twenty centuries ago.

No wonder the Holy Spirit used this apostle to warn the church against ignorance and failure of faith. How central to all we hold dear that God's people behave in dynamic obedience to all He proclaims in these blessed books.

A challenge for today and the new year:

> May the mind of Christ my Saviour
> Live in me from day to day
> By His love and pow'r controlling
> All I do and say.

> > > –A. Cyril Baring-Gould